the
science of
parenting

the
science of
parenting

Practical guidance on sleep,
crying, play and building
emotional wellbeing for life

MARGOT SUNDERLAND

LONDON, NEW YORK, MUNICH,
MELBOURNE, DELHI

Senior editor Esther Ripley
Senior art editor Anne Fisher
Project editors Becky Alexander, Ann Baggaley,
Kesta Desmond
Designer Jo Grey
DTP designer Sonia Charbonnier
Production controller Elizabeth Cherry
Managing editor Penny Warren
Managing art editor Marianne Markham
Picture research Myriam Megharbi
Jacket editor Adam Powley
Publishing director Corinne Roberts

The views expressed in this book are the author's
own. If you have any concerns about any aspect
of your child's behaviour, health, or wellbeing, it is
recommended that you seek professional advice.
Neither the author nor the publisher shall be
liable or responsible for any loss or damage
allegedly arising from any information
or suggestion in this book.

First published in Great Britain in 2006 by
Dorling Kindersley,
A Penguin Company
80 Strand, London, WC2R 0RL

A CIP catalogue record for this book is available
from the British Library

ISBN-13: 978-1-4053-1486-2
ISBN-10: 1-4053-1486-8

Reproduced by Media Development Printing,
Great Britain
Printed and bound by Star Standard, Singapore

Discover more at
www.dk.com

Contents

Forewords

"If we act upon what science can tell us about parenting, we can develop more benign societies."

THERE WAS A MOMENT OF SHOCK when I first realized how much impact the everyday interactions between parent and child can have on a child's developing brain. Yet the mass of scientific research on this subject was not getting through to parents or to the public arena. This is what fuelled my passion to write a book that would not be just one more opinion on parenting (we have quite enough of these already), but would rather empower parents to make informed choices for their children based on what we can learn from these scientific studies.

This book would not have been written without the ground-breaking research of Professor Jaak Panksepp, who has been studying the emotional brain in the US for more than 30 years. His findings are not only significant within the world of neuroscience but also have major implications for humankind. His work, and that of others, offers us joined-up thinking about why so many children grow up to be adults who suffer from depression, anxiety, or problems with anger.

If we are prepared to act upon what science can tell us about parenting, we can push forward to develop more benign societies with greater compassion, capacity to reflect, and respect for difference. Perhaps, too, society will begin to see that by nurturing parents, children will be empowered to thrive.

Margot Sunderland
Director of Education and Training,
Centre for Child Mental Health, London.

THIS SUPERB MANUAL FOR CHILD REARING describes how healthy minds emerge from emotionally well-fertilized brains. The quality of childcare has lifelong consequences for mental health. Children whose emotional feelings are cherished and respected, even their angry outbursts, shall live more happily than those whose early passions are denied. Both excessive distress and tender loving care leave lasting marks on the emotional circuits, and mentalities, of developing brains.

Modern brain research has clarified how neural structures and chemistries elaborate emotionality in our fellow animals. As a result, we can better understand the nature of social emotional urges within our children's brains. Margot has harvested and digested this abundant evidence and brilliantly highlights how this knowledge can guide better parental choices for children's lives.

The first three years of seeking and affectively engaging the world are critical for the future success of every boy and girl. It is important for them to get off on the right track both emotionally and intellectually. With *The Science of Parenting*, Margot Sunderland has given us a scientifically secure base for child-rearing practices in the 21st century.

"Here we have a scientifically secure base for child-rearing practices in the 21st century."

Jaak Panksepp, Ph.D.
Baily Endowed Chair of Animal Well-Being Science,
Washington State University; Head of Affective Neuroscience Research,
Chicago Institute for Neurosurgery and Neuroresearch, Illinois.

Introduction

What a gift to be given life. What an awesome thing that you didn't end up as one of the millions of sperms that didn't make it, or one of the eggs that ended up down the toilet. And on top of that, how incredible if you have been lucky enough to be born in a country not at war, or scared by persistent violence, so you don't have to live in fear. Yet despite all this, for many people there is a BUT. What if you didn't have the sort of parenting that enabled you to develop the capacity to live life to the full? What if, because of this, you have been troubled by depression, or persistent states of anger or anxiety? What if you never feel truly calm or able to find real generosity, kindness, or compassion in your heart, or have the drive, motivation, or spontaneity to do what you really want with your life? What if you never know what it is to love in peace?

For centuries we have been using child-rearing techniques without awareness of the possible long-term effects, because until now we simply could not see the effects of our actions on a child's developing brain. But with the advances of neuroscience, brain scans, and years of research on the brains of primates and other mammals, we no longer have the innocence of ignorance. For several years, science has

"Now we have a greater understanding of how to help children thrive, things can change for the better, in the family and in society, too."

been revealing to us that key emotional systems in the human brain are powerfully moulded for better or worse by parenting experiences. So while we can't protect our children from future unhappiness, we now have scientific information about the impact of different ways of parenting on a child's brain. We now know that millions of parent–child sculpting moments in childhood can set up systems and chemistries that will enable children to have a deeply enriching life, unblighted by the sorts of emotional anguish described above. In the past, it has been assumed that a child's developing brain can withstand all manner of stress, but

"To experience a warm world inside your head depends very much on special 'one-to-one' moments with your parents."

research is now revealing that it is in fact highly vulnerable. It is both awesome and sobering to discover that some common parenting techniques can have a direct effect on the wiring and long-term chemical balance in children's brains.

"So many grown-ups can't manage stress well. Because no one helped them enough with stress and distress in childhood, they never set up effective stress-regulating systems in their brains."

It is chilling to know that some accepted ways of being with children can leave them vulnerable to suffering from anxiety, depression, or rage in later life. The statistics are alarming: about 40,000 children in the UK are taking antidepressants, and the World Health Organization reports that depression in adults will soon reach epidemic proportions. More than half of all children have experienced bullying at school and 17,000 children in the UK are excluded from school each year for bad behaviour. In the search for causes, we have in the past pointed the finger at child neglect, child abuse, and the effects of financial hardship. This book goes deeper, harnessing research that shows how everyday parenting can contribute to this widespread misery.

Well, that's the sobering part. The good news is that we can use this knowledge to prevent unnecessary suffering. For example, I'll be showing you how certain styles of parenting can have positive effects on the stress systems in your child's brain and body so that whatever life throws up, your child will be able to manage stress well. Particular ways of responding to your child will establish pathways in his brain to enable him to manage emotions well, think rationally under pressure, and calm himself down without recourse to angry outbursts, attacks of anxiety or, in later life, alcohol, smoking and drugs.

In the early chapters we'll be using what we know about the structure of a child's brain to explore the potential to sculpt it for better or for worse. It is not a matter of genes as to whether a child develops the higher human capacities of problem-solving, self-awareness, the ability to react well under stress, empathy, kindness, and concern. But there are styles of parenting that can dramatically influence these crucial developments.

Parenting power can also affect children's ability to live life to the full, helping them to develop the will to follow things through from idea to reality. So many people go through life only pursuing short-term pleasures such as food, sex, and

"Parents can affect the chemistry in a child's brain to such an extent that, for the most part, her stream of inner thoughts will be self-encouraging rather than fraught with self-criticism."

material goods, because they haven't developed the capacity for long-term satisfaction in this way. We'll be exploring ways of parenting that enable your child to be moved and touched by people and events, able to stand and drink in the experience when faced with something remarkable, rather than always thinking of the next thing or the last thing. So many people go through life without feeling it fully. We'll be

"Parenting power means that your child will not lose her awe and wonder about the world as she moves into adulthood."

exploring how to help activate key systems in the brain to do with curiosity and drive, and build your child's enduring capacity to explore and embrace life. We'll also look at ways of fostering creativity. All too often, people put away their creativity and imagination in adulthood, and then fail to imagine more expansive ways of being or dream the dreams necessary to bear the richest fruit in their lives.

What happens when children test our patience to the limits? Again, science has some answers that have not been considered previously. Difficult behaviour in all its many guises is discussed in detail here, but always within the context of the extra insights we can glean from what is happening in a child's brain. Similarly, my tried-and-tested discipline strategies are chosen for their long-term benefits to the development of your child's social brain and emotional intelligence.

"Some children grow up with hearts big enough to feel the suffering of humankind; not just people in their close circle but those with different views, cultures, and beliefs to their own."

Parenting power can help nurture networks in a child's social brain, with all the skills needed for deep and enduring friendships. I'll be looking at the science of love within families – how it can empower a child to grow up to love in peace and enjoy the richest relationships. Lastly, my chapter "Looking after you" recognises that to do the very best by our children we need to cherish parents, too.

your child's
brain

Parents are not magicians. They can't guarantee their children happiness in later life, or protect them from loss and rejection. But they can dramatically influence systems in their children's brains that are key to the potential for a deeply fulfilling life, as we shall see throughout this book. Before we embark on this amazing journey, it is important to understand a few facts about the human brain.

The evolution of the brain

About 300 million years ago, reptiles had evolved on Earth. Mammals and finally humans followed much later. Amazingly, the structure of our human brain still bears witness to this history. What we ended up with were, arguably, three interconnecting brains, each with some particular functions.

BRAIN STORY

Our lower brains are very like those of other mammals but our higher brains, or frontal lobes, are much larger, so we can think more deeply than any other animal.

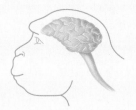

A chimpanzee has small frontal lobes (shown in pink), so it thinks mainly in the present.

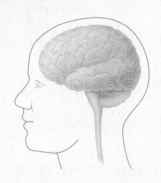

Our large frontal lobes allow us to imagine, reason, and solve problems.

Our brains are made up of a core reptilian brain, a lower mammalian brain, and – the crowning glory of evolution – a higher human brain. Each of these three "brains" or "brain regions" is connected to the others by a massive network of nerves, yet has its own special functions.

Sometimes the three brains work together in a beautifully coordinated way and, with the activation of some positive emotional chemicals, they bring out the best in humans. But at other times, particular parts of the brain or particular chemicals are in the driving seat. This can make people act in ways which cause all manner of misery to themselves and also to others. The incredible thing is that, as a parent, you can influence the activation of key functions and systems in your child's brain and the way in which the three brains interact.

Basic instincts

Humans might feel superior to other animals because we have the most developed higher thinking brain. But we are not superior in terms of the old reptilian and mammalian regions of our brain. In fact, these parts of our brains are very similar indeed, in overall organization (relative to size), to those of a mouse. These more ancient brain regions have mostly stayed the same over millions of years. As one scientist said, "It's like carrying around an ancient museum inside our heads."[1] What's more, our higher rational brain can easily be hijacked by these lower regions. When we feel unsafe, physically or psychologically, impulses from the reptilian and mammalian parts of our brain can hijack our higher human functions, and we can behave like a threatened animal. We can experience impulsive "fight-or-flight" reactions that make us lash out with rage or move into anxious behaviour. As a parent, you can have an impact on your child's brain so that his higher brain will be able, for most of the time, to manage these primitive lower brain reactions effectively.

How our brains grew

Over three million years ago, the earliest of our human relatives (hominids) had a brain about half the size of our own, and the brain remained small in the first upright man, *Homo erectus* (about 1.5 million years ago). By around 200,000 years ago the brain of our direct ancestors, *Homo sapiens,* had grown massively, matching our own modern brain in size and showing a connectedness that suggests an advanced ability to generate new ideas. Some 50,000 years ago humans were painting, making ornaments and jewellery, and adopting religion, but it still took a long time for humans to develop the capacity for sophisticated thinking that we enjoy today.

"The world is very old and human beings are very young."[2]

  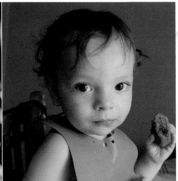

The reptilian brain evolved around 300 million years ago. It is instinctive, controlling body functions such as breathing and digestion, and has functions based on survival.

The mammalian brain evolved 200 million years ago, and with it new brain programmes for social behaviour – such as care and nurturance, playfulness, and bonding.

Humans have been around for 200,000 years and have developed highly sophisticated powers of reasoning, but we still have reptilian and mammalian areas in our brains.

Your child's three brains

You may think that your child has only one brain – but he has three! Sometimes the three brains act together in a beautifully coordinated way, but at other times one part is dominant. How you raise and respond to a child has a powerful influence on which part of the brain is activated most.

Your parenting will have a major impact on how these three brain regions (rational, mammalian, and reptilian) influence your child's emotional life on a long-term basis. Will your child be tormented by lower (reptilian) brain systems repeatedly triggering primitive impulses of defence and attack? Or will he feel so much hurt that he cuts off from the strong feelings of love and need in his mammalian brain, going through life in an over-rational way, unable to form close relationships? Or will his rational brain coordinate with the emotional systems in his mammalian brain in ways that allow him to enjoy the highest level of social intelligence with the deepest level of human compassion and concern?

THE RATIONAL BRAIN

This is the higher brain, also known as the "frontal lobes" or the neo-cortex. In evolutionary terms it is the newest part of the brain, amounting to about 85 percent of the total brain mass, and enveloping the ancient mammalian and reptilian parts. It is on the frontal lobes of a child's brain that emotionally responsive parenting has a dramatically positive impact.

Its functions and capacities include:
- creativity and imagination
- problem-solving
- reasoning and reflection
- self-awareness
- kindness, empathy, and concern.

This part of the brain has led to the greatest achievements of humans, but when cut off from the mammalian brain's social emotion systems, it is also responsible for appalling cruelties.

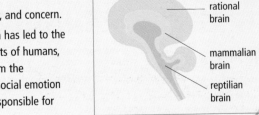

HOW THE BRAIN EVOLVED
This diagram shows a model of how the modern human brain evolved, building up layer upon layer with the ancient reptilian brain at its core.[3]

rational brain

mammalian brain

reptilian brain

cortex

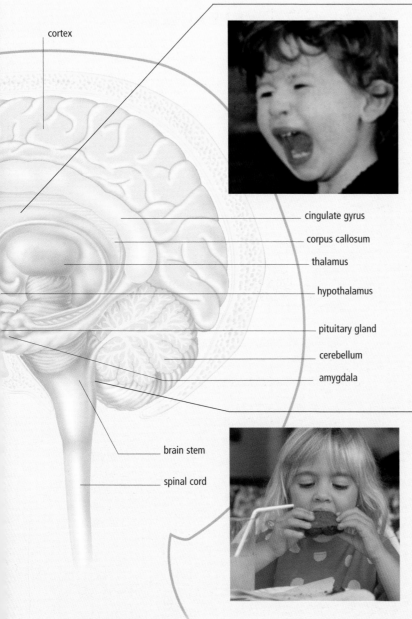

cingulate gyrus

corpus callosum

thalamus

hypothalamus

pituitary gland

cerebellum

amygdala

brain stem

spinal cord

THE MAMMALIAN BRAIN

Also known as the emotional brain, the lower brain, or the limbic system, this region has almost the same chemical systems and structure as in other mammals, such as chimpanzees. It triggers strong emotions that need to be managed well by the rational brain. It also helps to control primitive fight or flight impulses. This part of the brain activates:

- rage
- fear
- separation distress
- caring and nurturing
- social bonding
- playfulness
- explorative urge
- lust in adults.

THE REPTILIAN BRAIN

This is the deepest, most ancient part of the human brain, largely unchanged by evolution. We share this part of the brain with all other vertebrates. The reptilian brain activates instinctive behaviour related to survival, and controls essential bodily functions required for sustaining life, including:

- hunger
- digestion/elimination
- breathing
- circulation
- temperature
- movement, posture, and balance
- territorial instincts
- fight or flight.

THE MODERN BRAIN

A coloured diagram of the fully evolved brain shows the cortex and frontal lobes (purple), the limbic system (green), and the brain stem and cerebellum (brown).

Parenting the brain

For centuries we have been using child-rearing techniques without any awareness of the possible long-term effects on a child's developing brain. This is because, until now, we couldn't see the effect of our actions on what was going on inside a child's brain. However, we now know that the way parents interact with their child can have long-term effects on his brain functions and on the chemical balance in his brain.

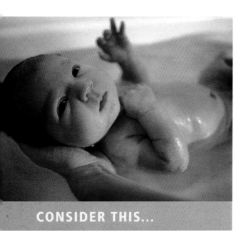

CONSIDER THIS...

Loss of brain cells (neurons) is part of the brain's natural "sculpting process", which continues throughout life. In the strengthening of key connections in the brain, unneeded or under-used cells are pruned away. At birth we have 200 billion brain cells but by the age of one we have already lost 80 billion of them. By the teenage years we have lost about 90 billion brain cells; by the age of 35, about 100 billion brain cells, and by the age of 70, about 105 billion. This is all because of what is known as "synaptic pruning". It's just the same as pruning back a rose bush to make it grow well.

With the advances of neuroscience, brain scans, and years of research on the brains of primates and other mammals (whose emotional brains have virtually the same architecture and chemical systems as ours), we now have vital information about the impact of different ways of parenting on a child's brain. Your approach to parenting can dramatically determine whether or not your child's brain systems and brain chemistries are activated in such a way to enable him to enjoy a rich and rewarding life.

Your child's unfinished brain

Much of the infant brain is developed after birth, so it is very open to being sculpted by both negative and positive parent–child interactions. At birth, your child's higher brain, in particular, is very unfinished, so much so that a newborn baby has been referred to as an "external fetus" (see page 36). When born, babies have in the region of 200 billion brain cells, but they have very few connections between these cells in their higher brain. These connections will be largely responsible for the emotional and social intelligence of your child, and it is over these connections that you have so much influence.

"Some adults remain stuck with the emotional development of a toddler."

This immaturity of your baby's brain is the result of a major evolutionary event. When the ancestors of modern man, namely *Homo erectus*, stood on two legs, humans were then free to use their hands; this led to a dramatic advance in intelligence, accompanied by an equally dramatic increase in the size of the brain. At the same time, standing on two legs produced a narrowed pelvis and birth canal in females. The bigger head and smaller pelvis meant the human infant had to be born very immature, with only 25 percent of final brain size, compared to, say, 45 percent in chimpanzees. [4]

"Most of the infant brain is developed after birth…your child's higher brain, in particular, is very unfinished."

■ **You have so much influence over how your baby's emotional brain develops because there are critical periods of brain growth in the first years of life.**
The infant brain starts to form connections at a very rapid rate during this time. In fact, 90 percent of the growth of the human brain occurs in the first five years of life. Over these crucial years, millions of brain connections are being formed, unformed, and then re-formed, directly due to the influence of your child's life experiences and in particular his emotional experiences with you.

Around age seven, this massive sculpting activity is slowed down. This is because more and more brain cells are being myelinated (myelin is a whitish material made up of protein and fats that surrounds the brain cells in sheaths, like a form of insulation). This enables better communication between brain cells. It also strengthens brain pathways, fixing them in place. Hence there is some scientific truth underpinning the often quoted Jesuit assertion: "Give me a child until the age of seven, and I will give you the man."

BRAIN STORY

Brain wiring from birth These diagrams show how a baby's higher brain forms connections at a very rapid rate as it is sculpted by experiences in the first years of life. At the beginning, brain cells are unconnected, like dangling wires in a computer.

A newborn baby has 200 billion brain cells, but few connections.

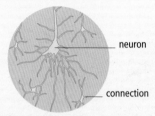

In a child of about one year, cells in the higher brain have developed many more connections.

In a child of about two years, the brain wiring has become more complex and synaptic pruning has begun.

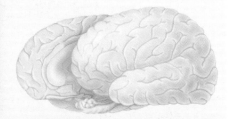
The parent–child connection

Everything your baby experiences with you as his parent will forge connections between the cells in his higher brain. The human brain is specifically designed this way so that it can be wired up to adapt to the particular environment in which it finds itself. This adaptability works for or against the well-being of a child. If, for example, a child has a bullying parent, he can start to adapt to living in a bullying world, with all manner of changes in brain structure and brain chemical systems, which may result in hypervigilance, heightened aggression or fear reactions, or heightened attack/defence impulses in the reptilian part of his brain.

So the way you listen to your child, play with him, cuddle him, comfort him, and treat him when he is being naughty are of real significance. It is these times with you as parent that can stack the cards so heavily for him thriving or failing to thrive in later life. With emotionally responsive parenting, vital connections will form in his brain, enabling him to cope well with stress in later life; form fulfilling relationships; manage anger well; be kind and compassionate; have the will and motivation to follow his ambitions and his dreams; experience the deepest calm; and be able to love intimately and in peace.

We need to understand the mammalian and reptilian parts of a child's brain.

In the first few years of life, because your child's higher rational brain is so unfinished, his lower brain will be in the driving seat. It is important in parenting that we recognize exactly what this means in reality. Basically, the emotional systems and primitive impulses in his lower brain will all too easily overwhelm him at times. Hence his intense bursts of rage, distress, screaming, and rolling around on the floor in a desperate state. This is not being naughty; it's just a fact about the immaturity of the human infant brain. Your child's higher brain has simply not developed enough yet to be able to calm these massive feeling storms naturally.

"I love my Mummy"

There is an amazing flow of emotional energy and information from your brain to your child's brain and from your body to your child's body. This is also true with other adults who play an important role in your child's life. Your emotional state, and what's going on in your frontal lobes, will have a direct and powerful impact on key emotional systems in your child's brain and key arousal systems in your child's body.

BRAIN STORY

When we experience feelings of fear, rage, or sadness, brain scans show large areas of activation (red) in the lower parts of the brain and deactivation (purple), largely in higher brain areas.

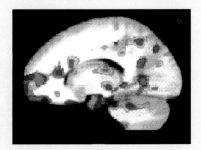

Fear produces activation in ancient structures in the lower and mid-brain.

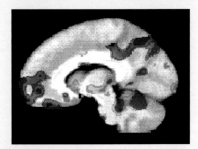

Anger produces activation deep in the brain stem.

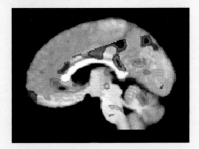

Sadness activates part of the lower brain's CARE system (see page 191).

There are several genetically ingrained emotional systems deep in the lower brain, and knowledge of these systems is key to good parenting. The systems are RAGE, FEAR, SEPARATION DISTRESS, SEEKING, CARE, PLAY, and LUST (which is not developed in children). We'll be looking at these throughout the book. Leading neuroscientists like Professor Jaak Panksepp, who has been studying the lower brain for over 30 years, have shown that these systems and their accompanying behaviours exist in all mammals and can be activated in mammals by stimulating specific areas of the lower brain.[5]

■ **The RAGE, FEAR, and SEPARATION DISTRESS systems are already set up at birth to support a baby's survival.**
They are designed to be so in order to save infants from being eaten by predators, and to keep them close to a parent. The potential dangers in the modern world are very different but, nevertheless, everyday events can easily trigger one or more of these systems in your infant's brain. For example, his FEAR system may be triggered when a door slams, or his RAGE system when you try to dress him, or his SEPARATION DISTRESS system when you walk out of a room. Infants keep getting overwhelmed by the triggering of these brain systems because there is so little higher rational brain functioning "on-line" yet, to help them to think, reason, and calm themselves down.

It is important to understand this when faced with a genuinely distressed, screaming baby or child. He needs your help to calm down. With consistently emotionally responsive parenting like this, your child's frontal lobes will start to develop essential brain pathways that will, over time, enable him to calm these alarm states in his lower brain.

■ **Some children never receive sufficient emotional responsiveness from their parents.**
When a child is not given enough help with his intense lower brain feelings and primitive impulses, his brain may not develop the pathways to enable him to effectively manage

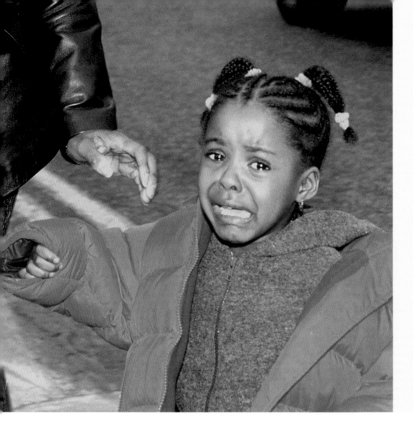

"I need to be calmed"

A distressed, upset child needs your compassion, soothing, and physical comfort to bring her dysregulated body and brain systems back into balance.

stressful situations. The legacy in later life is that they do not develop the higher human capacities for concern, or the ability to reflect on their feelings in a self-aware way. Brain scans show that many violent adults are still driven, just like infants, by their ancient rage/fear and defence/attack responses deep in the mammalian and reptilian parts of the brain. These brain scans show all too little activity in the parts of the higher brain that naturally regulate and modify raging feelings.[6] Just like toddlers, such adults can be regularly overwhelmed by powerful feelings without the capacity to calm themselves down effectively.

■ The chemistries in your child's brain are also affected by types of parenting.

The cells and pathways in the brain are activated by natural chemicals and hormones. Among a number of chemicals that are important in good parent–child relationships are oxytocin and opioids (see also page 87). Oxytocin is released at birth and helps mother and baby to bond. Opioids are hormones that give us a sense of well-being; these chemicals are produced when a child is lovingly touched or held by a parent or other

"Because your child's higher brain is so unfinished, his lower brain will be in the driving seat."

"The developing brain, in the crucial first years of life, is highly vulnerable to stress."

caring person. Warm attentive parents will repeatedly activate the release of these hormones, creating a secure bond with their child. If, however, parents do not understand their child's need for closeness – or worse, if they regularly respond to that child with criticism or shouting – the release of opioids and oxytocin is blocked. Instead, the child may then suffer from "hormonal hell" due to prolonged stress, which, as we will see later in the book, can cause permanent changes in the child's brain.

"Be excited with me"

In helping your child to establish effective stress-regulating systems in her brain, she needs to be deeply met in joy as well as in emotional pain. This is because joy is a stressful high-arousal state too. So meet her exuberance with your own. When children are not helped with the "stress" of joy, they can be frightened of the bodily arousal of excitement in later life.[7]

What science can tell us about stress

One of the biggest problems in the past has been the assumption that the child's developing brain is a robust structure that can withstand all manner of stress. Neuroscientific research has now found this to be a fallacy. Whilst children have some measure of resilience – and, genetically speaking, some more than others – the developing brain in those crucial first years of life is also highly vulnerable to stress. It is so sensitive that the stress of many common parenting techniques can alter delicate "emotion chemical" balances and stress response systems in the infant's brain and body, and sometimes cause actual cell death in certain brain structures.[8]

When a child is not helped enough with his intense feelings, the alarm systems in his lower brain can be over-active in later life.

This means that he may over-react to minor stressors, "sweat the small stuff", and live a life of worrying, and/or be angry or short-tempered for much of the time. As a parent, you can prevent your child from having to live like this. You cannot save him from life's inevitable sufferings, but you can have a dramatic impact on his quality of life by parenting in such a way that effective stress-regulating systems and anti-anxiety chemical systems are firmly established in his brain. There is a mass of scientific research showing that quality of life is dramatically affected by whether or not you established good stress-regulating systems in your brain in childhood.[9]

The brain's alarm system

One of the most important alarm systems in the lower brain is called the amygdala. One of its main functions is to work out the emotional meaning of everything that happens to you. If the amygdala senses that something threatening is happening to you, it communicates with another structure in the brain called the hypothalamus, and this part of the brain

ANIMAL INSIGHTS

All mammals have alarm systems, designed to protect them from danger. Even today, the lower human brain shares very similar anatomy and chemistry to that of other mammals. In ancient times, these alarm systems were very useful and protected humans from predators. Today, these systems register alarm when we feel psychological stress. We can feel irrationally frightened or anxious when, in fact, there is no real danger (physical or psychological).

"You can have a dramatic impact on your child's quality of life."

"I'm learning so fast"

There is a major growth spurt in the frontal lobes of a child's brain in the first two years of life. This time is a great window of opportunity for establishing nerve pathways that underpin learning and language development and also for establishing anti-anxiety chemical systems in the brain.

"Higher brain functioning can release anti-anxiety chemicals…so you feel calm again."

actions the release of stress hormones, which can then prepare your body for fight-or-flight.

The release of some of the positive arousal chemicals in the brain is blocked, to ensure your full attention is on the current threat. By this time you can be feeling awful. If, however, you have been helped in childhood with your intense feelings of anger, frustration, and distress, then your higher human brain will intervene effectively at this point. It can help you think clearly about the situation and work out what is best to do. It can also help you work out when you are over-reacting, and realize that what has happened is manageable.

All this higher brain functioning can quieten your amygdala, and release anti-anxiety chemicals in your brain, which relaxes the body so you feel calm again. On the other hand, if you were left in childhood to manage your painful feelings on your own, and without counselling or therapy in later life, your higher brain may not have developed the necessary wiring to be able to perform these wonderful stress-managing functions. As a result, you can stay feeling stressed out for hours, and sometimes days and even weeks. This can result in clinical depression.[10]

Not helping a child with his "big" feelings can mean that his brain's key response systems are in danger of being permanently wired as "over-reactive". This means that he can have real difficulties in turning off his over-sensitive alarm systems in his lower brain. As a result, his perception of events is coloured with feelings of threat or major difficulties.[11]

"When you help your child with his big feelings, a great number of cells in his higher brain start to form pathways..."

Helping children with their big feelings

When you help your child with his big feelings, a great number of cells in his higher brain start to form pathways connecting with those in his lower brain. These are called top-down brain networks or pathways. Over time, these networks will naturally start to control those primitive impulses of rage, fear, or distress in his lower brain, enabling him to think about his feelings, rather than just discharging them in some primitive action (such as biting, hitting, or running away). Ways in which you can help your child will be covered throughout the book, but here are some pointers:

■ **Take your child's distress seriously.** Recognize how your child is experiencing an event, even if it's very different from how you are experiencing it. Find age-appropriate words for your child's distress. Show that you have correctly understood the nature of his distress by telling him in a language he can

CONSIDER THIS...

If you don't consistently comfort and calm a child who is experiencing an amygdala alarm trigger in his brain, it can lead to enduring changes in his brain. These include serious disruptions to the fine chemical balances in his frontal lobes and to stress response systems in his body and his brain.

When any of the alarm systems – RAGE, FEAR, or SEPARATION DISTRESS are triggered in a child's lower brain, he will be in a state of emotional pain and intense bodily arousal, unless an adult helps him to calm down. This is because once one of the alarm systems has triggered, neurochemical and hormonal forces will be activated, which overwhelm the mind and body like wildfire.

Case study

understand: for example, "You are so angry with me that I wouldn't let you have the little red car in the toy shop", rather than, "Want! Want! Want! That's all you ever do."

Take, for example, Jack (aged 18 months) who is furious because his Daddy wouldn't let him suck a sweet that he found on the pavement. Jack's Daddy manages to move away from his initial thought of, "This is utterly ridiculous, of course you can't eat the dirty sweet", to being able to feel the level of Jack's distress. He takes the time to think and feel about what Jack is feeling. He tries to imagine the world as

"He needs to feel you are an emotionally strong parent who is clearly in charge."

Jack sees it in that moment, and he acknowledges Jack's feelings and their intensity. He says, "Jack, I can hear how cross you are with me about the sweet, not just a bit cross but very cross. You hated it when I took it away. You so wanted to eat it." Jack starts to quieten down and his Daddy picks him up and holds him. In so doing, Jack is further calmed.

Even a very young child will benefit from this kind of understanding. The parent's tone will get through, even if the child can't quite understand all the words. This helps to develop those essential top-down brain pathways that will enable Jack, as he grows up, to successfully manage the intensity of his big feelings and to be stable under stress.[12]

■ **Meet your child's feelings with the right voice and energy.** Meet your child's feelings with an energized rather than a flat voice. For example, if your child brings you a seashell with delight and enthusiasm, thank him with a similar energy of delight. If he is furious, make sure your voice and words acknowledge that energetically: "I can see you are very angry with me, not just a bit angry".

■ **Be calm and offer clear boundaries.** A key factor in your ability to manage your child's intense arousal states is managing your own. So take your own need for emotional support seriously, and find time to talk about your own feelings with an understanding other person. Be there for your child's feelings rather than burdening him with yours (for example, "I can't deal with this now. Can't you see how tired I am?"). Offer clear boundaries by saying No, firmly yet calmly, when appropriate. Dithering or trying to persuade your child or plead with him, for example, to put on his shoes, will make him feel emotionally unsafe. He needs to feel you are an emotionally strong parent who is clearly in charge.

■ **Use physical soothing.** Respond to your distressed child with calm, physical soothing. As we shall see later in the book, physical affection will release wonderful calming chemicals in your child's brain. If you feel the absolute opposite of calm in that moment, find another caring adult to soothe him instead, or step back and take time to calm yourself.

The long-term effects of not helping children

There is a mass of scientific research showing that quality of life is dramatically affected by whether or not good stress-regulating systems are established in the brain in childhood.[13] Research also shows that it can be very hard to reverse an over-reactive stress response system in the brain. It can be reversed, however, by powerful healing relationships in later life, such as counselling or therapy. Sadly, too many people do not take this option.

■ **It makes life such a constant struggle if we are unable to manage stress well, and there are so many people who just can't do it.**

We only have to consider the soaring numbers of children, young people, and adults who suffer from depression, anxiety disorders, or problems with aggression to realize that the problem is widespread. When we can't manage stress well, we end up shrinking from the world or doing battle with it.[14] People who are able to manage stress well, think well under

CONSIDER THIS...

Research shows that if your child has an over-reactive stress response system, he or she will be vulnerable to suffering from depression in later life, as a reaction to life's hard knocks. Last year, 19 million people in the UK were given a prescription for anti-depressants.

Seeking counselling or therapy in later life can be a real second chance to develop effective stress-regulating systems in the brain, but it can take a long time. It's so much easier to avoid problems with good parenting in childhood.

pressure, and can calm themselves down when the going gets tough, because they have developed effective stress-regulating systems in their brains, are the lucky ones. With such brain systems in place, it is possible to grow in wisdom from life's painful experiences, rather than to be damaged by them.

■ **People who have not established effective stress-response systems in their brains can suffer from all manner of problems.**

An overactive stress response system in the brain, originating in childhood, underlies a great many mental disorders and physical ailments.[15] These include:

- depression
- persistent states of anxiety
- phobias and obsessions
- physical symptoms/illness
- being cut off emotionally
- lethargy and lack of get-up-and-go
- lack of desire and excitement
- lack of spontaneity.

In addition, too many experiences become spoilt with a state of personal or social unease. Vital life forces are used up battling painful feelings rather than being channelled into creative, fulfilling relationships and endeavours. You can feel weary each day instead of invigorated by being alive.

What I hope to show in this book is that the brain-sculpting powers of parents are so amazing that you can prevent your child from having to live like this. You cannot save your child from the pain of life's inevitable problems, but you can influence how your child will respond to them.

"People who are able to manage stress well, can think well under pressure… they are the lucky ones"

Key points

■ **Human brains** contain primitive emotional alarm systems deep in the lower regions. Without emotionally responsive parenting, our higher brains can easily be highjacked by these systems.

■ **As a result** of certain forms of child-rearing, some adults remain stuck with the emotional development of a toddler.

■ **Everything** your child experiences with his parents will forge connections between the cells in his higher brain.

■ **It is essential** to help a child with his "big" feelings, to avoid future problems with stress and over-reaction.

■ **Your child** needs to feel you are an emotionally strong parent who can teach him how to be calm.

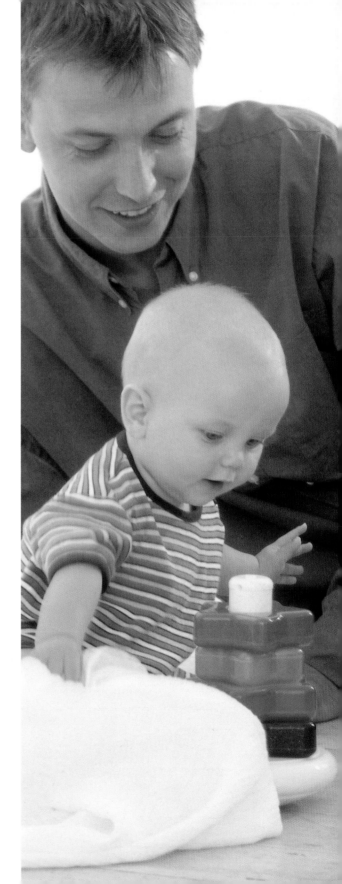

crying &
separations

Over the years, there have been many advocates of leaving babies and toddlers to cry. Mothers were told their babies were just "exercising their lungs" or that continually picking up a crying baby would "spoil him". More recently, spells of crying have been used to train babies to go to sleep and establish clear bedtime routines. There is no denying that these techniques work!

An uncomforted child will stop crying eventually if there is no response. But there are real costs. In this chapter we'll explore the research that reveals how stress from prolonged crying and separations can affect a baby's developing brain. We will also look at the wonderful long-term investment you make when you comfort your crying baby consistently.

All about crying

Babies are genetically programmed to call out for comfort when distressed. Crying is your baby's intense bid for you to help her with her overwhelming feelings and frightening bodily sensations because her brain is not yet developed enough for her to manage these on her own. Babies do not cry to exercise their lungs, to control you, or just for the hell of it. They cry when they are unhappy and need to alert you because something is really bothering them, either physically or emotionally. They are crying for your help.

ANIMAL INSIGHTS

All infant mammals, not just the human species, are genetically programmed to cry as a way of communicating their need for help with their painful separation distress. Research has shown that if a puppy is taken away from his mother, he can cry 700 times in 15 minutes.[1]

Why babies cry

Four million years ago, humans walked on two legs for the first time. Because this led to the freeing up of their arms to accomplish complex tasks, over time intelligence increased. The bipedal shift meant the human pelvis became narrower and, as intellectual capacities increased, the brain grew bigger. The evolutionary solution regarding childbirth was for the human infant to be born very immature because otherwise the enlarged head would never get through the mother's narrowed pelvis. So of all mammals the human is the most immature at birth. In fact, it has to complete its gestation outside the womb. Sigmund Freud was right when he said the human infant comes into the world "not quite finished". You need to think of your newborn as an external fetus.

■ **Yes she is that raw. Yes she is that sensitive. Yes she is that vulnerable to stress.**

Your baby will cry for many reasons. She will cry because she is tired or hungry or over-stimulated by too much adult fussing. She also moves easily into fear of threat and shock – the shock of the too bright, too harsh, too cold, too hot, too sudden. The amygdala in the lower brain, which functions as a detector of potential threat, is perfectly on line at birth.

Imagine her world. How can she know that the noisy liquidizer is not a predator that will come and attack her? How can she cope with the shock of being undressed and immersed in water when you lower her into a bath?

■ **At first it can be hard to work out what her crying means.**

But over time you will be able to read her cries more and more accurately. You will learn, for example, to tell a hungry cry from a tired cry. That said, there will be times when you will not know what the crying is about. This doesn't matter. What matters is that you calm her down and that you have the mental and emotional space in your mind to really hear and take seriously her panic and her pain.

■ **How long does all this crying continue?**

The first three months are often the worst. Crying usually peaks when the baby is three to six weeks old and then abates at around 12 to 16 weeks. Sheila Kitzinger suggests that

"Over time you will be able to read her cries more and more accurately."

crying lessens at this time because, by then, babies are more mobile and can grasp and play with things, so they no longer cry from boredom or frustration.[2]

Older babies and toddlers will still cry when cold, hungry, tired, or ill, although the shock of the world has dramatically lessened. But they are awash with new feelings. They suffer from states of panicky separation distress and are increasingly clear about likes and dislikes, what frightens them or displeases them. In the pre-verbal child, crying often means "no". "No, I don't want you to put me down; it makes me panic." "No, I don't want to be put on a stranger's lap; I was so settled in your arms." "No, I hate the feel of that jumper."[3]

"Help me cope with the world"

If you consistently soothe your child's distress over the years, and take any anguished crying seriously, highly effective stress response systems can be established in his brain. These will enable him to cope well with stress in later life. [4]

When a baby is left howling in her room:

● High levels of toxic stress hormones wash over her brain.

● There is a withdrawal of opioids (chemicals that promote feelings of well-being) in her brain.[6]

● The brain and body's stress response systems can become hardwired for over-sensitivity.

● Pain circuits in the brain are activated, just as they would be if she was hurt physically.[7]

■ **All this panic response means high levels of stress chemicals washing over a baby's brain.**

These chemicals are not dangerous in themselves, but as the following pages will show, it's a different story if they are left swirling round her brain for long periods in bouts of prolonged crying, and no one takes her panic seriously and comforts her. Distancing yourself from her distress, whatever some sleep training books may tell you, or even worse, an angry response to your baby's crying (although sometimes you may feel like it) is never appropriate.

Prolonged crying

Let's be clear at the outset – it is not crying itself that can affect a child's developing brain. It doesn't. It is prolonged, uncomforted distress. So I'm not advocating rushing to your child as soon as her bottom lip starts to wobble or after a short burst of protest crying that lasts a few minutes (perhaps because she couldn't have her favourite chocolate). Prolonged crying is the type of crying that any sensitive parent (or, for that matter, anyone sensitive to the despair of others) will be able to recognise as a desperate calling for help. It is the type of crying that goes on and on and on, and eventually stops when the child is either completely exhausted and falls asleep or, in a hopeless state, realizes that help is not going to come.

■ **If a baby is left to cry like this too often, a stress response system in her brain may be affected for life.**

There is a wealth of scientific studies from all over the world showing how early stress can result in enduring negative changes in a baby's brain. As we will see on the following pages, a child who has experienced periods of prolonged crying can develop an over-sensitive stress-response system that may affect her throughout life. This can mean that all too often her perception of the world and what is happening to her will be coloured by a sense of threat and anxiety, even when everything is perfectly safe.[5]

Q Can a baby manipulate or control a parent through crying?

■ Parents may wonder if their baby is using crying to manipulate them, especially when they hear comments from well-meaning friends and family such as "Just leave him. He's just trying to control you. Give in now and you will suffer later". We now know this is neurobiologically inaccurate.

■ To control an adult, a baby needs the power of clear thought, and for that he needs the brain chemical glutamate to be working well in his frontal lobes (see page 18). But the glutamate system is not properly established in a baby's brain, so that means he is not capable of thinking much about anything, let alone how to manipulate his parents.

■ Some parents cut off from their child's pain, and hear it as "just crying". This can be a result of their own upbringing. Because no one responded when they were babies, they are now unable to feel their child's distress.

What's happening in your baby's brain?

Parents would never dream of leaving their baby in a room full of toxic fumes that could damage her brain. Yet many parents leave their baby in a state of prolonged, uncomforted distress, not knowing that she is at risk from toxic levels of stress chemicals washing over her brain.

Earlier generations of parents let their babies cry because it "exercised their lungs", having no idea how vulnerable the infant brain is to stress. In a crying baby, the stress hormone cortisol is released by the adrenal glands. If the child is soothed and comforted, the level of cortisol goes down again, but if the child is left to cry on and on, the level of cortisol remains high. This is a potentially dangerous situation, because, over a prolonged period, cortisol can reach toxic levels that may damage key structures and systems in a developing brain. Cortisol is a slow-acting chemical that can stay in the brain at high levels for hours, and in clinically depressed people, for days or even weeks.

This micrograph shows the structure of cortisol, a hormone produced in response to stress.

GETTING STRESSED

As distress levels build up in a crying baby, a hormonal chain reaction is set in motion. It starts deep within the lower brain, in a structure called the hypothalamus: the body's general hormone controller. The hypothalamus produces a hormone that triggers the nearby pituitary gland to release another hormone called ACTH. This, in turn, stimulates the adrenal glands (just above the kidneys) to release the stress hormone cortisol. Cortisol then washes over the body and brain. This stress response system is known as the HPA axis.

A distressed baby has a highly activated HPA axis that keeps pumping out cortisol. This can be compared to a central heating system that can't be switched off. [8] Comforting the baby triggers the off-switch. Brain scans show that early stress can cause the HPA axis to become permanently wired for over-sensitivity.

HYPOTHALAMUS
This area of the brain produces hormones called "releasing factors" that control the pituitary gland. When a child experiences prolonged, uncomforted distress, the hypothalamus releases corticotropin-releasing factor (CRF).

pituitary gland

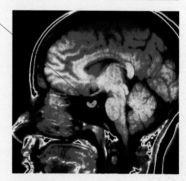

PITUITARY GLAND
This pea-sized gland in the brain has overall control of some of our most important hormones. When it is stimulated by CRF, the pituitary responds by releasing a hormone called adrenocorticotropin (ACTH), which travels to the adrenal glands.

ACTH is released by the pituitary gland

cortisol washes over the body and brain

ADRENAL GLANDS
These two glands are located one on top of each kidney. When they are stimulated by ACTH, they produce the hormone cortisol. In the short term, cortisol can help us to respond to stress by boosting the level of glucose in the blood. But if the brain is exposed to a prolonged high level of cortisol, cells in key parts of the brain may die.

Storing up problems

Increasingly, scientists are linking stress in infancy and childhood to the soaring numbers of people suffering from anxiety and depressive disorders from adolescence onwards. Integral to these disorders is an over-sensitive stress system in the brain. We have seen from the research how early stress can cause long-lasting changes in the stress response system in a child's brain.

In later life an over-sensitive stress system may lead to:

- fear of being alone
- separation anxiety
- panic attacks
- smoking addiction.

Wired for stress

What does an over-sensitive stress response system mean for a child as she grows up? It's a bit like having a faulty burglar alarm in her head, which keeps going off with the smallest thing. Her brain can react to small stressors, that other people take in their stride, as if they were big and threatening. Also, being wired for stress in early life can leave a child vulnerable to depression, anxiety disorders, stress-related physical illness, and alcohol abuse in later life.[9] This is particularly the case with children who were left to cry as babies and then experienced a childhood of strict discipline with little warm physical affection to compensate.

■ **Early stress can cause cell death in a very important structure in the brain.**

This structure is the hippocampus, found deep within the lower mammalian brain, which plays a role in long-term memory. In the brain scans of children who have suffered intense uncomforted distress, the hippocampus appears somewhat shrunken because of cell death within its tissues. We don't know exactly how much this cell death affects a child's working memory. However, adults with a shrunken

"An over-sensitive stress response system...is like a faulty burglar alarm."

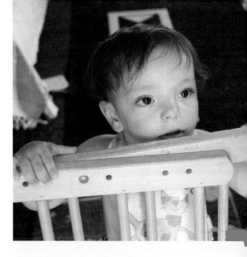

hippocampus score lower on memory and verbal reasoning tasks.[10] Brain scans have shown that the hippocampus of a very stressed child resembles that of an aged person. Some scientists regard stress in early life as a risk factor for accelerated ageing of this part of the brain.

■ Are all children affected the same way?

Science does not have a precise answer to this. Because each child is unique, the effects of prolonged crying cannot be predicted with any certainty. Some children may get away with developing a mild neurosis in later life because early stress has altered key systems in their brain, while others with genetic vulnerability and additional life stresses, such as suffering loss or being bullied, may later develop a full-blown anxiety or depressive disorder.

"The stress of unrelieved crying can leave an infant's brain in a disrupted state."

Studies on other mammals with lower brain structures and chemical systems like ours show that early stress can leave an infant's brain in a highly disrupted biochemical state. Essential systems involving the emotion chemicals opioids, noradrenaline, dopamine, and serotonin, which are still being established in an immature brain, may be badly affected, resulting in chemical imbalances in the brain.[11]

When dopamine and noradrenaline levels are low, this can make it more difficult for a child to focus and concentrate; this can lead to learning difficulties in comparison with other children. Low serotonin levels are one of the key components in many forms of depression and also in violent behaviour.

Opioids are vitally important for diminishing feelings of fear and stress, which is why deactivation of opioids in parts of the brain can lead to increases in negative feelings and stress, and decreases in positive feelings.[12]

Case study

Sleep training Billy
Bedtime had always been difficult for Billy and when he was ten months old, his mother was keen to try sleep-training.

When she left him each night, Billy cried for her desperately but she decided to tough it out for a week or two. Sure enough, over time, Billy stopped crying when he was put down and his mother counted this as a success. "He never cries now when I leave him," she said. Billy was also separated from his mother for much of the day, as she was at work. At his nursery, he had very little physical contact because the staff did not pick up the babies very often.

Billy has become less responsive during the day and other relatives now worry about his quietness. One family member has commented that "It's as if he isn't really there any more". Some people think babies and children are not capable of depression, but they are.

The science of comforting

In the stress of intense crying, your baby's autonomic nervous system, which automatically regulates the internal workings of the body, is thrown off balance. The result is physical and emotional upheaval. A small child cannot control her bodily arousal – but your love and comfort will.

BRAIN STORY

There is a key anti-anxiety chemical in the brain called GABA (gamma-aminobutyric acid) that naturally inhibits high levels of cortisol (see page 40) and calms the lower brain's threat-detection system (amygdala). Research shows that if young mammals are left alone or in a prolonged state of distress, this can have a marked influence on how the genes for GABA unfold in the brain. This can alter the brain's sensitivity to stress, resulting in an agitated attitude to life for much of the time. In the long term, an altered GABA system can lead to anxiety disorders and depression. Without an effective anti-anxiety chemical system, humans may feel:

• psychologically fragile
• prone to fear or anger (to a degree that is inappropriate to the situation)
• less able to calm themselves
• easily thrown by life's minor stressors.

An altered GABA system, resulting from too much uncomforted distress in childhood, may make adults prone to using alcohol for stress relief. This is because alcohol artificially regulates the brain's GABA system.[15]

What happens when your child cries

When your child cries in an intense, desperate way, her bodily arousal system, the autonomic nervous system (which is still maturing after birth), is way out of balance. While she is distressed, the aroused (or "sympathetic") branch of this system is overactive and the calm and centred (or "parasympathetic") branch is underactive. This means that your baby's body is primed for action, "fight-or-flight", as high levels of adrenaline are released. She is experiencing an increased heart rate; higher blood pressure; sweating; tense muscles; faster breathing; and suppressed appetite (because the digestive system is conserving blood and energy to prepare the muscles for action).[13]

It is up to you to bring everything back into balance. Your comforting activates the vagus nerve (see opposite), which belongs to the "slow down and relax" parasympathetic branch of the autonomic nervous system. The more responsive you are, the greater your regulation of her body arousal systems will be, and the more long-lasting the effects.[14]

The dangers of hyperarousal

When you soothe your distressed child, you regulate her autonomic nervous system. Research shows that if a child's need for comfort is not met with emotional responsiveness and soothing, this system can, over time, become wired for bodily hyperarousal.[16] This can make life a stressful and exhausting affair. It can also result in all manner of physical ailments in later life: for example, problems with breathing (such as asthma), heart disease, eating and digestive disorders, poor sleep, high blood pressure, panic attacks, muscular tension, headaches, and chronic fatigue.[17] There is also a wealth of research material (known as brain–gut studies) linking uncomforted stress in early life with irritable bowel syndrome. In a recent survey, less than 50 percent of the men and barely 30 percent of the women who took part had regular bowel habits.[18]

Many parents are simply not aware that a child's bodily arousal system is still developing after birth and that it is supersensitive to stressful experiences such as being left to cry. So leaving your baby "to settle herself" can have long-term adverse consequences for her body and brain. She cannot bring her autonomic nervous system back into balance; only you can do that.

"Many parents are simply not aware that their child's bodily arousal system is still developing after birth…"

BRAIN STORY – THE VAGUS NERVE

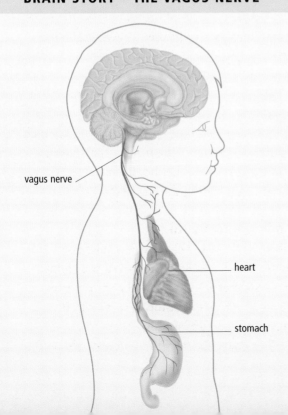

vagus nerve

heart

stomach

Comforting a screaming child activates her vagus nerve, which is found in the brain stem. This nerve, which is known appropriately as the "wanderer", regulates the function of major organs all over the body. As your soothing takes effect, the vagus nerve will rapidly restore order to key body systems disrupted by distress – rebalancing the digestive system, heart rate, breathing, and the functioning of the immune system.

One of the greatest gifts you can give your child is to help her establish good vagal tone. This means that the vagus nerve works well in all its calming, regulating functions. Research shows that good vagal tone is linked to better emotional balance; clear thinking; improved powers of attention; and a more efficient immune system. People with good vagal tone tend to be nice to have around.

How to soothe your baby

In order to activate the calm and centred branch in your child's autonomic nervous system, you need to quieten yourself down first. Breathing techniques are great. As soon as you do some effective deep breathing, your whole system will calm, and your body will start to send messages to your brain, telling it to stop pumping out high levels of stress chemicals. If you find this difficult, it's worth going to a meditation class that teaches breathing techniques.

Don't try and calm your baby at the same time as doing something else. For emotional and bodily regulation to take place, she needs to feel that her distress is the only thing on your mind.

If your crying baby is not in need of physical attention such as a feed or nappy change, then being next to your calm body will soothe her. Sometimes this works immediately, or it may take a while to happen. In effect, you are using your mature bodily arousal system to help regulate her very immature one.

■ **Do things that stimulate the anti-stress chemical systems in her brain.**

Three key comforts release the calming chemical oxytocin in a baby's brain in a way that can drop levels of stress chemicals back to base rate. These are touch and massage, sucking, and warmth.

■ **Touch and massage** Most babies will stop crying if they are picked up. Close bodily contact regulates their bodily arousal system, activating the calm and centred branch, as well as releasing oxytocin.[19]

If you want to use baby massage, go to a class to learn how. The wrong sort of touch is dysregulating and over-stimulating and will make your baby cry more.

■ **Sucking** Help your child to find her fist or thumb to suck. You can also offer your fingers. If your child is absolutely inconsolable, then, and only then, use a dummy. Never use it as a plug when she is not distressed. This is because the mouth is vital for communication and the forming of sounds pre-speech. It's also vital for oral exploration (such as putting toys in her mouth). You can end up feeling ruled by the dummy because the child won't go anywhere without it.[20]

■ **Warmth releases oxytocin.** Keep the room temperature at about 21°C/70°F. Hold your baby cuddled close to your body or snuggled in a flannelette sheet. You could get in a warm bath with a stressed-out newborn.

■ **Other strategies you can try.**

■ **Movement and rocking** Babies love rhythmical movement, particularly being carried around, being pushed in the pram, or being in the car. It is thought that the rhythm triggers associations of being carried around in the security of the womb. Make sure that you do not rock too hard, however, as this can have the same effect on the brain as shaking, which can cause burst blood vessels.[21]

"Most babies will stop crying if you pick them up. Close bodily contact regulates their bodily arousal system."

"Your touch helps to soothe me"

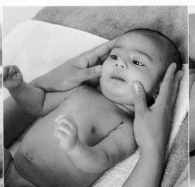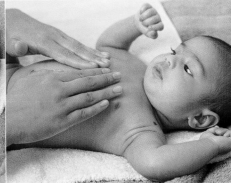

You can massage your baby from about two weeks old. It is a good way to comfort and calm him and to help strengthen the bond between you. Choose a time when he is awake and alert and you are both relaxed.

Lay your baby on a soft towel and make sure he is warm and comfortable. Starting at the crown of his head, massage very lightly across his cheeks and down to his shoulders.

Massage gently down his body using a downward motion. Talk to him as you massage, and engage in lovely eye-to-eye contact. If your baby loses interest, then try again another day rather than persist.

■ **Low sound** Let your baby listen to the washing machine or spin dryer, as the sound is evocative of the security of the womb. You could also play a recording of your heart beat, but this is often only effective if used from the start after birth.

■ **Provide novelty** This activates dopamine in the brain. If your baby is screaming with sheer boredom, think of ways to provide novelty. Keep small toys, such as a finger puppet, in your bag to amuse her on a journey.

■ **Avoid overstimulation** If you think your child is over-stimulated, take her with you into a quiet, low-lit room.

Hard-to-comfort babies

About one in five healthy babies is highly sensitive in the first few weeks. These hard-to-comfort babies can be like this due to genetic make-up, stress in the womb, or a difficult birth. Research shows that if a mother is repeatedly stressed in the last three months of pregnancy, high levels of the stress chemicals cortisol and glutamate can be transmitted through the placenta into the brain of the unborn child. So it's vitally important that you get as much soothing and comfort as you can in pregnancy. If you have lots of stress in your life once your baby is born, this can also result in a baby who cries more. If you have a hard-to-comfort baby, she will need a lot of soothing and comforting, and to do that well that you will need soothing and comforting, too, from family and friends.

■ **Make sure that you're not left in a desperate, isolated state with a screaming baby.**

Put your baby in her pram and go to the park, café, or a group with other parents. Isolation is extremely bad for brain chemistry. It can result in a dramatic drop in levels of serotonin (a key mood stabilizer), leading to aggressive impulses. It can also lower levels of dopamine (a positive arousal chemical), so you can feel awful over and above the distress you feel about your baby's screaming.[22]

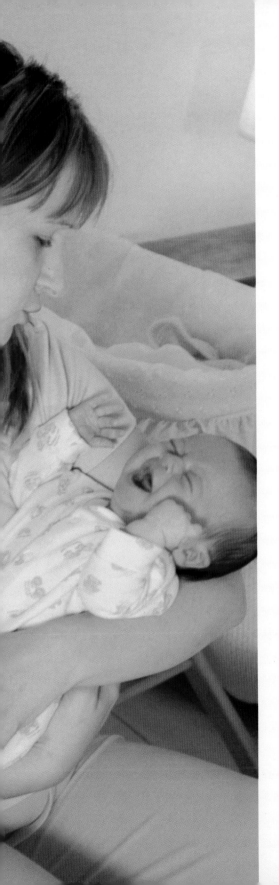

Q I have tried everything and I feel demoralized – what do I do now?

Let's be really clear. No one is disputing the fact that it can be totally exhausting when you are endlessly comforting a distressed child who just won't stop crying. When you have tried everything, you can feel impotent and demoralized, and want to burst into tears. The following may help:

■ Remember that "this too shall pass". This phase usually lasts for only the first three months, yet many worn-out parents think that it will be a life sentence.

■ Remember what a long-term gift you are giving your child when you calm her. All that calming time is an investment for the future, regulating her emotional and physical systems, which means that later she will have the ability to manage stress well.

Q Why do I feel like screaming when my baby is screaming?

Your baby's emotional states are so raw and primitive that they can easily trigger one or more of the three alarm systems in your lower brain: RAGE, FEAR, or SEPARATION DISTRESS. At the same time, your high levels of stress chemicals can block the release of your positive arousal chemicals, such as dopamine and opioids. You need emotional regulation. Ring a health visitor, join a parents' group, cry in your partner's arms, or get support from a counsellor or therapist (see also Looking After You, page 269).

Separations and time apart

When your baby reaches six to eight months of age, separation anxiety starts to kick in and often continues in some form until she is well over five years old. Early on, your baby will start to panic if you are out of her sight. Take her intense feelings seriously. Remember you are her world, her everything, you represent her very safety.

Eight-year-old Flint, one of the chimpanzees observed in the wild by biologist Jane Goodall, became depressed and lethargic after the death of his mother. Within three weeks he too was dead. Jane Goodall found that after the death of a mother, an infant chimpanzee, even though nutritionally independent, might be unable to recover from the pain of grief and so may die. The SEPARATION DISTRESS system in the chimp's lower brain has virtually the same neuroanatomy and chemical systems as that in a human brain.

A little bit of understanding

Your baby is not being "needy" or "clingy". The SEPARATION DISTRESS system, located in the lower brain (see page 24), is genetically programmed to be hypersensitive. In earlier stages of evolution, it was very dangerous for an infant to be away from her mother and if she didn't cry to alert her parents to her whereabouts, she would not survive. The development of the frontal lobes (higher brain) naturally inhibits this system, and as adults we learn to bring it under control with cognitive distractions, such as reading a book or watching TV.

■ If you are not there – how does she know you have not gone forever?

You can't tell her that you will soon return, because the verbal centres in her brain aren't on line yet. When she learns to crawl and toddle, let her follow you – yes, even into the toilet.

Prising her off you and shutting her in a playpen is not only very cruel; it can also lead to long-term adverse effects. She may move into panic, which means a dramatic and dangerous rise in those stress chemicals in her brain. This can lead to the wiring of an over-active FEAR system that may affect her later in life, resulting in phobias, obsessions, or fearful avoidance behaviour. Gradually, she will become more secure with you in the house, particularly as she becomes verbal. She will learn that if you go on your own to the toilet, she is unlikely to never see you again!

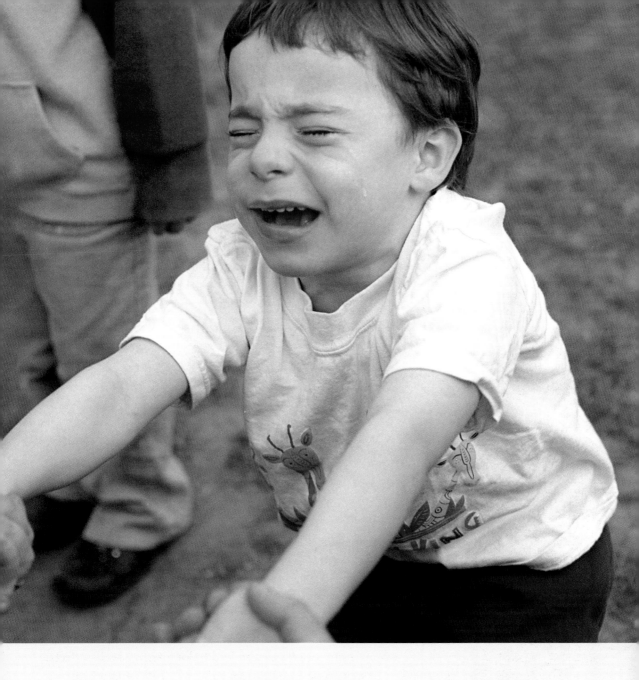

"When you leave me, it hurts so much"

When a loved person isn't there and a child is too young to understand, it can be extremely painful. You can't just say to a child who is missing his Mummy – "look, don't feel like that", yet adults often give that sort of message to small children. When we prise a distressed child away from his parent and urge him "not to be silly", we entirely underestimate the power of the massive hormonal reactions in his brain and body.

BRAIN STORY

This brain scan of a child from a Romanian orphanage shows what can happen to the brain when a child receives basic physical care but is deprived of love, affection, and comfort.

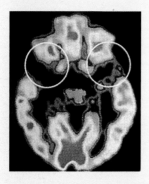

The black areas in this brain scan show inactive areas in the temporal lobes – part of the brain which is vital for processing and regulating emotions. Temporal lobe inactivity can result in poor social and emotional intelligence.

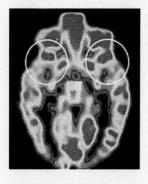

This is the brain scan of a child who has received loving parenting. In contrast to the brain scan of the Romanian child there are few black areas, meaning that the temporal lobes are fully active.[25]

▨ Separation hurts small humans in much the same way as a physical pain.

When a child is suffering because of the absence of a parent, the same parts of the brain are activated as when he or she is feeling physical pain.[23] So the language of loss is very much the language of pain. It does not make sense to comfort a physical pain, say from a cut knee, but not feel that it is necessary to address an emotional one such as separation distress. Yet sadly, that's what many parents find themselves doing. They are reluctant to take on board the fact that the emotional pain of their child is just as real. This is a neurobiological fact that should be respected by all.

▨ We sometimes push our children to independence long before they are ready.

Perhaps fuelled by a fear of our own dependency, our parenting traditions can push children into early separations. Sending children to boarding school at a young age is an example of this. A child aged eight can still be hypersensitive to separation distress and find it difficult to be away from parents for a long time. A child's emotional pain should always be taken seriously in key decisions about how long times apart should be, and how often and with whom the child should be left. The brain's GABA system (see page 44) is sensitive to very subtle environmental changes, such as separation from a parent. Studies link separation in early life to alterations in this anti-anxiety system.[24]

▨ Even short-term separations may do harm.

Some studies have found long-term changes in the HPA axis (see page 40) in the child's brain from even short-term separations, when the child was left with an unfamiliar carer. This stress response system is instrumental in how well we manage stress in later life. It is very vulnerable to being adversely affected by early stress.[26] Other studies link separation in early life with depression. Studies with higher mammals reveal that infants separated from their mothers stopped crying but then moved into a depressed response. Play with friends ceased and objects in the room were ignored. At the time of going to sleep, there was an increase in crying and agitation. If the separation continued, there was further withdrawal, leading to lethargy and a more entrenched depression.

In the 1960s, research showed that some children who were left with unfamiliar people for several days went into a full-blown bereavement response, which left them reeling from the trauma years later. The children in the study had been left with well-meaning adults or placed in a residential nursery for several days while their mothers were in hospital. Their fathers would come to visit, but basically they were left with adults whom they did not know.

One little boy, separated from his mother for just 11 days, stopped eating, cried endlessly, and repeatedly threw himself on the floor in despair. Six years later, he was still very angry with his mother. The researchers observed countless other children who had been left for several days and were in a state of yearning without end. Many would stare, for hours at a time, at the door through which their mother had left. They did not want to play; they just wanted to watch the door. This research, much of which is on film, changed attitudes throughout the world towards children visiting parents in hospital.[27]

■ But isn't stress good for you?

Some people justify leaving a child uncomfortable (for instance, during sleep training) by calling it "stress inoculation". But stress inoculation means introducing a child to moderately stressful situations to help her to handle stress better. For example, you might gently introduce a baby to a lovely warm swimming pool for the first time. People who say that a child screaming for a prolonged period is only experiencing moderate stress are deluding themselves.

"I'm addicted to Dad"

The brain chemistry of loving relationships is naturally addictive. When you hold your child, love him, soothe him, rock him in your arms, delight in him time after time, a very strong bond will develop between you. The bond will then mean that any tender loving contact with you will release natural opioids and oxytocin in your child's brain. When this happens, your child will be in a wonderful state of oneness and contentment.

The childcare question

There is a great deal of recent research showing improvements in cognitive performance (IQ) of a child who has attended a nursery before the age of five. Sadly, these positive changes have not been found to extend to emotional health and intelligence (EQ). Here we find that the opposite is true.

I believe all nurseries should have "emotional nurses", chosen for their calmness and emotional warmth.

These need to be people who frequently have opioids and oxytocin in dominance in their brain, probably because they were on the receiving end of warm parenting themselves, or good counselling or psychotherapy in later life.

In the UK, the almost phobic attitude to physical contact in schools (for fear of allegations of sexual abuse) is to the great detriment of children. We need a clear, well thought-out policy on touch that allows adults to comfort and hold young children in safe ways to activate their natural calming brain chemicals.

A problem with stress

Cortisol has its own natural peaks and troughs. It is naturally high in the morning and decreases as the day goes on. However, studies of children under five in nurseries have shown levels of cortisol rising rather than falling as the day goes on. What's more, as soon as the nursery children were with their parents again, their stress levels dropped dramatically. In one study, for 91 percent of children, cortisol rose at nursery, and for 75 percent of the children, it dropped when they returned home.[28] This research is worrying because a key stress response system in the brain can become wired for hypersensitivity early in life. Researchers found that toddlers in nurseries who played more with other children had lower cortisol levels than those who tended to play alone.

■ **Some parents think their child is fine at nursery, but her stress hormone levels may be very high.**

We know that a child can look fine and not be crying yet still be distressed. A famous research study called "The Strange Situation Test" showed that one year olds who didn't cry for their Mummy when she left the room had equally high levels of stress hormones as those who did. In other words, the one year olds had learnt at such a tender age to bottle up

"Cortisol is naturally high in the morning and decreases as the day goes on..."

"I don't want to be here"

Even a four year old may still be struggling with higher cortisol levels at nursery, so keep this in mind when you decide how long your child should spend there each day. Ideally don't lengthen the time away until your child has a good understanding of time frameworks and is confident that you will come back at the end of the session. Babies and toddlers can find long days at nursery particularly difficult because they have no sense of time and hence no notion of when or even if you will return.

their feelings. This is worrying because when small children do not appear to be upset they are very unlikely to get the comfort they need.[29]

■ **Nursery school children may become more difficult to manage later in childhood.**

The consequences of high levels of cortisol in nursery school children are already becoming apparent. Evidence suggests that when children are cared for extensively in a nursery early on, this can be associated with an increase in difficult relationships between parent and child and more aggression and non-compliance in the children.[30] It starts showing at age

"Toddlers who played more with other children had lower cortisol levels"

Q Sometimes I need to go away with work for a week or so. How will that affect my child long term?

It all depends on whom your child is left with. If your child is left with someone he knows and who is emotionally aware, such as a loving partner or family member, then your child will be fine. If this is not possible, there is worrying research to show that a child will react very badly if left with someone who is not able to provide emotional support.

two. The findings were particularly significant for babies who had spent 20 or more hours per week in nursery care during their first year.

The emotionally aware child minder

Leaving a child with a very good child minder or nanny during the day is fine, as long as that person is able to give emotionally warm one-to-one attention. But it isn't enough to give this attention to a baby or a child only when they are overtly showing signs of distress. Researchers have found that when nannies got on with something else, thinking that the child was fine (because she wasn't crying) the child's cortisol levels shot up.[31] So choose a nanny or childminder who adores little children, who is great at responding to both joy and distress, and who would rather talk to your child than read a magazine! When interviewing, ensure you sit in the

"Choose a nanny or childminder who adores little children and who is great at responding to joy and distress."

"I need to be comforted"

Anna hates it when her Mum leaves and is still crying in spite of all her mother's attempts to reassure her that she will be back to see her again at the end of the day.

Anna's child minder, Joanne, is ready to help her recover from her distress. She moves in quickly and lifts Anna into her arms, giving her all the time she needs to cry and grieve.

As Anna's sobs subside and she starts to feel safe, her cortisol levels fall and she begins to relax and play. Joanne stays with her to make sure she stays happy and content.

ANIMAL INSIGHTS

Touch is very important when an infant has been separated from its mother. In a study with monkeys, researchers found that the infant animals would choose the comfort of clinging to a cloth dummy over taking food when their mothers were absent.[32]

background and watch the carer interact and talk with your child for at least 30 minutes. Your personal observations will be worth a million references. Is there is laughter, delight, and a real feeling of warmth in the room between the prospective carer and your child? If so, then she is likely to be a source of opioid and dopamine activation, both of which are wonderful for the development of your child's social and emotional brain.

▪ Your child needs to be held in familiar arms when you are not there.

There is all the difference in the world between leaving your child with an unfamiliar minder and leaving her grieving for her "gone mummy" in the care of a calm, warm, loving person with whom she feels safe. If there are no loving arms for your little one, you are risking the activation of high levels of stress hormones in her brain. These hormones will deactivate the positive arousal hormones and your child will end up feeling awful. If your child is still crying when you leave, lift her into the arms of her minder. A good nanny or child minder should be able to soothe her painful feelings and amplify the positive ones. Holding and soothing will bring down her cortisol levels and activate a more positive chemistry in her brain.

▪ Early separations and depression may be linked.

The alarm response in the brain of a child stressed by separation from her mother is the same as that found in adults suffering from clinical depression – an illness reaching epidemic proportions in many parts of the world.[33] As we are not born with a gene for clinical depression, we need to look closely at the long-term effects of stressful childhood experience.

Amazing studies have been carried out into the brain chemistry of infant monkeys separated from their parents. Researcher Harry Harlow found that the unmothered infants became severely stressed and depressed. Many became abusive and neglectful mothers in their turn. In the worst cases, some failed to mother their own infants in later life.

"Mummy's gone, but I'm safe"

This little girl feels secure because the adults who care for her know that she needs help to manage separation from her Mum and Dad. When she is playing happily and seems fine, they give her the same attention as when she is crying or upset. They know that plenty of warm, emotionally responsive interaction and cuddles will help prevent her cortisol levels rising while she is separated from the people she loves.

The need to cling

Young mammals (animals and humans) cling to a secure adult whenever they feel unsafe. Some human parents get irritated about clinging, but animal parents don't. They don't have higher brains like ours, which question whether we should stop a child from doing it.

If a child clings to you, he is trying to bring down his high bodily arousal level and high levels of stress chemicals. He is also trying to activate the lovely brain chemicals that produce feelings of well-being (see page 86). He can't do any of this without you, as you are his secure neurochemical base. A child is not being naughty or "attention-seeking" by clinging to you; he is feeling unsafe, and needs your support. In clinging to you, he is trying to change the emotion chemical balance in his brain to a calmer and more positive chemistry.

What research tells us

Studies have shown that by the end of the first year, mothers who had attended promptly to their crying babies had children who cried much less than those whose mothers had left them to cry.[34] Although some people think that a child becomes clingy because he has been cuddled or loved too much, or "spoilt" by attention, there is no evidence that supports the theory that anxious attachment is a result of excessive parental affection or attention.

Prolonged clinging is far more likely where a parent has not handled the child's dependency needs well. The parents may have pushed the child to be more independent (often by

"A child is not being naughty by clinging to you – he is feeling unsafe."

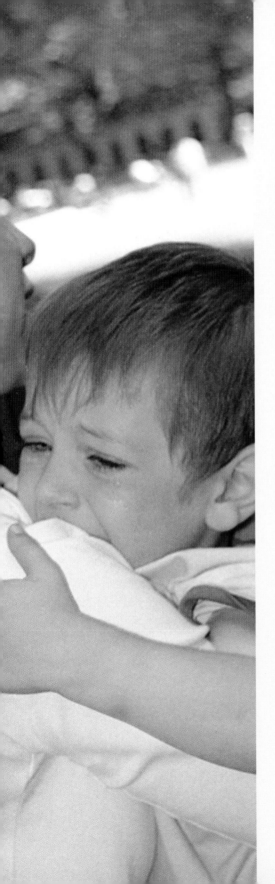

Q What should I do if my child clings to me at the school gates?

The best thing to do is to avoid a quick getaway when he's screaming for you to stay. Rushing off will make matters worse by sending your child's stress chemicals and stress hormones sky-high.

■ Try to have quality time with him before you leave. Hold him really close. This will activate oxytocin and opioids in his brain and will make him feel calmer. It also means that he "finds" you before he "loses" you. When you leave, he will have a memory of a calm, soothing mother, rather than one who rushes away.

■ Activate his SEEKING system (see page 94), for example, by showing him the sandpit and encouraging him to start exploring. Take time to introduce him to a friend.

■ Make an arrangement with a warm, kind teacher whom he knows, and who he likes to pick him up in her arms, and use distraction to activate his frontal lobes; for example, by showing him a butterfly. Slip away quietly, knowing that you have given him that vital opioid fix in his brain before you go.

■ If your child is repeatedly distressed when you leave, give him something to remind him of you, such as a scarf that smells of you or a warm, loving message on a Dictaphone so he can play your voice whenever he chooses.

"When children feel safe in the world, they will turn to it naturally"

CONSIDER THIS...

If you respond with compassion and patience to the clinging phase, it is a great investment for your child's ability to be independent in later life. If each time he has wanted to cling, you have picked him up and held him, he will start to feel very safe in his being-in-the-world. As he develops, he will then naturally start to turn away from you and explore the world for ever-increasing lengths of time. He will be just fine spending longer and longer times away from you with his friends, knowing that you are always there as a secure base, to which he will always return for emotional re-fuelling before going off again.

literally pushing him away when he felt the need to cling to them) when he was still in this genetically programmed dependent stage of his development.

When the clinging stops

Parents often worry that their child's grief at partings and goodbyes will never end. But who ever heard of a teenager who bursts into tears when his parents announce that they are going to the cinema for the evening? As your child grows up, the SEPARATION DISTRESS system in his lower brain naturally becomes far less sensitive. This is largely because the development of the higher brain naturally inhibits this system. Then, in puberty, the increases in testosterone and oestrogen suppress the system even more. So when people say, "If I give into his clinging now it will never end", it is inaccurate in terms of a child's body-brain development.

Some children whose clinging has not met with an emotionally responsive reaction can move into a false independence. It is extremely shame-inducing for a child to be in a state of desperate need and meet with a rebuff or criticism, or to be told to be a big boy. As a way of dealing with the pain, some children take a "I don't need my Mummy!" stance, successfully hardening their hearts and moving into an emotional numbing against attachment needs. This can cause all manner of misery, loving in torment, and fear of closeness in adult relationships (see The Chemistry of Love, pages 182–215).

So when you have a clinging child, remember what an investment you are making in his long-term mental health if you respond with empathy and soothing. Remember the long-term anti-stress effects of repeated activation of oxytocin in the brain from all that physical affection. Remember the studies with other mammals that showed that if infants received loving touch, they were better able to handle stress, had a far less fearful response to life, were psychologically stronger, and even aged better!

Key points

■ **Parents can be trained** out of their instinct to comfort a child, and a child can be trained out of his instinct to cry ... but science is now showing us the costs.

■ **Prolonged uncomforted** crying can adversely affect key systems in the brain and body, leading to a vulnerability to depression, anxiety disorders, and other physical and mental illness in later life.

■ **Being left to cry** means a child learns that he is abandoned just at the time when he needs help.

■ **Early in a child's life** separations must be considered carefully. When they are necessary, parents should always leave their child with an emotionally responsive, warm adult.

sleep &
bedtimes

Sleep training or co-sleeping? The debate has
been raging passionately over the decades and
the level of emotion it stirs up in people can be
truly intense. Maybe a child's cry as the bedroom
door closes contributes more than we realize to
people not being able to reflect calmly on their
options. This chapter presents the latest scientific
thinking on the subject of where and how your
child should sleep, and looks at current research
into SIDS. I hope it will help parents to make an
informed choice about what to do with their
children at bedtime and during the night.

Getting your child to sleep

At bedtime, you should have one clear aim: to make your baby or child feel that all is well in his world. If you are successful, you will prevent stress chemicals being activated in his brain and leave him feeling very safe and loved as he drops off to sleep. There are things that can help you to achieve this, whether you choose to co-sleep or settle your child in his own bed.

CONSIDER THIS...

If your baby has difficulty sinking into a blissful sleep, bodily contact with you will help him to relax. Ideally, you should lie quietly next to him until he drops off. If your baby is still sleeping in a cot, stay close and offer him calming contact by keeping a soothing hand resting on his body.

The facts about children and sleep

First – babies are awful sleepers. When we accept this, maybe we will stop seeing a wakeful baby as some kind of parental failure. Research into the sleeping patterns of babies and young children has established that:

■ **Babies are prone to wake far more than adults,** as their average sleep cycle lasts only 50 minutes, compared with our 90-minute cycle.

■ **Persistent or recurring infant sleep problems** in the preschool years are very common.

■ **Approximately 25 percent of children** under five years old have some type of sleep problem.

■ **Up to 20 percent** of parents report a problem with infant crying or irritability in the first three months of life.[1]

Calming the brain at bedtime

Your primary aim at bedtime is to bring your child down from a superalert awake state, by activating the calming brain chemical oxytocin and the sleep hormone melatonin. The most likely way of achieving this is by establishing a soothing routine. Whenever this is repeated, there is a chance that it will activate the same calming chemicals in the brain.

"Babies are awful sleepers...they are prone to wake far more than adults."

▥ Whatever you do, stay calm.

If stress chemicals are being strongly activated in your own brain you can't expect to bring your child down from an aroused state. Your tone is everything, and if you are tense, uptight, irritated, or angry your attempts to be calm will be false ones. All too easily, your stress and anger can activate the alarm systems in your child's brain, making him feel too unsafe to go to sleep. On the other hand, if your brain is strongly activating opioids, and your voice is gentle, quiet, and soothing, this can be deeply reassuring for your child and he is likely to respond brilliantly to you.

"Your primary aim at bedtime
is to bring your child down from
a superalert state."

▥ Snuggle up and read a story.

While you read, your body contact with your child will activate oxytocin in his brain, which can make him feel sleepy. Listening to the story will engage your child's frontal lobes (higher brain), the part that naturally inhibits motoric impulses – such as the desire to jump about on the bed.

Try and set up a magical atmosphere. Dim the lights (the dark will activate melatonin) or use safe candles. You could also play soothing music, which can lower bodily arousal levels.

▥ Don't give food that will keep him awake.

Avoid giving your child protein food, such as meat or fish, in the two hours before bedtime, as it activates dopamine (a brain stimulant). Chocolate is not a good idea either, as it contains the stimulant drug caffeine. If your child is hungry, offer him a carbohydrate food such as a banana, as it activates serotonin in the brain, which can help to make him feel sleepy.

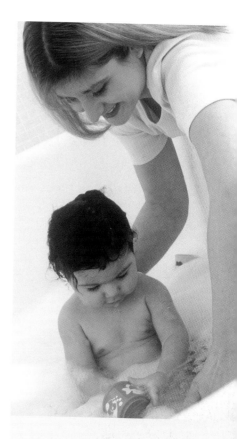

"I know it is
getting close
to bedtime"

A winding-down routine before bedtime, with a bath followed by a story, will help to regulate your child's bodily arousal system. She is also highly dependent on you to regulate her brain chemistry in a way that prepares her for sleep.

"Once his feelings are out in the open, you can find ways of soothing him."

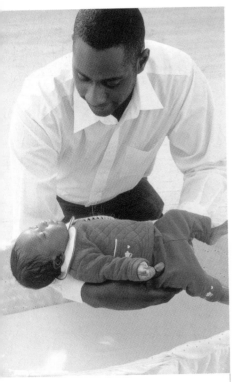

Having a baby with all his erratic sleeping patterns is hard work for a parent, but it is not true that you can never have an evening to yourself. Let him fall asleep in your arms and then quietly tiptoe away.

◼ Avoid activating the FEAR system in your child's lower brain.

If your child is frightened of the dark, keep a nightlight in the room. You could call it the "safe fairy" who will watch over the child as he sleeps.[2] Take his fears and anxieties seriously and reassure him. If you don't, his brain may keep triggering high levels of glutamate, noradrenaline, and CRF (corticotropin-releasing factor), moving his body into a state of hyperarousal. When this happens, no human being will feel at all sleepy.

◼ You may choose to lie down next to your child while he goes to sleep.

If you do this, there should be no talking. Pretend to be asleep yourself; concentrate on your own deep breathing. The skin-to-skin contact will regulate your child's bodily arousal system and strengthen the bond between the two of you. The more calm you are, the more calm he will be. Consider the brain chemicals involved. Body contact activates the release of opioids and oxytocin – and oxytocin can promote sleepiness. Once your child is sleeping, you can leave to have your evening.

◼ If your child is too anxious to let you go, it's worth asking him why.

An anxious three year old who is suffering from the activation of the brain's FEAR or SEPARATION DISTRESS system is likely to ask for another drink, a pee, or his dummy, when he is really trying to say that he is frightened. Ask him what he is afraid of, or what he thinks might happen when you leave the room. Once his feelings are out in the open and talked about, you can find ways of soothing him, such as giving him an item of your clothing to go to bed with, tucking him up in a special way, or reassuring him with words and cuddles. Use your emotionally warm presence to activate opioids in his brain, as these chemicals naturally inhibit SEPARATION DISTRESS.

Q I have to resettle my child continually, every night –
  what am I doing wrong?

If you are finding it difficult to get your child off to sleep night after night, you need to ask yourself some questions. First, are you being calm enough, still enough? The human brain is acutely sensitive to emotional atmospheres and to picking up emotions that you may be feeling strongly but are trying not to show.

Is there an atmosphere of peace and safety in his room, with dimmed lights to activate the sleep hormone melatonin? Is your child tired enough? Has he recently eaten protein or chocolate, or had a fizzy drink, all of which will wake him up? Is he getting enough physical activity during the day? Make sure that he plays outdoors during the afternoon whenever possible; the more daylight he gets, the better he will sleep at night.[3]

Is something at home or school disturbing him, so that he doesn't feel safe enough to sleep? Do you tell him off a lot? Does he shout at you a lot? If he feels the relationship with you is wobbly, he can be scared to let you go.

Sleeping with your baby

Sleeping in close physical proximity to a parent provides a baby with a sensorially rich environment because of all the movement, touch, smells, and sounds. Skin-to-skin contact throughout the night has been shown to regulate a baby's immature body and brain systems, and can play a key role in maintaining his long-term mental and physical wellbeing.

ANIMAL INSIGHTS

All primates except humans co-sleep with their young as a matter of course. After all, infant mammals are tasty morsels for a predator if left in the dark, unprotected by their parents. Leaving a baby sleeping on its own (solitary sleeping) is only a very recent shift for humankind. For most of their 2 million years of evolution, humans have co-slept with their babies.

Extensive scientific research shows that safe co-sleeping can be a real investment for your child's future physical and emotional health. Sleeping with your baby can positively influence his physiology, and all those extra hours of body contact can bring you together better, as bonding goes on at night at well as during the day.[4]

■ **Close physical contact with you will regulate your baby's body systems.**

Skin-to-skin contact with the mother is the genetically programmed natural environment for a human infant. When a newborn baby is placed on his mother's chest, something amazing happens. If the baby is a little too cold, the mother's temperature will rise two degrees to warm him; if the baby is a little too warm, the mother's temperature will lower by one degree to cool him. This is called "thermal synchrony" and is just one of the extraordinary phenomena that result from close bodily contact between mothers and infants. Being next to your body will also synchronize your baby's sleep patterns with yours and regulate his:

- arousal patterns
- body temperature
- metabolic rate
- hormone levels
- enzyme production (increasing the strength of antibodies in the baby's system and thus his ability to fight disease)[5]

"I feel so calm and safe"

Sleeping next to your baby can help to regulate his breathing. Studies have shown that sensory stimulation (such as the rocking of the mother's body as she walks, and the sounds she makes) keeps the unborn child "breathing" rhythmically using practice breathing movements that begin up to three months before birth. It is thought that the stimulation of sleeping next to a parent after birth keeps a child breathing regularly through the night.

- heart rate
- breathing
- immune system (the anti-stress effect of close body contact releases oxytocin, which boosts the baby's immune system). Babies sleeping "skin-to-skin" with their parents appear to be less likely to have a serious illness in the first six months after birth.[6]

Co-sleeping means hours of extra body contact. There is a mass of scientific evidence to demonstrate that the more touch a child gets in childhood, the calmer and less fearful he is likely to be in adulthood. This is because physical contact helps to regulate the stress response system in the brain – which, without this regulation, can become hard-wired for oversensitivity. When this is the case, it can

"The more touch a child gets in childhood, the calmer he is likely to be as an adult."

Extra hours of body contact each night can bring about better bonding between mother and child. Mothers who maintain this prolonged skin contact have also found it easier to produce breast milk for an extended period.

"Even when asleep, mothers appeared to be aware of the baby next to them."

be very difficult for a child, as he grows up, to calm himself down when stressed.[7] Sleeping with a child in early life means an extra eight hours or so of stress-relieving skin-to-skin contact.

Some studies show that children who have never slept in their parents' bed are harder to control.

Such children also tend to cope less well with being left alone, and are more likely to have tantrums and be fearful. This makes sense in terms of them getting less bodily and emotional regulation, and having less opioid and oxytocin released in their brains. (As we will see, optimal levels of these chemicals are strongly linked to psychological strength.)[8]

There are some practical benefits of co-sleeping with your baby, too.

Getting up in the night to attend to a crying child in the next room can feel awful. However, if your child stirs and you are lying next to him, he can be comforted quickly and you don't need to become properly awake. Research shows that if you are awake for less than fifteen seconds you can usually quickly drop off to sleep again.[9] You will definitely be fully awake if you have to get out of your bed to go to the baby in the next room, and you will soon be exhausted if you have to do that several times throughout the night.

But are there risks with co-sleeping?

Some parents worry about co-sleeping because they have fears about suffocating their baby by lying on top of him – overlaying, as it is known. Research indicates that these fears are unfounded, as long as no one in the house smokes, or the parents are likely to sleep so deeply – because they have been consuming alcohol, are on medication, or are simply exhausted – that their vigilance is impaired.

In fact, in many cases, co-sleeping seems to bring a higher degree of maternal vigilance. One study of around 800 hours of video material of mothers and babies showed that even when asleep, mothers appeared to be aware of the baby next to them. No mother rolled on her infant, however close they were to each other.[10]

Research has also shown that when co-sleeping, parents and babies tend to spend most of the night facing each other. And remember, babies don't just passively let themselves be smothered. Even newborn babies will struggle and cry in response to something preventing them from breathing.

▥ If you intend to sleep with your baby, you need to know about SIDS (sudden infant death syndrome).

SIDS (often known as "cot death") is a problem with immaturity of heartbeat, breathing, or blood pressure during sleep. The heart–lung system of your baby matures only after birth. Until it matures, your baby's respiratory system is not at all stable. In fact, the heartbeat of a perfectly healthy baby can be very irregular. This puts babies at risk of breathing problems, especially during sleep.[11] In the UK, 500 children a year die of SIDS and 90 percent of SIDS babies die before they reach the age of nine months. Research makes it clear that certain sleeping conditions carry a significant risk, particularly in the first three months of life, which is the most vulnerable period (see Key facts, right).

▥ Research around the world shows very low rates of SIDS in countries where co-sleeping is common.

Where and how a child sleeps raises very passionate feelings only in some parts of the world. In many areas, it is not at all controversial – co-sleeping just happens as a matter of course. This is largely to do with the fact that putting a baby or child in another room is not an option for many families around the world, because they simply haven't got a spare room. Solitary sleeping for babies is very much a Western middle-class phenomenon. One study showed that only four percent of Asian babies sleep alone.[12]

KEY FACTS

To minimize the risk of SIDS, you should adhere to the common sense safety rules listed below.

- A baby should not be laid to sleep face down (in a cot or his parents' bed).
- A baby's head should not be covered while he sleeps (whether in a cot or his parents' bed).
- A baby up to 11 weeks old should not sleep in a room on his own.
- If you or anyone in the house smokes, you should not co-sleep with your baby.
- If you have been consuming alcohol, you should not co-sleep with your baby.
- If you co-sleep with your baby, do not cover him with the duvet.
- Do not let your baby sleep on a pillow, or in close proximity to a pillow.
- A baby should not co-sleep lying between two people.
- A baby should not co-sleep on sofas, water beds, or with other children.
- Do not co-sleep with your baby if your vigilance is impaired by exhaustion.
- Never leave your baby unattended in or on top of an adult bed.

Studies have shown that the majority of babies in South East Asian families sleep with their parents at night. Some researchers believe that this factor may be linked to the low incidence of SIDS (sudden infant death syndrome) in South East Asian populations.

In China, where co-sleeping is taken for granted, SIDS is so rare it doesn't have a name. One key childcare researcher found that no one in China knew what he was talking about when he spoke about SIDS. They simply didn't understand his description of a young baby dying suddenly for no apparent reason.[13]

SIDS is also uncommon among the populations of South East Asia, such as those of Vietnam, Cambodia, and Thailand, where nearly all babies sleep with their parents. In Hong Kong, where high-density living makes co-sleeping the norm, rates of SIDS are among the lowest in the world.[14] In a five-year study period, there were only 15 cases of cot death. In Western countries, with the same number of babies, 800–1200 cot deaths might have been expected over this same period. Research in Japan has shown a direct correlation between increases in co-sleeping and decreases in SIDS.[15]

A recent international childcare survey team, the SIDS Global Task Force, found that "cultures practising the highest co-sleeping and bed-sharing rates experienced ... the lowest SIDS rates of all".[16] As a result of such studies, many researchers think that higher rates of SIDS in Western populations may be the result of long periods of lone sleep.

■ The SIDS debate continues to arouse controversy.

The best sleeping arrangement for babies and children continues to be a subject for study and heated debate. Depending on the "spin" put on a particular piece of research, one study can appear to contradict another.

A study from the Department of Child Health, University of Glasgow, published in 2005, suggests that there is no risk in co-sleeping with a baby over 11 weeks of age. However, in babies under 11 weeks old, they did find a risk of SIDS, not only from co-sleeping but also from a baby sleeping in a separate room, but their conclusion that co-sleeping with very young babies is risky contradicts the research carried out among populations in other parts of the world (see above).

What's more, the Glasgow researchers did not include the following factors in their study:

■ **Bedcovers and co-sleeping.** In their previous study into infant death, they found that over 80 percent of the babies who died from co-sleeping were covered by a duvet.

■ **Parental exhaustion** (and therefore loss of vigilance). The lack of clear definition as to what is safe and what is unsafe co-sleeping makes this study misleading. It is vital that any research should include details of the co-sleeping environment, so that there can be no confusion between the general and the specific.

■ So let's go back to the science of SIDS.

As we have seen, SIDS is caused mostly by unstable breathing and an immature cardiovascular system. It is known from scientific studies that separation from the mother's body means the baby moves into a primitive defence mode, which can result in wildly irregular breathing and heartbeat. After six hours, a baby separated from his mother has stress hormone levels twice as high as a baby whose mother is close by. In contrast, being in close bodily contact with the mother stabilizes a baby's heartbeat and breathing.[17]

That said, there will be many parents who remain anxious about sleeping in close contact with their babies. If you feel uncertain about the issue, you can place your baby to sleep in a cot right beside your bed, where you can instantly reach out to him when he cries.

Co-sleeping and sleep problems

It seems that while in some cultures co-sleeping is pretty much problem-free for parents, in other cultures, it is not. One research study showed that in the experience of many Japanese families, co-sleeping was not associated with any increased sleep problems. In contrast, the same study showed that American children who co-slept had problems not just with sleeping but during their waking hours.[18]

> "In some cultures, co-sleeping is pretty much problem-free for parents; in others, it is not."

ANIMAL INSIGHTS

Other primates don't share our human dilemmas about whether to co-sleep or not. They follow their instincts (the same instincts we have, unless we over-ride them). Many infant apes and chimpanzees sleep with their parents until about the age of eight, although they will leave the parental bed earlier if another baby comes along.

It seems, therefore, that whether or not co-sleeping works for a family without disruption of sleep is down to many factors. It probably includes things such as attitudes towards bedtime, parental expectations, the parents' calmness, their ability to establish soothing routines at bedtime, and, not least, the size and comfort of the bed. It needs to be big enough to accommodate you, your partner, and your child comfortably. If necessary, you could try a large mattress on the floor, with accompanying side mattresses.

If you can't get the sleep you need with a child in your bed, the secure bedtimes and safe sleep training ideas in this chapter may better suited to you. Your sleep is vital if you are to be an effective emotional regulator for your child during the day. If you are tired, your brain is far more likely to activate a negative brain chemistry, which will do your child no good. By co-sleeping, you are helping him to regulate his emotional and physiological systems during the night, but you are likely to fail him during the day if loss of sleep has made you irritable, agitated, and lacking in interest.

When do you stop co-sleeping?

There are no rights and wrongs about when to stop co-sleeping. If you are considering getting your child to sleep in his own bed, you should first ask yourself whether you want to do this. Or has someone suggested you should? If you and your child are getting enough sleep, and you and your partner have enough physical intimacy, then there is no reason to give up co-sleeping. You may cause a lot of stress at bedtime by pressurizing yourself to meet some fictitious norm.

Studies show that the majority of preschoolers need an adult next to them until they fall asleep, and most come to their parents' beds regularly for comfort.[19] Such is the power of the lower brain's FEAR and SEPARATION DISTRESS systems in early childhood. Parents who are emotionally responsive accept this natural stage of infant brain development and don't try to over-ride genetic programming.

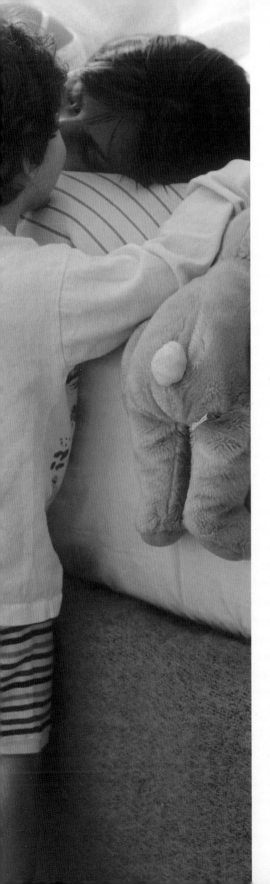

Q If I let my toddler co-sleep, will he ever settle in his own bed?

When parents worry about their children being dependent, clingy, and in their bed forever, they should take comfort in the fact that the SEPARATION DISTRESS system in a child's brain becomes far less sensitive over time. This is largely because the child's rapidly developing higher brain naturally starts to inhibit this system. Also, as your child moves towards puberty, increasing levels of testosterone (in boys) and testosterone and oestrogen (in girls) have a further inhibiting effect. Neuroscientists don't really know why this happens. Some think it is because we are genetically programmed in adolescence to move away from parents to relationships with peers. As your child gets older, separation from you at night will not trigger the emotional pain that affected him when younger.

Q What about our needs as parents? We want some privacy.

You need to weigh up your needs as adults with all the psychological and physiological benefits co-sleeping can have for your child. Of course, there are costs if you choose co-sleeping, but many parents take a creative attitude. They have sex at other times, or start off the children in their own beds and then allow them to come into the parental bed in the middle of the night for that vital emotional and bodily regulation. If you are at the end of your tether and desperate for time away from your children, then these feelings must also be considered when you make decisions about sleeping arrangements.

All about sleep training

Some children go to sleep happily in their own beds, without ever having been trained to sleep or left to cry. They have built up a very strong association between bedtime and feeling completely safe in the world. But for many children, bedtime activates primitive alarm systems in the brain and body and they need gentle help to calm down.

Babies are programmed to be highly dependent, and they need us to regulate their distress states. A child left alone to cry for hours will eventually go to sleep, but only from exhaustion, or because he's given up crying for help.

Beginning sleep training

Most parents begin training because they and their child are in need of better sleep. A child of one to three years of age needs 12–14 hours sleep a night; from three to five years, he needs 11–13 hours, while children from five to twelve years old need 10–11 hours. Sleep is vital for physical growth (the growth hormone is released only during sleep). The effects of sleep deprivation can include poor performance at school, lack of attention, and hyperactivity.[20]

If you do decide to sleep train, make sure that you don't use a method that involves prolonged crying, even for a few nights (see page 81). As the higher brain develops, children grow out of SEPARATION DISTRESS, but until they do, it's vital that you meet their frightened or distressed states with reassurance and comfort. See it from their point of view; the thought of being parted from you at night and being put in a dark room on their own can provoke extreme anxiety.

■ **Some experts advocate leaving a child to "cry it out".**

The theory is that after a few nights of fruitless crying, a child will go to sleep without fuss. Often, however, this entails prolonged periods of crying of an hour or more, and for many nights, not just a few. The technique is effective from the parents' point of view, but it can never be considered as a worthwhile achievement. And what is the cost for the child?

▥ Babies cannot calm themselves down.

A baby is not capable of settling himself to a state of inner peace and well-being. What he can do, however, is eventually give up in the absence of response and go to sleep after endless exhausted, unanswered cries for help. And going to sleep stressed from all that desperate calling means he may wake up frequently in the middle of the night, just as adults would if they had gone to sleep in a very stressed state. This cannot be counted as successful sleep training; it's simply what happens with any mammal (human or otherwise) whose cries are ignored by its parent. The most determined infants with the strongest wills will cry the longest.

A baby who is trained out of his instinct to cry on being separated from a parent should never be mistaken for being in a state of calm. His stress levels will have gone up, not down. Studies show that after being left to cry, babies move into a primitive defence mode. This results in an irregularity

"A baby is not capable of settling himself to a state of well-being."

in breathing and heart rate, both of which can fluctuate wildly, and high levels of cortisol. Infants who have been trained not to cry can often be seen staring into space with a fixed stare. Allan Schore, a neuropsychoanalyst, calls it "the black spot in going-on-being" or "conservation-withdrawal". [21] In attachment theory, when a child starts to bottle up his feelings rather than express them, the process is known as PROTEST—DESPAIR—DETACHMENT.

Without your help, your baby cannot bring his stress hormone levels down to base rate, or adjust his bodily arousal states, or change his brain chemistry so that relaxing oxytocin and opioids flood in. To make these things happen, your baby needs you next to him, soothing him and regulating his immature brain and body systems.

BRAIN STORY

Children can be highly sensitive to separation at bedtime. If a child feels anxious about being alone, the pituitary gland in his brain sends a hormone (ACTH) to his adrenal glands, which respond by producing high levels of the stress hormone cortisol. Studies of other infant mammals showed that the longer an infant was left for, the greater the increase in the level of cortisol.[22] Even when external signs of distress such as crying and restlessness decreased, the level of cortisol stayed high or increased.

The possible long-term effect of repeated separation anxiety is an extreme sensitivity to stress. Adults with this hypersensitivity find it difficult to calm themselves down.

A child who receives reassurance and calming touch at bedtime, however, is likely to have oxytocin and opioids washing over his brain and helping him to sleep peacefully.

The stress response

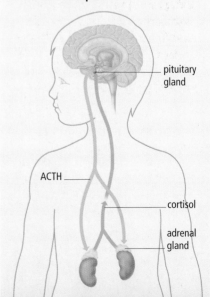

pituitary gland

ACTH

cortisol

adrenal gland

Q Bedtime has become a battle with my toddler – why?

Sadly, scenes at bedtime are all too often mistaken for a battle of wills rather than the activation of pain and panic in a child's brain. When children cry for their parents not to leave them at night, they are acting as other infant mammals are genetically programmed to do when left on their own. It is not about control; that's an adult interpretation of events. It's the effect of a powerful hormonal system in the lower mammalian part of the brain.

Q My child is desperately clingy at bedtime. What should I do?

If your child needs to cling to you to get to sleep, then let him. Children cling if they feel very unsafe. They also cling to you to change their negative brain chemistry (high levels of stress chemicals) to a positive one. Body contact with you can activate opioids and oxytocin in the brain, naturally lowering levels of stress chemicals. Sometimes a child's anxiety is increased because something has made his little world feel insecure. One way to help him is for you to tell him the story of his day, which will help him process all the emotional ups and downs he went through. As adults we can't get to sleep when worries and concerns keep swirling round our minds, because no one has helped us to manage them. It's just the same with children.

Kind sleep training

Of course, not all sleep training is bad for the brain. Here are some safe no-cry options.

If you have done everything to settle your child in his own bed, but he follows you out of the room, turn round immediately and put him back into bed. Reassure him that he is safe and that you will see him in the morning. Don't leave him to cry, and don't just plonk him in his bed like a sack of potatoes and walk away. If you do, you are giving him an experience of rupture, which can activate his lower brain SEPARATION DISTRESS system. Tell him again that he is safe and loved and give him a cuddle. Keep doing this every time he gets out of bed.

If he gets distressed, this is not the right technique for him right now (bearing in mind those so vulnerable immature brain systems). Instead, you can sit by his bed until he feels safe enough to fall asleep.

"Reassure him that he is safe and that you will see him in the morning."

■ **Avoid sleep training that is based on a deal to leave the door open.**

This is the technique where you tell your child that if he gets out of bed to follow you, you will close the door – but if he stays in bed, you will leave the door open. This method works because it activates the FEAR system in the child's lower brain. The fear of the door being shut (and completely cutting off access to you) is so awful the child stays in bed. But in using this method, we are back to those worrying levels of cortisol (see page 40). For centuries, people have got children to behave by activating the brain's FEAR system. But studies show that repeated activation of this system in childhood can lead to anxiety disorders in later life.[23]

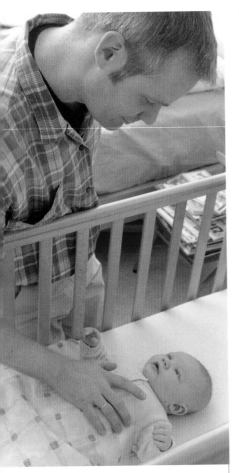

Daytime naps are important for babies and very young children, but it can also be very tempting to go on putting a child down for a sleep simply for your own benefit. There is no point in insisting your child has a nap if he has long outgrown the need. Children will catch up on sleep anywhere – on the sofa, in a pushchair, or in a car seat – if they are really tired.

▪ When it's time for your child to sleep on his own, use science to inform your methods.

Studies with other mammals show that the acoustic presence of the mother (in other words, the sound of her voice) can effectively bring down stress chemical levels in a baby separated from its mother.[24] Give your child a tape recording of you saying something like: "Hi, little one, you are really safe. I love you very much." You could also make a recording of you telling one of his favourite stories. Then, if he gets into a state of painful opioid withdrawal in the night, he can just switch on the tape recorder by his bed.[25]

Your smell can also trigger powerful positive feelings in your child's brain. Give him something to hold in the night that smells of you – for example, a piece of your clothing. With a baby, placing near him a soft piece of cloth with the smell of your breast milk can be highly effective in settling him down. This is because the olfactory bulb in the brain, which registers scent, is right next to the amygdala, the part of the brain that triggers strong emotional associations.

We know that opioids can be activated in the brain when someone enters a familiar, cosy place. So make your child's bedroom a really special sanctuary where he loves to be.

"Make your child's bedroom a really special sanctuary where he loves to be."

If your child is older, he can help you design it, choose the bedding, pillows, posters for the walls, and so on. Research shows that preschool children who received massage before bed experienced less difficulty falling asleep and better sleep patterns.[26] Encourage your child to have a cuddly toy. This may also activate comforting brain chemicals. Try a reward system: each time your child sleeps in his bed the whole night through, he gets a sticker. Agree with him that a certain number of stickers means a little present.

Key points

■ **Most babies are** terrible sleepers. Your parenting is not inadequate just because your baby won't settle at night.

■ **Co-sleeping** is the norm in many parts of the world; fears about the level of risk appear to be unfounded, provided parents follow all the safety rules.

■ **Skin-to-skin contact** and close physical proximity during the night can play a key role in maintaining the mental and physical health of your child, regulating his immature body and brain systems.

■ **Leaving a child to** cry himself to sleep is putting him at risk of adverse changes to his immature brain systems.

■ **Sleep training** doesn't have to involve tears. The gentle approach will work without having damaging long-term effects.

the chemistry
of living life
well

As a parent, you have a major influence over whether your child will grow up to live a fulfilling life or one spoiled by persistent states of anger, anxiety, or depression. Hormones and brain chemicals powerfully influence our feelings, perception, and behaviour, and your child's early life experiences have a direct influence on which emotional states will become commonplace to her. What is more, the way you are with your child has dramatic effects on her brain's key systems for drive, will, motivation, and zest for life.

The power of hormones

Hormones are powerful chemicals produced in the body and brain that can make us feel wonderful or awful. We tend to think of hormones only in relation to our sexuality, but there are many different types that affect us in all manner of ways – influencing our feelings, perception, and behaviour.

CONSIDER THIS...

Touching base is when little kids run about happily then, all of a sudden, sit on Mum or Dad's lap or lean on them or touch them in some way. This can last a matter of seconds or minutes. Then off they go to run about happily again. This is called "emotional re-fuelling"[2] and it serves to create a lovely chemical balance in their brains. If your child is doing this with you, it's a real compliment – she is experiencing you as a source of natural brain opioids.

Hormonal heaven

Neuroscientist Candice Pert says, "Each of us has his or her own … finest drugstore available at the cheapest cost – to produce all the drugs we ever need to run our body and mind."[1] The natural hormones and neurochemicals that we have in our bodies and brains can not only make us feel just great, but also enable us to thrive. The problem is that because of too much relational stress in childhood, some people may never gain access to the finest chemicals "in the drugstore of their mind".

■ **When opioids and oxytocin are in dominance in the brain, the world feels like a warm, inviting place.**
When they are strongly activated in combination, these neurochemicals can bring us the deepest sense of calm and contentment, with the capacity to take life's stresses in our stride. If you provide your child with lots of early experiences of loving calm, she will repeatedly experience oxytocin and opioids being in dominance in her brain. This will make her feel very calm, safe, and warm inside. She is likely to be better able to enjoy:
■ the capacity to savour
■ the capacity to linger in the moment
■ the capacity to drift and let go.
Through experiencing these neurochemical states on a regular basis, she will start to greet the world with interest and wonder, rather than with a sense of fear and threat.

What's more, she will also be building up resilience to deal well with painful and stressful times in life, which no human being can avoid.[3]

Hormonal hell

If a child repeatedly feels fear and rage in childhood, say from a strict parenting style that regularly involves shouting at her, or lots of commands, criticisms, and angry facial expressions, it can block the release of opioids and oxytocin in her brain. Unrelieved by calmness, comfort, and warm physical affection, her body and brain can then become accustomed to high levels of the chemicals cortisol, adrenaline, and noradrenaline, which are pumped out by the adrenal glands in times of stress. This can make her feel threatened and unsafe at all times.[4]

"A child's sense of being fundamentally unsafe in the world can become her way of knowing herself and other people."

▨ **When the hormone cortisol is activated in the brain and body at high levels for too long, the world can feel like a hostile, attacking place.**

High levels of cortisol can make us feel overwhelmed, fearful, and miserable, colouring our thoughts, feelings, and perceptions with a sense of threat or dread as if everything we need to do is far too hard.

Adrenaline and noradrenaline can also strongly affect our mood, both telling the heart to pump faster and harder, the liver to release glucose, the fat stores to release fat, and the muscles to mobilize energy stores. With optimal levels of these hormones, we can feel alert with clear thinking, but when strongly activated, just like cortisol, they make us feel anxious or angry or both. We become intensely focused on

BRAIN STORY

Opioids are brain chemicals with many functions. One is to relieve pain. The name of one type, endorphin, comes from "endogenous morphine"– morphine that is made naturally by the body. However, opioids also give us a general sense of well-being.

Oxytocin is vital for contributing to feelings of comfort and safety in children. It also inhibits the action of the stress response system (see page 40). When oxytocin is released by the pituitary gland, there is a cascade of chemical reactions. One of their effects is that the adrenal glands, on top of the kidneys, release less of the stress hormone cortisol.[5]

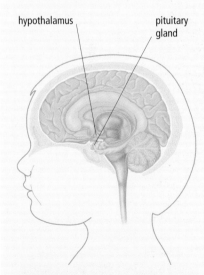

hypothalamus   pituitary gland

Opioids are released by a group of cells in the hypothalamus, and there are opioid receptors all over the brain. Oxytocin is released by the pituitary gland.

ANIMAL INSIGHTS

Research with other mammals has shown that:

● The more physical contact the mothers gave to their babies, the less fearful and more courageous their babies grew up to be, and this effect lasted a lifetime. Baby mammals who experienced lower levels of touch from their mothers showed more fearfulness in adulthood.

● The more physically demonstrative the mother, the more mentally healthy the infant in later life. In adulthood they became confident, attentive mothers with calmer infants.

● Babies who experienced physical contact also aged better, with fewer degenerative changes in their brain; and they were less anxious when placed in a new environment, and explored more.

● They also coped well with stress.[9]

a feeling of threat, real or imagined, and our bodies move into a state of hyperarousal, activating all manner of lower brain fight impulses (aggression) or flight impulses (withdrawal and avoidance). Research shows that a child's early experiences of parenting are extremely influential in determining whether stress chemicals are strongly activated on a regular basis in later life.[6] If they are, they can leave her in a sort of hell on earth in a persistent state of hyperarousal. She may feel threatened for much of the time. Tragically, this sense of being fundamentally unsafe in the world can become her way of knowing herself and other people. As a result, she may move into living her life in a chronic state of mistrust and take one of two fundamental positions; either "shrinking from life or doing battle with it".[7]

"When lying next to your calm body, your child will have oxytocin and opioids cascading all over his brain. This will feel delicious and satisfying for both of you."

Warm physical contact

The problem is that you can't just inject children or adults with oxytocin, as it doesn't travel to the brain. And you can't give it orally as it just gets digested. These chemicals can only be highly activated in the human brain through warm human connection! In short, if we want children to grow up able to feel calm and safe in the world, and at ease with themselves and other people, we need to ensure that safe physical contact and physical comforting of distress is integral to their lives.[8]

■ **Any form of warm physical contact between parent and child can have a positive effect.**
Cuddles and hugs, affectionate little squeezes, baby massage, and falling asleep in your arms can all have a wonderful effect

on your child. All these "one-to-one" moments with a loving parent will activate opioids and oxytocin in your child's brain. When she is lying next to your calm body, your child is likely to have oxytocin and opioids cascading all over her brain. This will feel delicious and satisfying for both of you. For this to happen, it is important that you are in a calm state, as this is when opioids and oxytocin are in dominance in your brain. Monitor your mood because lying next to your child when you are anxious or tense will release stress chemicals.

■ Don't forget to cuddle your over-fives as well as your little ones.

The amazing brain effects of touch are just as powerful with older children. What's more, if you keep lots of lovely cuddles going right through into adolescence (as long as the young person still wants them from you, of course), there can be far less tension in your relationship when your children become teenagers. This is because the oxytocin from the cuddles will keep the opioid bond with your child alive for far longer.[10]

"These wonderful emotion chemicals are nature's gifts to us." ~ Jaak Panksepp

"Please pick me up"

Only body-to-body contact releases wonderful stress-relieving chemicals. It is such a common sight to see a baby in a pushchair screaming in spite of all attempts at rocking and jiggling to soothe it. Once picked up, he often becomes quiet within seconds.

Joy juice

Some people have such a delightful sense of fun, play, humour, and spontaneity. They are lovely to be around, and their vitality is often infectious. Others are somewhat lifeless in comparison and never seem to enthuse about anything. They live for most of the time within a narrow band of safe emotions. They can, of course, be very likeable, but you can never really go "flying" with them.

What I mean by flying is experiencing precious shared moments of intense joy when you feel incredibly alive. By and large, the "flyer" who wants to live life to the full is likely to have been parented in ways that have repeatedly activated intense positive brain chemical and bodily arousal states. Loss and trauma can send a flyer into the depths of despair, but because such a person has experienced the power that warm, loving parenting exerts in terms of sculpting their brain for strong positive arousal states, they will eventually bounce back and experience the heights of joy once more.

Activating joy

In the brain there is a foundational genetic system for joy, but how it unfolds depends on the interaction of those genes with social experiences. By and large, it is not possible to access the brain's "joy juice" naturally without emotional connection with others. It is possible to experience pleasure, but not real joy.

Joy is also a bodily state. To feel heights of joy, as opposed to just pleasure, we have to be moved from the very depths of us. This means that, alongside the activation of the brain's joy juice, the body's arousal system (called the autonomic nervous system) has activated high levels of adrenalin, which surges around the body. We can feel this adrenalin boost as our heart rate goes up, we breathe faster, and our appetite is

"We have fantastic times together!"

Joy is the result of human connection. With high levels of bodily arousal, optimal levels of adrenalin rushing through the body, and optimal levels of dopamine and opioids cascading over the brain, we feel intensely alive, wide awake, and with masses of energy to do what we want to do. "When lots of dopamine synapses are firing, a person feels as if he or she can do anything."[11]

The difference between people who can let themselves experience excitement and those who seem to defend against it is a direct result of parenting. Parenting affects whether a child's brain and bodily arousal system will be set up to bear intense states of joy and excitement in later life. It's not automatic.

Intense feelings of joy produce lovely chemicals in the brain but also high levels of bodily arousal and activation of stress chemicals. So an essential parenting function is to help your child to handle "the stress of joy", so that she does not feel overwhelmed by it. You will be doing this every time you meet your child's joyful energy with your own joyful energy. So if your child runs up to you in a state of true delight with a picture she has drawn, or when she is exhilarated when on the trampoline, try to match her delight with your own facial expression, tone of voice, posture, and movement. If you are engaged in joyful play with your child and then have to stop abruptly to answer the phone, her joy levels may plummet. Her level of bodily arousal may be just too intense for her to cope with alone, which can lead to tears and upset.[14]

suppressed. Dopamine and opioids in combination have to be activated at optimum levels in the brain if we are to feel joy. The repeated activation of these brain chemicals in childhood can enable your child to access many other wonderful human gifts – namely, to be spontaneous, to have the drive and hope to follow a dream, and to feel awe, wonder, and sheer delight in response to the beautiful and amazing things in the world (as opposed to the low-key responses of non-flyers). This particular brain chemistry also promotes resilience in the face of stress, making minor stressors feel manageable. This solid foundation is likely to make a child far more able throughout life to maintain, or quickly regain a sense of:

- hope
- optimism
- a "Yes I can" attitude to life.

Joy juice for babies

Some people are of the opinion that babies can't enter into any real dialogue until they can walk and talk, yet the first six months can be one of the most sociable times of a child's life.[12] During these early months, babies are usually far more interested in faces than toys and you can have a fabulous conversation with your baby from about three months onwards, using sounds, words, and a variety of facial expressions and movements.

Sadly, some parents miss out on these vital face-to-face communication times in the first year of their child's life. As a result, the child misses out on early vital brain development time and the regular activation of "joy juice".[13] So the next time you are enjoying time with an adult friend, remember to talk to your young baby too! Your baby will enjoy "joining in" with the laughter and conversation, far more than playing on her own in the buggy.

One-to-one conversations with a baby have a pattern that is somewhat different to adult conversations. Pick a time when your baby is wide awake and not hungry. Make eye contact, and give her time to make her own response (see below). Be sensitive to her cues. She will find the communication very stimulating, and will need lots of breaks. All babies need to look away from time to time, and when she is ready, she will look back.

Infant researcher Beatrice Beebe found that some parents did not read these "let's have a break" cues and tried to keep their baby looking at them and engaging with them. The babies began to "chase and dodge", moving their heads from side to side and finally breaking contact by becoming still and staring into space. This not only switches off the positive chemicals that have been activated in their brain but also switches on high levels of stress chemicals.[15]

> "The first six months can be one of the most sociable times of a child's life."

"I love talking to you!"

John holds three-month-old Mabel a short distance from his face and starts a one-to-one conversation. Babies are wired to respond to familiar faces from day one.

Babies respond to communication much more slowly than an adult or child, so John is patient while Mabel works up her response.

It may be a smile, a copycat expression, a wave, or a little whoop of delight. Then Mabel pauses and waits for John to reply to her.

The joy juices in Mabel's brain are fully activated and vital brain connections are being forged. This is baby play at its finest.

Seeking life's satisfactions

Like other mammals, we enjoy a host of short-term pleasures, such as eating, drinking, playing, and socializing. But what differentiates us is our higher brain functions, which enable us to make plans, seek out new pleasures, and find satisfactions that are far more long-term and profound.

Your child's interest and curiosity about the world will come from you. Encourage him to explore and experiment from an early age. This will serve him well into adulthood. The SEEKING system (see right) "coaxes animals and humans to move energetically from where they are presently situated to the places where they can find and consume the fruits of the world".[17]

The capacity to achieve long-term satisfaction means:

■ **You can follow through dreams** to make them a reality.

■ **You can pursue a goal** in the service of something far greater than merely gain for yourself.

■ **You get a sense of satisfaction** or self-worth from using yourself well and making a positive impact in the world.

■ **You have the ability to produce ideas**, and the drive and motivation to go after them. If your ideas involve others, you have the social skills for successful joint creative ventures.

Everyone looks for that sparkle in friends and lovers to "make things happen". Most of all, everybody is looking for energy within themselves: the motivation and drive to get up and do something, and the endurance, stamina, and resolve to carry through.[16]

The source of curiosity

The lower brain contains a SEEKING system, one of the seven genetically ingrained systems in the brain (see page 19). When this system is stimulated in other mammals, they explore and investigate their environment with curiosity. In humans, the SEEKING system can activate an appetite for life, an energy to explore the new, and an eagerness to seek out whatever the world has to offer. It also stimulates curiosity or intense interest in something and the sustained motivation and directed sense of purpose that help us to achieve our goals. When the SEEKING system is working in a well-coordinated way with the frontal lobes, it means you can enjoy the necessary drive to transform the seed of an idea into an amazing reality. This is vital if we are to live our lives to the full. This creative union between the lower and upper brain is responsible for many activities, from a child's desire to build a magnificent sandcastle, to an adult turning a dream into a successful business.

▨ Dopamine is the big "light-switch".

There are many chemicals in the SEEKING system, but dopamine is the one that turns things on. It cascades all over the frontal lobes, enabling a person not only to have a great

> "Everybody is looking for energy within themselves: the motivation and drive to get up and do something"

idea, but also to have the directed purpose to see it through to completion. The SEEKING system is like a muscle – the more you use it, the more it will work for you, in the sense that the more curious, creative, and motivated you become. In contrast, when adults loll about in front of the TV for hours on end, or spend entire holidays on a sunlounger, their brains' SEEKING system can be underactive. The resulting low levels of dopamine can lead to procrastination, uncreative thinking, and few, if any, new ideas.[18]

For many people, it is hard to activate a drive for life in adulthood if it has not been awakened in childhood. If a person faces a crisis or shock in life (such as a period of serious illness or the loss of a job that appeared to offer long-term security) or meets a vibrant new person, it can act like a wake-up call and he or she can be encouraged to use the "muscle" of the SEEKING system, often for the first time. For many adults, however, this does not happen and they never use their lives well.

Case study

Life passing by

Howard follows the same routine day after day. He works each day and returns home to his family in the evening. He watches television and then the whole thing starts again the next day. Each year, Howard goes on holiday to the same place.

Howard is not satisfied in his job, but doesn't really know what else to do. When asked about his job, he often replies, "Well, it brings in the money". Once Howard started a novel, but now it sits in a drawer. He never seems to find the energy to get on and finish it. Mid-life, Howard asks himself, "Isn't there more to life than this?"

Howard's life isn't bigger than it is because he doesn't have enough drive and energy to make it into a bigger life. Howard's SEEKING system is not activated strongly enough. In many ways, therefore, Howard is no longer developing as a human being.

Howard's childhood was very quiet. He spent a lot of his out-of-school-time watching television or doing homework. These activities failed to strongly activate his SEEKING system, and this legacy has stayed with Howard for life.

The importance of play

To encourage your child to strongly activate her SEEKING system, you will need to repeatedly offer her interesting experiences. This can set her up for life with the inquisitiveness, drive, motivation, and focus to be able to use her life well. It will empower her to engage with people and places, and walk through many open doors – or, if doors are closed, find the energy to open them. Children who loll about all day tend to have an underactive SEEKING system.

Children with strongly activated SEEKING systems will find opportunities for play wherever they look! Parents, carers, and teachers can inspire this by providing an "enriched environment" with space, toys, equipment, and, most of all, ideas.

One of the most powerful ways to activate your child's SEEKING system to work in creative union with her higher brain (frontal lobes) is to provide her with richly stimulating environments for imaginative and explorative play.

The enriched environment

Providing your child with places to explore, imaginative and creative toys to play with, and friends to interact with all contribute to an "enriched environment". There is no need to go to great expense; playing outside or with water can be enough to stimulate a young child.

The benefits of creative play within such an environment are many. Research with both humans and other mammals demonstrates that it can lower stress chemicals, enabling us to deal better with stressful situations.[19]

In one fascinating study, rats were given an enriched environment with "climbing tubes and running wheels, novel food, and lots of social interaction". Two months later, the rats had an extra 50,000 brain cells in each side of the hippocampus (one of the key memory and learning centres in the brain).[20]

Another research study found that if deprived, at-risk children were given a nutritional, educational, and physical exercise-enriched programme between the ages of three and five, they were far less likely to develop criminal or anti-social

"We're going to the moon"

Encourage children in creative play by starting them off with a few ideas and providing objects with creative potential to play with. Show them how to fly to the moon on a broom, look for elves, or build a castle. They will soon be captivated. Simple "toys" such as pots and pans, a bowl of water, or a tray of sand are usually all children need to get started. There is no need to provide an array of expensive, manufactured toys. Children enjoy finding their own way to play once the game is underway.

"You can do a great deal for your child by providing lots of stimuli to trigger her imagination"

behaviour in early adulthood.[21] Environmental enrichment during adolescence has also been shown to compensate for some of the adverse effects of prenatal stress and the stress of postnatal maternal separation. There were clear improvements in social behaviour and a lowering of stress chemicals in the brain. The adolescents also had lower levels of anxiety. In short, environmental enrichment can go some way to reverse the damaging brain effects left by adversity early in life.[22]

How parents can help

Whereas some routine is lovely for a child, when a family settles into the same routine each week, this can lead to an underactive SEEKING system in the child's brain. So as parents, it's important to provide your child with lots of

"Let's build a dam together"

Children of all ages enjoy the space and sense of freedom they get from being outdoors. Show them how to explore and search for fun in their environment.

They may need suggestions to get them started, such as "Can you climb that mound?" or "that bush looks like a little house". Once inspired, they can be occupied happily for hours.

For over an hour these two boys have been building a dam in a stream to make their own rock pool. Totally absorbed in their project, they no longer need adult help.

new stimuli to trigger her imagination, making sure she can play with friends regularly rather than, say, relying on the television for entertainment. You may need to help your child get started. Once you start to show her how to play with new things, her SEEKING system will be activated. After a while, step back, so she can explore in her own way. Here are some ideas to try:

■ **Make a den** using chairs and sheets and fill it with toys to play "houses".

■ **Help your child to gather and play with natural things** like leaves, flowers, sand, water, and snow when it's available. Put on waterproofs and boots and go puddle-splashing in the rain.

■ **Build a fantasy world**, providing such things as small cars, a bowl for a lake for boats, and a watering can to make it rain.

■ **Take your child on a trip** into the countryside, where there is access to earth, water, and soft green grass to roll around on. If you are by a brook, show her how to make a dam, stepping stones, or small boats out of twigs and leaves.

Parents usually end up marvelling at the productivity of a child when her brain's SEEKING system has been activated. However, don't expect her to know how to start off these activities without using you as a springboard for ideas. It's like lighting a spark. But once you've triggered her absorption, curiosity, and explorative urge, make sure that you don't take over or lead her play. Stand back and let her ideas and her creativity come to the fore. Follow rather than lead. Teaching a child how to use her SEEKING system is a vital parental function.

Choosing the right toys

There are certain toys on the market that strongly activate a child's SEEKING system because they grip a child's imagination and open the door to free play. This is play where a child can develop an idea in any direction she wants.

■ **Choose a landscape**, world, or environment which she can develop imaginatively; for example, a zoo, a sweet shop, a

Case study

Getting started at the beach
When Ted takes his son, Jake, to the beach, he gets out his newspaper and tells Jake to amuse himself. Jake sifts the sand through his hands, picks up a few rocks and hits them together, then stands in the sea. After 15 minutes, he tells his father he wants to go home. Without a few ideas from Dad on how to use a beach well, the SEEKING system in Jake's brain is poorly activated. He needs help to get started.

Another time, Sally, a friend of the family, comes to the beach too. Sally makes sure she takes a bucket and spade. She shows Jake how to make sandcastles and how to dig a large crater and make a sand car to sit in. She has also brought a few little lorries. Jake picks them up eagerly and drives them on a track around his sandcastles. When Jake is really engrossed in his play, Sally can relax and read her newspaper for a while.

"Choose toys that grip a child's imagination and facilitate free play."

castle, a circus, or a doll's house. Events begin to "happen" in these places with the addition of a few key figures (for example, miniature animals and people). Environmental toys such as these can be far more stimulating than those that facilitate only structured play. For example, board games and toys that rely on a physical skill are good for many reasons, but are unlikely to activate the SEEKING system as well in ways that allow the development of a creative idea.

■ **Art and modelling activities** are also great for allowing a child to develop her own ideas, worlds, and fantasies. Sit back and let her experiment rather than insist that she draws recognizable pictures or makes a neat model. Although colouring books are enjoyable, they don't allow free rein to the imagination, in the way that spontaneous art activities do.

If parents put effort into activating a child's SEEKING system before school, they lay down vital foundation stones

Q How do computer games and television affect my child's brain?

The results of over 4000 studies suggest a connection between high rates of television-viewing in children and aggressive and violent behaviour, lower academic performance, and stereotyped behaviours in matters of sex, race, and age. While watching violent television, the motor programming parts of a child's brain are often activated, which means that the child is rehearsing the violence he is watching. Parts of the brain that detect threat can also be activated, and the memory of a disturbing film can be laid down in the brain in the same way as the memory of a traumatic event in real life. As far as we know, playing solitary computer games does not result in the highly positive brain events activated by play, fun, and laughter with another human being.[23]

in terms of capacity for exploration, absorption, curiosity, and self-belief. This the very stuff of love of knowledge and the will to learn.[24]

Blighting your child's SEEKING system

Isolation, insecurity, fear, anger, and SEPARATION DISTRESS can all kill a child's urge to play. You can blight your child's SEEKING system in many other ways, too:

■ **Being critical** of noise, mess, and lots of running about (see page 137). If you tidy up too quickly, or become cross if the timing and location of the play does not suit you, your child may learn to inhibit her desire to explore and create, as it becomes associated with too much fear.

■ **Allowing your child to spend long periods bored** and understimulated. A child can adjust herself all too easily to low arousal states and boredom. Regular states of lethargy can become part of who she is. When children like this reach adolescence, exasperated parents often call them "lazy slobs", but underneath a child can feel depressed, with a sense of "Is this all there is?" [25]

■ **Expecting your children to keep quiet** on journeys or sit through adult meals with nothing to occupy their brains and with no conversation directed their way (see pages 141–145).

■ **Providing very little adult-child** "one-to-one" adventure time with you.

■ **Allowing your children to make television their main source of recreation.** Statistics show that, on average, children spend 21 hours a week in front of the TV and only 38 minutes in meaningful parent–child interaction.[26]

■ **Over-timetabling** your child's leisure time with adult-led, structured activities, such as violin lessons, French lessons, chess clubs, riding lessons, and ballet lessons. These activities are fine, but not if they rob your child of precious child-led free-play time. What is more, structured activities with a dominating teacher can mean suffering the blight of over-direction: "No dear, that's not quite right. Let me show you".

TRY THIS...

Talking to your child about new and interesting things can also be brilliant at activating her SEEKING system. This is because your interest, curiosity, and your own strongly activated SEEKING system will activate optimal levels of dopamine in your child's brain. On outings or in the garden, take the time to talk to your child about what you see. Tell her about your hobbies and interests; you will be amazed at how much she will absorb.

"As you walk into a primary school you can often feel a natural urge for knowledge that is totally lacking in the classrooms of secondary schools."

■ **Shaming or discouraging** a child's natural creative, explorative impulses.

Older and teenage children with an underactive SEEKING system can find boredom and low arousal so painful that they often try to counteract it by moving into high-arousal incidents like violence, vandalism, or drugs. They need to do drastic things in order to feel any interest or excitement.[27]

What schools need to do

Some truly inspiring teachers have such strongly activated SEEKING systems themselves that they are likely to strongly stimulate their pupils' brains. Such teachers are passionate about their own subject and continue to spend countless hours acquiring further knowledge about it – not because they have to, but because they are fired by an intense, unstoppable desire to know more.

However, to be a good teacher, a person also needs to be "embodied", which means being able to speak from the heart

"I can do this myself now"

Good teachers can encourage children to try new skills for themselves, and foster a sense of independence and achievement. Schools that focus too closely on a curriculum may fail to inspire children with a love of knowledge and learning.

and from the gut. Some teachers are cut off emotionally, with low levels of bodily arousal. As a result, they speak in a dry, dull way. This kind of teacher is far less likely to be able to activate a child's SEEKING system.

Schools that focus only on the confines of a curriculum, and on tasks which are exclusively about facts and figures, are not allowing the child enough opportunity to develop her own ideas. This may fail to inspire a child's love of knowledge. Similarly, assessment-focused learning at too young an age can kill that vital desire to know and discover more. Some schools are centred on teacher-directed learning rather than child-directed exploration, leaving too little room for the child's own "seeking behaviour". Some schools in Finland start teaching reading far later than in the UK, allowing the child more years for explorative learning through play. Children in these Finnish schools are way behind in reading at age seven, compared with schools in the UK, but way ahead during adolescence. This may well be due to the increased years of explorative free play learning, leading to a more active SEEKING system, and resulting in a stronger appetite for knowledge.

If a child comes to school already rather bored with life, with no desire to seek knowledge, a school that fosters free play and exploration can give that child's SEEKING system a real second chance. However, if that same child goes to a school that is all about fitting into tight assessment schedules and rule-bound tasks, he can be left with his appetite for learning seriously dampened.

Primary schools are often much better at activating a child's SEEKING system than secondary schools. There is a misconception that secondary school-aged children have grown out of the need for free play and child-directed explorative learning, so there are all too few resources for this in the secondary school. As you walk into a primary school you can often feel a natural urge for knowledge that is totally lacking in the classrooms of a secondary school.

A child with a lack of positive parenting may have a transformative relationship with a very warm, calm adult such as a relative, teacher, or counsellor, who will activate positive chemicals and hormones in his brain.

"To be a good teacher, a person needs to be able to speak from the heart."

Rough and tumble

There is a PLAY system deep in the mammalian part of the human brain, and, as we shall see, it's just a great system! It's very powerful, and it has a key role in your child's social and emotional intelligence and general mental health. This system is activated by rough and tumble or gentle and tumble play, body against body.

Physical interactive play increases the activation of a very important "fertilizer" in the higher brain (frontal lobes) called brain-derived neurotrophic factor (BDNF). This helps to programme the regions in the frontal lobes that are involved in emotional behaviour. Research shows that there is increased gene expression of BDNF in the frontal lobes after play.[28]

If you have lots of physical playtimes with your child, it's highly likely that you are enhancing the development of her higher human brain, with all its amazing functions, including better management of emotions and stress.

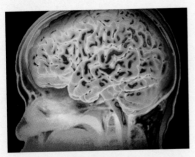

The emotion-regulating areas in the brain's frontal lobes (on the left in this scan) are stimulated by physical play.

The importance of play

Research points clearly to the fact that, for many reasons, physical interactive play is very important for long-term emotional health. This form of play has natural anti-stress effects, and because it strongly releases opioids it promotes powerful positive emotional states. Interactive play can enhance the emotion-regulating functions in the frontal lobes, helping children to manage their feelings better. Children in orphanages have been seen to make dramatic developmental progress after programmes of play.

Rough and tumble that activates the PLAY system can be between adult and child or between children. It is boisterous play, which can transport children into states of joy and often results in a child bursting into squeals of laughter or delight. You engage in this form of social play with your child when you blow a raspberry on her tummy, or toss her up in the air, spin her round, or tickle her. Face-to-face play that includes touching is this sort of play, and so are spontaneous, unpredictable, humorous moments with your baby, as when you say, "Oops, I may have to eat your foot!" and then pretend to do it. Or you pretend to be a postman and say to the child, "Ah, a parcel has arrived!" and you pick her up and plonk her into another adult's lap. Child-to-child rough and tumble or gentle and tumble play involves all manner of delightful rolling on the floor, toppling over each other, and play-fighting. It is so physically free that it can sometimes tip into hurting if an adult is not there to keep watch.

"This is good for my brain!"

It seems hard to believe, but tumbling on the grass with a friend is essential for healthy brain development. Not only is this type of play an outlet for primitive motoric impulses, such as the urge to run and climb, but it also enhances higher brain development. In later life, these boys may be better able to manage their emotions and cope with stress as a result (see page 20).[29]

■ What happens if children don't get enough rough and tumble?

We ignore play at our peril. Research shows that if mammalian infants don't get enough socially interactive play, they will make up for lost time and play harder, often at all the wrong times.[30] In other words, their play impulse comes out inappropriately. This is what happens with some children labelled as having attention deficit hyperactivity disorder (ADHD). One study found that children deprived of playtime at school developed ADHD symptoms and were unable to sit still and focus their attention.[31]

"Children deprived of playtime at school developed ADHD symptoms."

Hyperactivity – or not enough play?

Children with attention deficit hyperactivity disorder (ADHD) have symptoms of hyperactivity, impulsiveness, and poor attention. They find it hard to concentrate, to keep their minds on tasks, to follow instructions, to organize anything, and to listen. They often run about and climb on things inappropriately as if driven by a motor. They are easily bored, and get extremely frustrated if they can't manage a learning task. They frequently fidget and squirm about, and may lash out impulsively at other children. A child with ADHD can talk excessively at you, and can find it very hard to wait his turn – interrupting, intruding, and being disruptive. Sadly, all these types of behaviour mean that she can find it hard to make friends. For a diagnosis of ADHD, 75 percent of these symptoms must be present for at least six months and in more than one setting (for example, at home as well as in school).

Some children suffer from ADHD due to neurological problems (sometimes caused by maternal stress during pregnancy, or by prenatal exposure to cigarettes, alcohol, or drugs, birth complications, low birth weight, premature birth, malnutrition in infancy, or environmental toxins). But these reasons certainly do not apply to the 5 to 7 percent of the entire child population who have been diagnosed as having ADHD. Many children are misdiagnosed. Some of them have suffered a trauma that has left them with feelings that they can't manage and which are too painful to bear, so they move about manically instead. Other misdiagnosed children are able to concentrate, be calm, and interact perfectly well when given good quality adult–child interaction time, and lots of encouragement and praise in place of nagging and shouting.

In ADHD, one major problem is that the frontal lobes are not yet fully "on line". As we have seen, interactive play can develop a child's frontal lobes and enhance their regulating functions. This helps an ADHD child to naturally inhibit her primitive "motoric impulses" (all that rushing about, wanting to hit you) and manage stressful situations.[32]

Q But I've never been very good at play – how do I start?

If you find it difficult to play with your child, the first thing is to stop giving yourself a hard time – it doesn't come naturally to everyone. One possible reason is that in your own childhood you may never have been on the receiving end of high-quality one-to-one parent–child play.

Here are some ideas for playing with a child under five. Sit on the floor opposite your child. If you feel uncomfortable, get some props to help you. For example, start by blowing bubbles, or taking turns to throw a bag of feathers in the air to see who can catch them before they fall. Have a mutual face-painting session. (There are lots more ideas in the chapter on the Chemistry of Love, page 182.) It's vital to keep your voice light and fun. If it all gets too serious, your child is not going to want to play with you.

Although play is a genetically ingrained impulse, it requires the right environment for expression), which means your child has to feel psychologically very safe with you. Once you have managed to activate the PLAY system in your child's brain, her squeals of delight will soon be so reinforcing that you will both want more playtimes like this.

If play remains awkward for you, make sure there are some people in your child's life (including other children) who can give her social play for about an hour a day.

Parents who have never experienced playful human interaction themselves can benefit from being on the receiving end of such interactions in adulthood, whether via play classes or on a one-to-one basis. There is wonderful work going on by clinical psychologist Sue Jenner, who uses what she calls the Parent–Child Game to teach parents to interact with their child in a playful way. In this method, a therapist tells the parents, via an earpiece, what to say or do while they are actually in a situation with their child.

▉ Why drugs may not be the answer.

Some people, unaware that interactive play can develop the regulating functions in the frontal lobes, think that the only answer to hyperactivity is drug treatment with methylphenidate, which has the brand name Ritalin. Methylphenidate is an amphetamine, like cocaine. This drug has common side effects including headache, nausea, insomnia, and loss of appetite. Parents and teachers often report that children on methylphenidate seem to lose their fun, sparkle, and ability to play.[33] The result of stopping the drug can be a "rebound effect", which includes agitation, depression, and exhaustion.

What's more, the latest research shows that when methylphenidate was given to pre-pubescent mammals, they had life-long reductions in brain dopamine activity. This is because the drug puts a great deal of strain on the brain's developing dopamine system. Parkinson's disease results from a reduction in the brain's dopamine, although we do not yet know whether pre-pubescent children taking methylphenidate are at particular risk of developing early Parkinson's disease.[34]

Research with mammals shows that interactive play can be as effective as mild doses of methylphenidate.[35] Many children also stop being hyperactive if they take fish oil rather than drugs. Fish oil can increase levels of serotonin in the brain, which naturally inhibits impulsiveness.

Play well and live life well

The activation of the brain's PLAY system is key to living life well. When this system is optimally activated in childhood, it is likely to set vital foundations for the ability in later life to be able to bring fun and a sense of play into relationships. The "play urge" can be channelled into vital social capacities. Also, in adulthood when the PLAY system works in combination with the higher verbal brain, it is likely to result in new forms of play, such as humour and the play of ideas, a kind of "playground in the mind".[36] Humour is a vital capacity for mental health in the face of adversity.

Key points

■ **Providing your child** with calm and comforting physical affection is likely to strengthen her immune system and have a long-term effect on her brain's stress-regulating systems.

■ **Lots of joyous** and playful times one-to-one with your child can activate positive arousal chemicals in her brain as well as her brain's PLAY system. As a result, zest for life can become one of your child's personality traits.

■ **As parents,** we can easily crush joy by squashing a child's excitement or by using frightening or shaming discipline.

■ **If you provide** your child with lots of imaginative, explorative activities, you will activate the SEEKING system in her brain. When this system is working, your child will have an appetite for life, curiosity, and the drive and motivation to make her creative ideas into a reality.

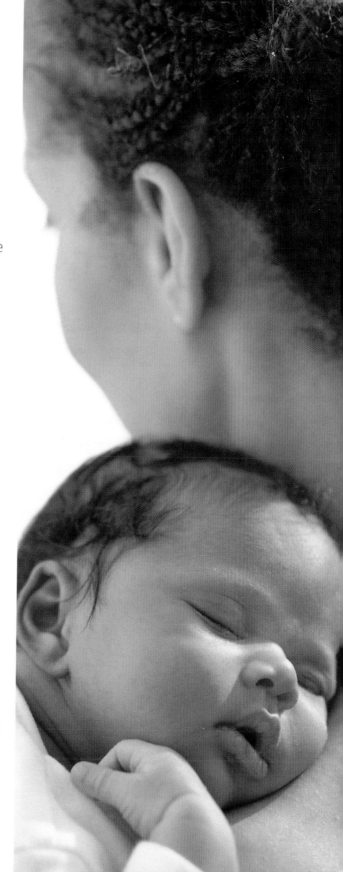

behaving badly

All parents experience challenging behaviour from their children at some time. This chapter is all about empowering parents with the scientific and psychological explanations for bad behaviour. It also focuses on temper tantrums – a time when most parents feel that they could do with practical help. Some child behaviour specialists advise ignoring a tantrum, but this is not always the best advice. In this chapter I will explain why looking only at a child's behaviour, rather than his distress levels and his needs, can fail a child.

Why children behave badly

When your child is being horrid, he is not just a bundle of naughtiness – although it may feel like this at times. He is a little person with highly complex emotional reactions, and psychological and physiological needs. What's more, if we reduce everything to a matter of behaviour, we can all too easily forget to think about what's causing the behaviour.

"Children can be horrid when they are hungry because hunger disrupts their hormones."

Parents can do a great deal to prevent their children from behaving badly. This chapter aims to empower parents by explaining what is going on inside a child's head when he is being naughty and how they can help to avoid or resolve troublesome episodes. It shows how, when addressing challenging behaviour, we need to hold in mind a child's feelings and relationship issues as well as just the behaviour. Whenever your child is behaving badly it is due to one or more of the following six reasons and knowing what they are will help you to respond to your child appropriately.

"Sorry, I'm just fed up"

When a child is being naughty, it can be difficult to think about why. Children are highly complex beings, yet they do not have the maturity to communicate these feelings effectively. This can lead to outbursts of bad behaviour. If you take time to talk to your child about her behaviour, in an attempt to understand the underlying causes, her real feelings often come out, and you can find a creative way to resolve the situation.

Reason one: tiredness and hunger

Children often behave badly when they have an unmet physical need for sleep or food. Consuming certain foods or drink may also play havoc with their brains and bodies.

Research shows that sleep deprivation is associated with imbalances in the autonomic nervous system (see page 44), which regulates bodily arousal. When this system is balanced, natural calming mechanisms come into play to help stabilize mood. When we are short of sleep, these mechanisms may no longer function well and the arousal branch of the system is left in the driving seat, often tipping the child into states of over-arousal.[1]

Sleep loss also intensifies negative emotions when we are under stress. In addition, it can cause imbalances in blood sugar levels, with consequent effects on mood – including aggression, anxiety, and depression.[2]

■ **But you can't blame tiredness for everything.**
Because it's easier to look for a physical cause for bad behaviour than it is to reflect on the complexities of emotional and relationship needs, many parents too easily blame tiredness when their child is being horrid. If the child is not tired and is feeling awful for another reason, this incorrect labelling means a painful experience of misunderstanding for the child and the missing of an opportunity for real resolution of the problem.

■ **The hunger monster plays havoc with the brain.**
Children can be horrid when they are hungry because hunger disrupts their hormones. If your child's blood sugar level falls too low, his body will respond by releasing stress hormones from the adrenal glands. These hormones include cortisol and adrenalin, which are designed to raise blood sugar levels. However, the strong activation of adrenalin and cortisol means that your child may then suffer from any of the following: anxiety, agitation, aggression, feelings of panic,

CONSIDER THIS...

Research shows that missing breakfast can result in hyperactive behaviour. A proper breakfast improves a child's academic performance, psychological well-being, and behaviour. When children who didn't eat breakfast started eating it, they had a far more stable mood for the rest of the day.[3]

"Chocolate and sweets eaten on an empty stomach send a child's sugar levels sky high."

Research on infants shows that DHA (one of the omega 3 fatty acids) from fish oil is essential for normal brain development, thinking, and concentration. It also boosts serotonin levels. One study shows that low levels of DHA were associated with more:

- temper tantrums
- sleep problems
- behaviour problems
- learning problems.[5]

and confusion. These painful feelings may be discharged in a temper tantrum.

Low blood sugar (technically known as hypoglycaemia) also deprives the brain of glucose, which can lead to out-of-control behaviour, similar to the way people behave under the influence of alcohol.

Sugar and sweets may cause bad behaviour.

Chocolate and sweets eaten on an empty stomach, instead of a proper meal (or without the presence of adequate amounts of protein), send a child's sugar levels sky high. The child gets an energy boost within 10–15 minutes, but then, because blood sugar levels rise too high, insulin kicks in to drop the blood sugar back to safe levels. After about 30 minutes, the child experiences a dramatic drop in blood sugar that is lower than before he ate the sweets. This can lead to hypoglycaemia, which in turn leads to aggression, anxiety, and hyperactive behaviour such as rushing about and climbing up things.[4]

This same child can play very well for some time if he eats a proper meal, which boosts levels of the mood-stabilizing chemical serotonin in his brain. If you do give snacks, a piece of toast with honey or a banana is better than chocolate. These foods will not cause a dramatic drop in blood sugar, and they also raise levels of serotonin.

Food additives can impact on the brain.

Children are particularly vulnerable to food additives because their bodies and brains are so immature. Some additives reduce levels of dopamine and noradrenaline in the brain, resulting in hyperactive behaviour in some children. So, if your child has just had an ice-cream or fizzy drink, and starts being hyperactive, you'll know why. Watch out for:

■ **E110,** which is used in some biscuits. It is carcinogenic when fed to animals.

■ **E122,** found in some jams. It is also carcinogenic when fed to animals.

"I'm being hyperactive!"

Food additives in processed foods such as biscuits, sweets, and soft drinks can have mood-altering effects on a child's brain and are common triggers of bad behaviour. Sometimes this is the reason why children's parties end with at least one overexcited child in tears. Try to choose appealing, healthy alternatives that are low in additives, colouring, and sugar.

- **E127** is used in some sweets. It is also a dopamine and noradrenaline inhibitor, and can lead to loss of concentration and behaviour such as ADHD (see page 106).
- **E150** is added to some soft drinks and crisps.
- **E210-E219** is used in some soft drinks, jam, and salad cream, and is linked to asthma and childhood hyperactivity.
- **E220-227** is in some desserts, biscuits, and fruit juices.
- **E249-252** is added to some cured meats and some cheeses. It causes headaches and is linked to cancer in human studies.
- **Sweeteners** are added to some soft drinks and sweet foods. They can reduce levels of tryptophan, which is vital for the brain to make the mood-stabilizing chemical serotonin. Low tryptophan levels are linked to both hyperactive and aggressive behaviour.[6]

"Children are particularly vulnerable to food additives because their bodies and brains are so immature."

"Young children can't naturally inhibit their primitive impulses to run about and climb up things."

Reason two: an undeveloped emotional brain

Children are sometimes criticized for bad behaviour that they simply can't be held responsible for, because their emotional brains are too immature for them to behave better. In young children, the higher brain is still very undeveloped, which means that they can't naturally inhibit their primitive impulses to lash out, or run about and climb up things all the time.

There is much unfair punishment by parents and in schools due to lack of understanding about immature brains.

▪ **One in five parents** thinks it is OK to smack a toddler for throwing a tantrum.

▪ **One in ten parents** thinks it is OK to smack a toddler for refusing to get into a buggy.

▪ **More than 85 percent of parents** shout at their children.[7]

"I feel really angry"

There are many reasons why a child may behave badly at school or nursery. Tiredness and hunger may play a part, but there may be emotional reasons, too. Difficulties at home can have a dramatic influence on a child's relationships with her peer group and with carers and teachers.

Some people hit a baby or lash out in anger at a toddler, because they think the child is being deliberately naughty. In other words, they read intention into what the child is doing. Many previous generations of parents have subscribed to the view that to "give in" to a crying baby will "spoil" him or that children can have their parents "wrapped around their little finger". However, we now know that a baby's or young child's brain isn't developed enough to be clearly defined thoughts about manipulating adults (see box, right).

Reason three: psychological hungers

The three psychological hungers – for stimulation, recognition, and structure – were originally defined by a psychologist called Eric Berne. He found that, over time, if one or more of these hungers remains unsatisfied, people can become emotionally unwell and even, in the long term, be affected by mental and physical ill health.[8]

"If a child is not experiencing enough incidents, he will make his own."

■ **Understimulation is a pain in the brain.**

The brain registers understimulation as stress. To change this painful state, people will do something to increase their arousal state and to change the chemical state in the brain. Adults, for example, may turn on the radio or light a cigarette; infants may start head-banging; children might start running around screaming. Because children have fewer resources than adults, the stimulation they choose is often aggressive, noisy, or destructive – such as hitting a sibling or pouring juice all over the table. Part of stimulation hunger is incident hunger. Again, if a child is not experiencing enough incidents, he will make his own, perhaps by fighting his brother or throwing a temper tantrum (see page 120).

BRAIN STORY

There is a chemical system in the frontal lobes of the brain called the glutamate system, which enables us to have clearly defined thoughts and intentions – including destructive ones. The glutamate system is not properly established in babies and small children, which means that they lack the sophistication to be deliberately naughty or manipulative. Some parents mistakenly interpret behaviour that results from immature brain chemistry as rudeness or defiance, and they respond by punishing the baby or child. The glutamate system starts to develop during the first year of life.

frontal lobes

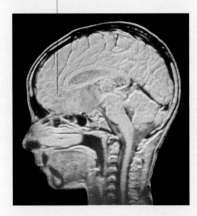

An MRI of a baby's head shows the cerebrum (yellow), the main part of the brain. The glutamate system is very undeveloped in a newborn baby's frontal lobes.

"Children need lots of attention for healthy brain development."

We are all attention-seeking, but children especially need lots of attention for the healthy development of their brains, and they are generally far more overt about their recognition needs than many adults. Children don't know about the psychology of recognition hunger, but they soon discover that bad behaviour guarantees getting attention.

Recognition hunger makes a child seek attention.

Recognition hunger is the genetically programmed human need for attention, which means having an impact on someone in a way that makes them respond. We all have a fundamental psychological need to feel that we can have an impact on the world, because, "If I have an impact, I know that I exist."[9] If a child feels that good behaviour does not impact on his parent, he resorts to bad behaviour instead.

Bad behaviour that stems from recognition hunger comes from an inner scream of "Please don't ignore me". If your child thinks the only way to get your attention is to be naughty or to scream or cry, then this is what he will do. Of course, for all children lovely attention is better than angry attention, but if angry attention is all that is available then this is what children will seek.

Structure hunger can lead to bad behaviour.

We all have a psychological need for structure. Lack of structure can make adults feel depressed, anxious, or angry or lose focus and meaning. A society without structure is an extremely fertile ground for bad behaviour. Without the structure of rules and the law, we would have a breakdown in civilization. It's just the same with children. They need the structure of clear house rules and clear routines.

Think of the structureless time for a child of waiting in a queue or following you around a shop. Your child suddenly becomes horrid. But when you do some structured activity with him, you have a great child!

Reason four: needing help with a big feeling

Sometimes children behave badly because they are discharging tension from a very painful emotion. They may be angry or frustrated with someone; they may be being bullied at school or jealous of attention being paid to a sibling; they may be struggling with some event, such as the loss of a relative, a friend, or a pet. A big painful feeling activates stress chemicals in a child's brain and body, so ear-piercing outbursts are often a child's way of relieving tension. A child does not have the words to express his emotions, so he vents his feelings in a scream or a shout. Some parents immediately punish their child for this rather than treating it as a cry for help. If we help children with their painful feelings (disappointment, jealousy, loss, frustration) rather than criticizing them for their lower brain-triggered emotional outbursts, we can help their higher brain to develop the nerve pathways essential for naturally regulating such feelings.[10]

Reason five: picking up on your stress

A child's behaviour is often a barometer of parental stress, depression, anger, or grief. Persistent screaming and raging in a child can be a way of discharging his parents' emotions.

Parenting is one of the most stressful jobs there is, and the more stressed you are, the more likely your children are to behave badly. Why? The right prefrontal part of a child's brain can pick up emotional atmospheres in milliseconds. Just as some dogs are susceptible to the emotions of their owners, so children are deeply affected on a bodily and emotional level by stress or unhappiness in their family. If you are relaxed, the chances are your child will be calm. If the atmosphere at home is tense, your child can be horrid.[11]

Reason six: you activate the wrong part of your child's brain

Your way of relating to your child may be activating the wrong part of his brain. For example, if you shout and issue endless commands – "Do this, don't do that" – you could be unwittingly activating the primitive RAGE and FEAR systems deep in the mammalian and reptilian parts of his brain. In contrast, lots of play, laughter, and cuddles are likely to activate the brain's PLAY system and CARE system. These systems trigger the release of lovely calming opioids. So hey presto, you have a calm, contented child.[11]

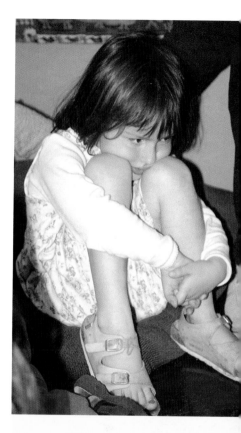

"You're being horrid."

One of the main reasons why children behave badly is because the way a parent is relating to a child is activating the wrong part of a child's brain. You will have a horrid time with your child if you activate her lower brain RAGE, FEAR, or DISTRESS systems (see page 24). You can have a delightful time if you activate her lower brain PLAY or SEEKING systems (see pages 94 and 108) or her CARE system (see page 190).

Temper tantrums

Temper tantrums are intense storms of feeling. They usually happen because a child's higher brain is not sufficiently developed to deal with powerful feelings in more socially acceptable ways. As we shall see, many tantrums are the result of genuine emotional pain, which should be taken seriously: the pain of impotence, deep frustration, loss, disappointment, and feeling misunderstood. Only some tantrums are primarily motivated by a wish to have control over a parent.

"There are two types of tantrums and each needs a specific response."

Because of their intensity, temper tantrums are often not only frightening to the child himself, but also leave the parent feeling lacking in skills, helpless, overwhelmed, or ready to explode. This is particularly true when parents' own intense feelings were not handled well in their childhood. It can be a real art for a parent to manage their own feelings during a child's tantrum. It's vital that the whole thing doesn't turn into a matter of winners and losers, but instead involves a parent staying calm and thinking of rational or creative ways to manage the child's feelings.

Conflict with parents over food and eating accounts for around 17 percent of toddler tantrums. The reasons are often complex (see page 143).

Being strapped in a car seat or high chair can activate the lower brain's RAGE system, and accounts for more than 11 percent of tantrums.

Getting dressed restricts a child's movements in much the same way as being put in a pushchair, and accounts for about 11 percent of tantrums.

Why tantrums are important

Temper tantrums are key times for brain sculpting. This is because the emotional regulation of a child's feelings during storms of feeling enable him to establish essential brain pathways for managing stress and being assertive in later life.

The too-good child who does not have tantrums may have learned early on that when he expressed big feelings, he elicited a frightening parental response, and that the price of parental love and approval is total compliance. The too-good child misses out on the vital brain sculpting that he gets from his parents when he expresses big, dramatic feelings. This means that when he faces frustration in later life, he may respond with angry outbursts or struggle to be assertive.

▨ Not all tantrums are battles for power.

Many tantrums are about genuine emotional pain. It is a mistake to think that rage is always just about control. There can be terrible pain in some rage, as, for example, in the rage of failing to get your beloved parent to understand something that is deeply important to you.

▨ When faced with a potential conflict, ask yourself if this is worth fighting over.

Imagine you are two years old and the people in your life have control over everything you do. Wouldn't it make you mad? Work out what it is worth fighting about (for example, behaviour that is dangerous) and areas where you can give your child some slack.

▨ There are two different types of tantrum.

I call the first type a "distress" tantrum and the second a "little Nero" tantrum. It is important to know what's happening to your child's brain during each type, because each needs a specific response. With little Nero tantrums you need to move away from the child, and with distress tantrums you need to move towards the child with comfort and solace.

"It's not fair!"

One of the two types of tantrum is the "distress" tantrum. It can be triggered by strong feelings such as disappointment, loss, or frustration and can make the child feel hugely upset. This type of tantrum needs sensitive handling, and an understanding that the child cannot handle these big feelings without your help.

Distress tantrums

A distress tantrum means that one or more of the three alarm systems in your child's lower brain has been very strongly activated. These alarm systems are RAGE, FEAR, and SEPARATION DISTRESS (see page 24). As a result, your child's arousal system (see page 40) will be way out of balance, with excessively high levels of stress chemicals searing through his body and brain.

Case study

A tantrum at breakfast
James has a distress tantrum because the family has run out of his favourite breakfast cereal. He is not being naughty, but he is disappointed. He needs to discharge the bodily arousal caused by the frustration, and he needs a compassionate response.

James' dad scoops him up in his arms and uses understanding words that will enable James to start to develop stress-regulating systems. This approach is more effective than trying to reason with a young child.

Distress tantrums happen because essential brain pathways between a child's higher brain and his lower brain haven't developed yet. These brain pathways are necessary to enable a child to manage his big feelings. As a parent, your role is to soothe your child while he experiences the huge hormonal storms in his brain and body. If you get angry with a child for having a distress tantrum, he may stop crying, but this may mean that the FEAR system in his brain has triggered, over-riding his SEPARATION DISTRESS system. Or he may simply have shifted into silent crying, which means his level of the stress chemical cortisol will remain sky high. As we have seen throughout this book, uncomforted distress can leave a child with toxic levels of stress hormones washing over the brain.

■ **Children can't talk or listen well when distressed.**
The dramatic brain and body changes of a distress tantrum hijack your child's thinking functions and the verbal centres in his higher brain that control the comprehension and expression of speech. It is important to understand this because trying to talk to your child during a distress tantrum, or expecting him to talk about his feelings, is a waste of time. All he can do is discharge his emotions.

■ **A distress tantrum needs sensitive handling.**
It is important that you take a genuine distress tantrum seriously and meet your child's pain of loss, frustration, or

acute disappointment with sympathy and understanding. When you do this, you will be helping your child to develop vital stress-regulating systems in his higher brain (see pages 27 and 29). Repeatedly getting angry with a child's genuine distress can mean that the child never develops inhibitory mechanisms in his higher brain. Picture a man who often loses his temper in a restaurant, or violently kicks a faulty vending machine – in early life he may have missed out on the parenting that would have helped him manage rage.[12]

"Your role is to soothe...the huge hormonal storms in his brain and body."

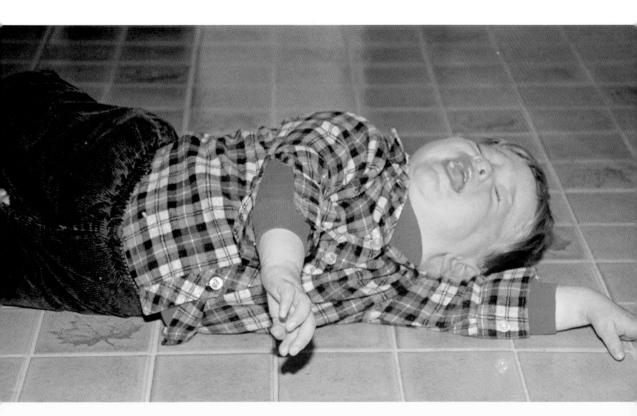

"Life is so terrible."

When a child has a "distress" tantrum, you can see real anguish in his face. Two-year-old Ben, writhing on the shop floor because he had set his heart on shoes that did not fit, is in emotional pain. One of his brain's alarm systems has triggered, and stress chemicals and hormones are flooding his body, making him feel dreadful. He needs comfort.

"Help me to handle this"

If your child is experiencing a distress tantrum, she will need your help to quieten down again. If you hold her in your arms, your mature bodily arousal system (see page 40) will help to calm her immature one.

Speak to her softly, using simple, soothing words. Your child will begin to feel very safe as she realizes that you can help her with her big feelings. This will prevent her becoming angry or withdrawing from you.

When your child feels better, try to distract her with something fun, such as a toy, or point out something interesting nearby.

▧ **Regulating childhood distress is a key task for all parents, teachers, and other childcarers.**

Receiving help to manage intense feelings of rage, frustration, or distress means that a child can develop the brain pathways that enable him to calm himself down when under stress. If we don't respond to a genuine distress tantrum and, instead, adopt a fixed approach to all tantrums, we lose a vital opportunity to sculpt a child's brain in a positive way. It is deeply reassuring to a child to know that an adult can calm and understand the volcanic storms that rip through his body and brain. It is most disturbing to a child that when he is in terrible emotional pain his Mummy gets angry or just walks away from him.

How to handle distress tantrums

Your role is to give YOUR child a sense of safety, comfort, and reassurance when he is having a distress tantrum. These techniques can all help to calm your child.

▪ **Use simple, calm actions** or provide a simple choice. For example, if your child is upset about getting dressed, ask him whether he wants to wear his blue or his brown trousers.

▪ **Distraction is a wonderful,** often under-used technique. It activates the SEEKING system (see page 94) in your child's lower brain and makes him feel curious and interested in something. It can naturally override the brain's RAGE or DISTRESS systems. It also triggers a high level of dopamine, a great positive arousal chemical in the brain, which reduces stress and triggers interest and motivation.[13]

▪ **Hold your child tenderly.** Sometimes it really helps to hold a distressed child, but you must feel calm and in control yourself. Being next to your calm body will bring his over-aroused body and brain systems back into balance and release natural, calming oxytocin and opioids. Say simple words such as, "I know, I know". (Words alone, however, will not strongly release these wonderful chemicals.) If his RAGE system has been triggered as well as his DISTRESS system, and he is

CONSIDER THIS...

It is very common for children to have nightmares after they have had a distress tantrum during the day. Intense feelings may well be symbolized by monsters in the nightmare.

"We are deeply feeling and deeply biological creatures ... we must come to terms with the biological sources of the human spirit."

~ Jaak Panksepp

Getting a young child dressed can be a common area of conflict. Offering your child a choice, or engaging her brain with a distraction, can make the process less stressful for both of you. If you try to hurry a child, a scenario along the following lines is all too likely to occur:

Parent: "Time to get dressed, please."
Molly: "No."
Parent: "Come on. It's time to go out."
Molly: "Shan't! No! No! No!"

The RAGE systems in both child's and mother's lower brains are triggered as cascades of horrid hormones and stress chemicals flood out. Before this turns into a tantrum, try activating a child's frontal lobe by giving her something to think about. Offer her a choice, such as

"Do you want to wear a dress or trousers today?"

You could also try distraction as you get your child dressed. Point out a toy, or sing a song, using a lovely, playful tone of voice. This engages your child's higher brain and makes the whole process much more enjoyable.

throwing things around the room or hitting or biting, you will need to use the proper holding technique (see page 177).

■ **Sometimes a child will feel safe and contained** just by you sitting down calmly next to him and talking gently. Some children find this preferable to being held, as it allows them the freedom to move.

■ **Avoid using the time-out technique** during a distress tantrum. You wouldn't walk away from your best friend or send her to a time-out room if she was writhing and sobbing on the floor, so this is certainly not appropriate for children, who have far fewer emotional resources than adults. Using time-out for a child in distress would also mean missing a vital opportunity for rage and distress regulation and establishing effective stress-regulating systems in the brain.

■ **Avoid putting a child in a room on his own** during a distress tantrum. Although the child may stop vocal crying, he may continue to cry internally – something that research shows is more worrying.[14] Whereas vocal crying is a request for help, silent, internal crying is a sign that the child has lost faith that help will come. In some people, this tragic loss of faith can stay for life.

■ **Remind yourself that a child's distress is genuine.** A two year old who is screaming because his sibling has snatched a toy car is not just making a fuss. Research shows that a sense of loss activates the pain centres in the brain, causing an agonizing opioid withdrawal.[15] Because small children have been in the world for only a few years, they don't have a clear perspective on life. As adults, we have a backdrop of events and experiences that tell us that the loss of a toy car is a minor disappointment. But for a small child this loss can mean everything. If a child is repeatedly punished for grief-fuelled tantrums (grief often includes rage), the lesson he learns is: "Mummy cannot manage or understand my grief." As a result, he is likely to cut off from feelings of hurt because they are no longer safe to have. This has consequences for how a child manages his feelings in adulthood (see page 205).

Q It feels as if I'm giving in when I distract her with a game. Am I "spoiling" her and encouraging more tantrums?

Starting a game of pat-a-cake or launching into a song is a very good way of distracting a toddler who is building up to a tantrum. Research shows that distraction can work very well at this stage, whereas it often doesn't once a child is deep into a full-blown distress state.[16]

Using distraction to avert a tantrum is not "spoiling" your child. Young children do not have an adult perspective on life, and not being able to do or have something they want can activate a full-blown grief reaction. Throwing a tantrum is not naughty, but is a result of immaturity. As a parent, you need to use compassion and understanding to help your child manage her feelings.

Little Nero tantrums

The Little Nero tantrum is very different from the distress tantrum in that it is about the desire to control and manipulate. A child having a Little Nero tantrum doesn't experience or show the anguish, desperation, and panic that characterizes the distress tantrum, and he doesn't have stress chemicals flooding his brain and body.

BRAIN STORY

The brain activity during a distress tantrum is very different from that in a Little Nero tantrum. During a distress tantrum, your child can't think or speak rationally because his upper brain functions are hijacked by primitive emotional systems in his lower brain. By contrast, a child who is having a Little Nero tantrum is using his frontal lobes or "upstairs brain" to produce behaviour that is calculated and deliberate.

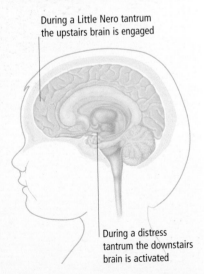

During a Little Nero tantrum the upstairs brain is engaged

During a distress tantrum the downstairs brain is activated

A Little Nero tantrum is about a child trying to get what he wants – attention, a particular toy, or food – through bullying his parents into submission. A child who has frequent Little Nero tantrums has learned that shouting and screaming produce results: "If I cry and scream, I know that eventually they'll give me that bar of chocolate."

Children who have Little Nero tantrums need to learn that they can't always receive the gratification they want at the time they want it, and that it's not OK to bully or control people to get what they want in life.

The problems of giving in

If you reward frequent Little Nero tantrums by giving in to your child's demands, you are in danger of setting up a trigger-happy RAGE system in your child's brain. This is because the mere experience of rage without the capacity for reasoned thinking can result in rage becoming a part of your child's personality.[17]

Some children, whose Little Nero tantrums have not been handled well, not only win the battle at the age of two but are still winning at six, eight, and ten years old. They then grow up to be power-seeking, bullying adults who think they can rule the roost at work and at home. Such people are developmentally arrested – Little Nero two year olds in adult bodies – and they can bring abject misery to the people who have to live with them or work with them.

"Give me what I want – now!"

A Little Nero tantrum is very different from a distress tantrum. There is usually an absence of tears and the child is able to articulate her demands, and to argue when you say "no". A child uses this type of tantrum because she has learned that it will get her what she wants. The more you reward this type of tantrum with attention and giving her what she wants, the more she will continue to adopt this behaviour. This can train your child to become a bully in later life (see page 160).

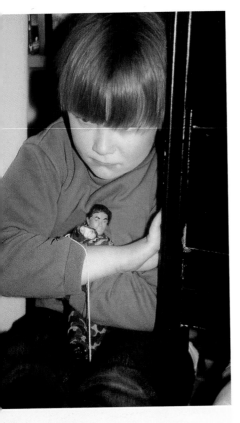

"Well, that didn't work!"

If you ignore a Little Nero tantrum, you are helping your child to develop important social skills. It is essential that you do not humiliate your child, though; he should lose the battle gracefully and with dignity. Reward your child with your attention as soon as his behaviour improves.

Techniques for handling Little Nero tantrums

Little Nero rages need a very different sort of response from a distress tantrum. The following key techniques will help you to be the one in charge, rather than your two year old being in control of you.

■ **Don't give your child an audience.** A Little Nero tantrum must be a solo performance. If you are absolutely sure your child is not having a distress tantrum, simply walk out of the room. If you ignore a child's Little Nero tantrums, he will stop. It's no fun if there is no-one watching.

■ **Don't try to reason, argue with, or persuade** your child. Attention and words reward his negative behaviour.

"Pay no attention to your child while he is using control and dominance."

■ **Don't "kiss it better".** This approach gives your child the message: "If you go into a rage, I will give you lots of love."

■ **Don't negotiate.** If you do, you are rewarding controlling, angry behaviour. If a child discovers that rage works well in manipulating his parents, he may continue to use it in his adult life. Consider the following nightmare. You have always rewarded your child's wish to control you with attention. Now, at 16, he is still hitting you and kicking doors. Because he's bigger than you, you can't just put him in his room and make him do Time Out (see page 174).

■ **Give clear, firm "nos"** and try to manage your own rage. No human being likes feeling controlled.

■ **Deal firmly with your child's commands.** Give a clear, firm message about commands being unacceptable as a way of getting what you want. For example, if your child is shouting and screaming for a biscuit, try saying: "I'm really happy to talk with you about what you would like when your voice is as quiet as mine." Then get on with what you are doing until your child is calmer and says "please". Pay

absolutely no attention to your child while he is using control and dominance as a way of requesting something. Carrying on any conversation with him while he is still issuing you with commands rewards his rage and power-seeking behaviour, and goes one step further towards setting up a hot temper as a personality trait.

■ **Give information about social charm.** This works better with an older child, whose higher brain is more developed. You could say: "If you order people to do something, they won't want to help you. So if you want something, can you think of a way of asking that will unlock my kind feelings? If you need help with that, let me know."

Or try a really light and clear response: "Hey, Toby, that really won't work for me."

■ **Use humour and play when appropriate.** This can deflate a Little Nero's power bubble. Mirror him back to himself. The underlying message is that your child will not get away with a "power over" transaction with you. Try something like: "You really do want to boss me about, don't you? Let's do it together to this can of peas. 'Can of peas – get me that biscuit now! Or, I know, let's boss the toothbrush around...come here toothbrush!'" By now, your child will be looking at you as if you are mad. But the ploy serves to upstage him, stop him in his tracks, move you both into the realm of humour and play (whether he likes it or not), and mirror him back to himself. It will also show that you do not take bullying seriously.

■ **Use Time Out as a last resort.** It's appropriate only if your child is hurting someone by biting, hitting, or kicking (particularly if your child is over the age of five). Take him to a time-out room and say: "I am putting you in here because you bit me. It is never OK to hurt someone." (Time Out is explained on page 174.)

■ **Distinguish between a Little Nero tantrum** and a distress tantrum. Sometimes this is difficult because one tips into the other. Obviously, you should never reward statements such as: "Go to the shops to get me white bread NOW", but if he

Case study

Out of control Emma

If Emma didn't get her own way, she would scream, kick, cry, and throw herself on the floor. She was often bossy, saying things like: "Don't go out, stay with me." She deliberately damaged her doll because she wanted a new one. Emma's mother tried to reason and plead with her – the worst response to Little Nero behaviour. Emma got worse. When she began to pull light fittings off the wall to make her mother do as she asked, Emma was referred to a therapist. Her mother confessed that she although she loved Emma, she didn't like her any more.

Emma was very well-behaved at school. When asked why she was so different at school, she said: "You aren't allowed to be naughty at school." When Emma's mother went to parenting classes, she learned how to set clear boundaries and consequences. At age nine, Emma lost a two-year-long battle – but better late than never!

"Ask yourself if there is enough parent–child play in your house."

moves into a grief reaction when you say "no" (and you sense the pain is genuine rather than a magnificent act) he will need help with his feelings. The message you need to give your child is: "I don't respond to commands, but I will help you if you are in pain." All mammals, including human infants, are genetically programmed to react with rage if they don't receive an anticipated reward, and do not have the frontal lobe development to override these feelings.

Feelings and physical states linked to tantrums

As we have seen, certain physical and emotional states are responsible for bad behaviour in general. Similarly, there are well-recognized tantrum triggers. Hunger, tiredness, and tension are among the most common. You could also check to see if the following painful states are turning your house into a persistent scream zone.

■ **Boredom.** If children are suffering from stimulation hunger (see page 117), then screaming and shouting can become very appealing. Ask yourself if there is enough parent–child play in your house. Screaming is common in families who don't play together. A classic example of boredom is the tantrum in the supermarket. If you give your child interesting tasks and activities, the tantrums usually stop (for more on this, see page 140).

■ **Frustration.** Children aren't good at finding words for frustration. You may need to help them express their feelings: "It's so hard to share sometimes, isn't it? You just start playing with that toy and your little brother came and took it."

■ **Disappointment.** Loss and disappointment activate the pain centres in the brain. As adults, we are able to say "never mind" and distract ourselves with something else, but when children are disappointed they find it overwhelming and may burst into tears. Children need help to manage their painful feelings and for you to acknowledge that disappointment can hurt a lot. Ignoring or getting angry with a disappointed child will simply add to his pain.

Understimulation or boredom is a painful state in terms of low bodily arousal. To satisfy the human psychological hunger for stimulation, your child may resort to screaming and tantrums. Learn how to play together as a family, and find your child plenty of rewarding tasks to do.

Key points

■ **There are six triggers** for bad behaviour: tiredness and hunger; an immature brain; unmet psychological needs; intense emotions; parental stress; and a parenting style that activates the alarm systems in a child's lower brain.

■ **A child having a** distress tantrum is in genuine pain and needs lots of calm, compassionate support from you. Ignoring or punishing distress can be damaging.

■ **Although distress tantrums** can be challenging, they present a great opportunity to help your child develop essential brain pathways that enable him to manage stress in the future.

■ **Little Nero tantrums** should be ignored. Children who are rewarded for rage often continue to use it as a technique as they grow older. Rage can become an ingrained personality trait.

the trying times

Focusing mainly on the under-fives, this chapter looks in depth at what is happening in the brains of young children when they are behaving badly. Most parents will be familiar with the common situations covered here – from bouncing on beds and rioting in restaurants to "I want" scenes in toyshops and fighting with siblings. What parents may not know is that such behaviour happens at a stage of development when children's brain systems are not mature enough to take control.

Getting out of control

Adults don't particularly want to jump up and down on beds or run around shops. Why not? It's because the frontal lobes of our brains are mature enough to naturally inhibit our "motoric impulses" – urges to run, jump, and climb. Small children have not yet developed such controlling mechanisms, and so simply asking them to comply with adult behaviour is unlikely to work.

CONSIDER THIS...

In children, the brain's dopamine and noradrenaline systems are slow to mature. These systems are vital for concentration and sustained, focused attention. This is why your child is often:

- easily distracted
- impulsive
- unable to focus
- unable to filter out distractions
- prone to lots of manic behaviour.

When they just say "won't"

While we need to give a child clear boundaries, rules, and consequences for unacceptable behaviour, we also don't want to damage her will. A child's strong will is a great life resource. Saying "won't" at two or three years of age is the precursor for the capacity to stand up for yourself, the passion to know what you want in life, and the drive to follow it through. Children who move into total compliance at the toddler stage often suffer in later life from not having developed a separate self. They may be very skilled at adapting to the needs and feelings of others, but with little or no notion about they want and feel. This can happen with over-strict parenting where an infant is too frightened to protest, or with parenting which employs all manner of subtle forms of withdrawal of love and approval to get obedience. The latter happens with parents who delight in the placid, dependent baby but then can't allow the stroppy toddler to have any autonomy or protest. A parent's love and approval is a basic need for a child, and if the price of that is total obedience, the toddler may decide, well so be it.

If you have a toddler who often asserts her will in very trying ways, give yourself credit for the fact that whilst you obviously need to be clear about boundaries, you have not moved into obedience training. As parents, we need to think very carefully how to respond to a child who says "no". This chapter offers many resources and ways forward.

Trying times when they bounce about

Bouncing on beds and running about is not being naughty. Unless under-fives have been frightened by obedience training, which triggers a freeze response on naturally spontaneous behaviour, they will find it extremely difficult to put the brakes on their behaviour. This is because their higher brain has not yet formed key pathways which connect to their lower brain. These pathways will naturally inhibit the urge to bounce about. Also, infants have very immature noradrenaline and dopamine systems in their higher brain, which also results in impulsive "can't sit still" behaviour.[1] The answer is to find a channel for their energy.

"Children who move into total compliance often suffer later in life."

If you are worried about your bed or sofa, give your child something else; for example, provide a small trampoline in the garden, or take her to the local playground. There is no need to lose your temper; just say in a gentle voice, "It's not OK to jump on this bed. Let's go outside". If your child will not get off the bed, pick her up gently and take her outside.

Trying times in public places

Because of your child's uninhibited impulses, it's wise to consider carefully which public places you can visit. Small children and five-star restaurants are, by and large, a very bad mix. Parents can get very angry and disappointed when their child's brain can't act like an adult's, and an outing is ruined. If they think of places to go to that cater well for a young child's motoric impulses, they will probably have a great time.

▨ **Find a space to run around.**

If you are visiting a public place such as a gallery, restaurant, or hotel, look around for a large space where your child can

CONSIDER THIS...

In one sense, all young children have ADHD (attention deficit hyperactive disorder), which means impulsive behaviour and poor concentration on one thing for any length of time. Instead, they run around, climb, move constantly, and fidget. This is a natural developmental stage and the result of an immature brain. It is also considerably harder for boys to sit still than girls because the maturation of the higher brain (frontal lobes) is slower in boys than in girls.

Young children need a lot of time in the day for running about. If they don't get it, they tend to be highly active at times that don't always suit you.[2]

"I just can't keep still!"

If children understood their own brain processes and had the powers of sophisticated speech, they would explain that they simply haven't got the brain wiring yet to curb their restless impulses. They might impress on you the need for some space to let off steam, such as a trip to a play centre. The novelty of a fresh environment and new toys will activate calming dopamine in their frontal lobes.

run about. The fewer other people around the better, then your child can be as noisy as she needs to be. After running about to her heart's content, she will be more inclined to behave quietly again inside.

▤ Boredom often breeds bad behaviour in cafés and restaurants.

Consider the following scenario. Mia, aged two, has been taken to a café for tea, and she's getting bored. So she bangs her spoon loudly on the table, causing heads to turn. She starts to spurt her blackcurrant drink over the table and dabbles her fingers in it. Then she pours sugar everywhere and plays at dive-bombing her mother's cup of coffee. What is going on in Mia's brain?

Mia isn't being naughty; the immature systems in her brain are making her act like this. She's been told to sit quietly but, like any small child, she's bored stiff by the adult conversation going on over her head. Mia's boredom means she is in a state of low arousal, which can activate painful stress chemicals in her brain, making her behave in an even more trying way. Her behaviour at the table is her attempt to satisfy her stimulation hunger. Coupled with this are Mia's motoric impulses, which her brain is too undeveloped to be able to inhibit naturally.

Of course, a toddler messing about like this is very trying. Parents may at this stage move into punishment. (Out of ignorance about a child's developing brain, some parents will lash out at children at such times.) But there is a way forward.

If we give Mia a toy to play with or a colouring book, it is very likely to engage her higher brain in a coordinated way with her lower brain's SEEKING system.[3] This system releases dopamine and opioids, brain chemicals that will enable Mia to focus on the activity, and in so doing, naturally calm her motoric impulses. If we don't bring things for children to do in cafés and restaurants, it is very likely that they will make their own entertainment.

"Of course, a toddler messing about is very trying. But there is a way forward."

The cafe is boring and Mia needs something to lock her attention onto – otherwise the outing may well end in tears.

"Sitting with nothing to do is extremely stressful for children."

■ **Turn the shopping trip from hell into an exciting treasure hunt.**

A long trip to the supermarket with nothing to do is often too hard to bear for a young child. To avoid a trying time, it is important to engage your child in what is going on. Without an activity such as a task-focused game, a child can feel very bored, with unmet structure and stimulation hungers (see page 117). She will also experience low bodily arousal states,

"I'm fully engaged"

We need to provide entertainment for a child when visiting public places or immaculate homes where children are not always made welcome. If you don't give a child alternatives, such as a fascinating toy or a drawing book, he will find his own entertainment, such as playing with cutlery, blowing bubbles in his drink, and exploring where he shouldn't.

which, as we have seen, can trigger pain centres in her brain. This means that you are right on target for a shopping trip from hell, with your child running up and down the aisles and crashing the shopping trolleys.

Before all this happens, move into the playful part of your brain for a moment or two, and think up a game for you and your child to enjoy together while shopping: a "let's do something together" game. This will satisfy her stimulation and structure hungers. A good example is "Champion Shoppers", which can go something like this:

"Let's play a game. Have you heard of 'Champion Shoppers'? No? Well, here is how it works. When we get to each aisle, I will whisper in your ear an item of shopping we need for the trolley and you can go and look for it. When you've found it and brought it back, I'll whisper something else. If you find everything, you are a Champion Shopper and deserve a Champion treat. You can choose it yourself!"

TV Supernanny Jo Frost has a really creative version of a "let's" game for supermarkets. At the beginning of each shopping trip, the children are given a board with pictures of foods they have to find. The boring shopping trip is instantly turned into a treasure hunt.

Trying times on train and car journeys

If a child has to sit in a car or train or other form of transport for a while, her motoric impulses will become very strong, leading to fidgeting and restlessness. As adults, our mature frontal lobes inhibit such impulses, so we are happy to keep still, especially with a book or conversation to occupy us. Sitting with nothing to do is extremely stressful for children.

■ **To enjoy a journey, give your child something interesting to do to engage her frontal lobes and activate her SEEKING system.**

If you do this, it will naturally calm those primitive impulses to run about. You could initiate a guessing game, or give her

Neil, aged four, has been given the task of looking for items of shopping. He's become helpful instead of rioting. The structured activity has engaged his higher brain and his lower brain's SEEKING system, which will dramatically improve his ability to focus and concentrate. When a child's higher brain is not engaged because there is no structured activity on offer, his bodily impulses to run wild, shout, and scream can have a field day.

"If you forget to bring something to play with, don't be surprised if you have a stressful journey."

some paper and crayons. The more you join in with your child's play – for example, by initiating a game that involves you both or paying attention to her drawing – the more your mature brain and body systems will be emotionally regulating her immature systems.[4] Your calmness will have a direct calming effect on her. You can increase her settled state by letting her sit on your lap and cuddling her. This will release oxytocin in her brain, which is a calming anti-stress chemical.[5]

By taking on board these simple facts about brain science, and fully catering for your child's immature brain systems, you can turn a potentially difficult journey into a delightful time together. If you forget to bring something to play with, or some creative activities to engage her higher brain, don't be surprised if you have a stressful outing.

"We're bored and stressed in the car!"

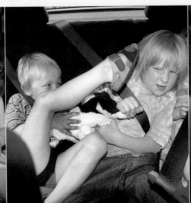

Sitting in the back of a car for ages is very stressful for children. It activates negative arousal chemicals in the brain. To change this painful brain chemistry, children will find their own amusement.

Kicking your sister (which is what happened here) seems like a good activity to fill the time. And if your sister cries or hits you back, then you have live entertainment to lift you out of your boredom.

To inhibit their motoric impulses, give them something to read, make, or draw. This will shift negative to positive brain chemistry, enabling them to lock their concentration onto more peaceful activities.

▨ Take a break from the road.

If you are on a long car journey, find time to pull off the road and head for the nearest playground or open space. This will give your child a much needed chance to let her motoric impulses rip for a while.

Trying times with meals

Why does your child prefer to play games at the table, swooping like a seagull or a bomber pilot, rather than sitting nicely and eating her food? If she's excited about something, her highly aroused body (the autonomic nervous system; see page 44) will be suppressing her appetite. An excited child is not being naughty because she's refusing to eat her food properly. It's just that human bodies are genetically programmed to have no interest in eating when in a state of high excitement. Once again, you will have a trying time if you attempt to fight against these facts about your child's bodily arousal system.

Some parents can get into a very negative pattern at mealtimes, trying to make an excited child eat. This can cause considerable relational stress for the child, which is bad for her developing brain (see page 32). If you wait until her high arousal level has come down again and she is calm, she will start to feel hungry again.

Similarly, if a child is anxious or fearful, she will lose her appetite. Some parents get very agitated around mealtimes, and the child picks this up and doesn't want to eat. The more uptight the parent gets, the more anxious the child becomes, and the less interested in her food. The more laid-back a parent can be around eating times, the better.

▨ If a child has become anxious about food, undo any negative associations between eating and place.

In all mammals, high levels of stress or fear can block hunger and close down natural digestive processes. So if your child picks up on your anxiety about her not eating enough, or

Benjamin has been on the train for half an hour and his impulses to move are very strong. His natural brain and body responses are urging him to clamber all over the seat rather than sit on it.

about the mess she is making (you can give this away by madly wiping away any mess round her mouth or spills), she may not want to eat. Parental anxiety and intrusive feeding can be a major cause of eating problems in children. The right frontal lobe is amazing at picking up emotional atmospheres. So when you are worried about her not eating enough, this part of your child's brain will be picking up in milliseconds your anxious facial expression, agitated voice,

> "The important thing is to avoid squashing your child's wonderful creativity and imagination."

or tense body. Try to activate your child's lower brain PLAY system at meal times, so she starts to associate food with fun instead of fear. Give her patterned plates, and allow her to play with food to explore new textures and colours.

Trying times with making a mess

The house has gone strangely quiet. You go to look, and then you discover the mess. The children have laid waste to the bathroom, making a river out of toilet rolls. What do you do? You can let it trigger the RAGE system (see page 24) in your lower brain, or you can pull yourself back from the brink and think of how to make your response a positive, rather than negative, relational experience for your child. The important thing is to avoid squashing your child's wonderful creativity and imagination. Imaginative, cooperative play is a real developmental achievement for young children, and it helps to develop their higher brains (frontal lobes).[6]

Cooperation, planning, thinking about what to do next, and listening to each other's ideas can form all manner of new neural connections and pathways in your child's higher brain. Such activities must be applauded and encouraged, not

TRY THIS...

If a child has got into an anxious lock with food because she has picked up on your anxiety about eating, try the following suggestions.

● Change where the child eats, in order to undo any negative associations between eating and place.
● Cook together, so your child becomes interested in food. Let her do some playtime with foods where she can explore new textures with her fingers and make a mess with food.
● Don't punish poor eating. Ignore it if you can. Instead, reward good eating and sitting well at mealtimes. Use stickers and stars when your child eats properly. Give the sticker immediately so there is a clear association in the child's mind between nice feelings and eating well at a table.
● If a child isn't eating well, and you are convinced it's not because of your anxiety, make sure there aren't lots of super little snacks available so she's quietly grazing throughout the day.

punished. That said, it is also important not to give the message that your child can create whatever havoc she likes all over the home and expect you to clear it up.

■ Make tidying up into a game.

With a small child, try making tidying up a "let's" game. Say, "Let's see who can put the most toys away in the box. I bet I can beat you...ready, steady, go". Let your child win! Afterwards say, "Wow, you are a champion toy tidier".

If your child refuses to tidy up, you may need to move into the technique called "choices and consequences" (see page 167). Not only does this stop the nagging; it activates the decision-making part of your child's higher brain. Take her hands, look calmly into her face, and say: "There's a rule in this house that whoever makes a mess clears it up, so you

"Cooperation, planning, thinking about what to do next can form new neural connections in your child's brain."

have a choice. You can tidy up your toys now or I can tidy them up. But each toy I tidy, I will take away from you and keep in a box until you have shown me you understand the tidying. Let me know what you've decided". With lots of children, this will be enough for them to start tidying. If the child ignores you, avoid nagging or persuading and just carry on as you said you would. Tidy up the toys and take them away. She can earn them back by helping you tidy up something else in the home.

Trying times and toy wars

Why do children get so heated about possession of a toy? There are several brain factors involved here. First, emotional attachment to an object releases opioids in a child's brain.

"What a mess!"

The toilet has become a river made from eight rolls of toilet paper, and the mess and waste are appalling. You could let your RAGE system take over, but you could also control the situation (and keep the creativity going) by saying something like:

"Let's see if we can find a better way of making a river without lots of paper. Help me tidy up and we'll see what's in the garden".

"If children come up with a solution, give them masses of praise, because negotiation and compromise are sophisticated human skills."

These give the child a sense of well-being when she is playing with a toy. But if the toy is taken from her, she may move into a state of opioid withdrawal in her brain, which causes emotional pain,[7] hence the distressed crying.

Furthermore, to a child, the toy is her territory. Any animal is likely to respond with rage to an invasion of its territory; it is an instinct triggered in the ancient reptilian core of our brain. The brain chemical vasopressin, which is linked to aggression, is released when animals guard their territory. Together the pain and the rage and the territorial brain chemicals can cause your child to descend rapidly into primitive fight behaviour. As your child is in real pain and her brain and body are awash with strong hormones, she needs help and compassion when having to share a toy, and not an angry response. The good thing is that the pain can be short-lived, especially if you are skilled at distraction.

"This toy is all mine!"

Sonia has taken possession of the rocker at play school. Two of her playmates would like to join in, and grab the handles. There's plenty of room for all of them.

Sharing the rocker doesn't suit Sonia at all. She wants it all to herself and because she sees the plaything as her territory, she defends it passionately with screams of rage.

A playworker steps in. She explains about sharing, providing vital emotional regulation. Sonia, now calm, can re-engage her higher brain and her anger is short-lived.

■ Who gets the toy? Help them to find a solution.

If your child's higher brain (frontal lobes) is not yet developed enough for solution-finding, you need to find a solution for her. Use a calm voice, and never punish a child for the immaturity of her brain. With older children, whose frontal lobes are better developed, give them support as they try to negotiate. You could teach them about trading or taking turns: "So you both want to play the dragons game at the same time? Shall I help you to take it in turns?" You can help them to say something to the other child like, "I'll trade you time with my boat for time with your car". You could also devise some family rules over sharing toys.

If it gets "reptilian" again, take away the toy and say something like "OK you two, I am taking this away until we have found a way to share the time with it". If the toy is no longer there, children can often move from intense feelings to thinking. If they do come up with a solution, give them masses of praise, because negotiation and compromise are sophisticated human skills.

■ If a child throws a tantrum or cries after losing a game, it is down to her immature higher brain.

If a child cries or rages because she has lost a game, you have to ask whether it is fair, at her age, to put her through an experience when she might lose. In terms of a child's underdeveloped brain, losing a game can be very painful, so it is unfair to punish her or accuse her of being a bad loser. Young children are not good at putting things in perspective. The memory store in their brain is still relatively empty, so they have no layers of experience from which to realize the relative insignificance, in the grand scale of things, of losing a game. Also, a child can throw a tantrum on losing because she may have anticipated feeling the delight of winning. All mammals (including humans) experience anger or rage at the frustration of anticipated rewards. At the thought of winning, dopamine, a positive arousal chemical, can be activated in the

CONSIDER THIS...

Allocate a shelf for toys that siblings are not ready to share. The child is allowed to put a limited number (you decide what the number is) of toys on this shelf. They cannot be shared without the owner's permission. This can also develop ownership skills and care of special things, which is particularly great if your children share a bedroom.

A child aged over five has more mature frontal lobes and will respond well to choices. Introducing her to pocket money is a vital part of this development. You can say: "You have a choice here. You can use your birthday money to buy the toy or put it towards the bicycle that you want". This engages her higher brain.

brain, whereas with losing, there can be a decrease in levels of dopamine. This decrease can bring about a low mood state in adults and crying in infants. So if your child goes into distress or rage states at losing a game, think of choosing cooperative games until she is a bit older and so able to get the whole thing more in perspective. It's far kinder.

Trying times and wanting something

Imagine your child in a toyshop. First, she won't leave, and then she runs out of the shop, and tries to take a toy with her. Toyshops can activate the SEEKING system in the child's lower brain. This system, which is to do with curiosity, exploration, will, drive, expectancy, and desire, activates optimal levels of dopamine and glutamate, making your child extremely

> "A good strategy is to pay no attention whatsoever to any pleading."

aroused and focused. If you do not let her have the toy she wants, her desire is deeply frustrated, so her RAGE and SEPARATION DISTRESS systems can be triggered. A child's higher brain is not developed enough to moderate these powerful lower brain systems naturally, hence tears and rage.

■ Managing under-fives in a toyshop means taking a firm stance.

A good strategy is to pay no attention whatsoever to any pleading. Give a clear "no", accompanied by an empathic response to all that desperate yearning; for example, "I really hear how much you want that doll, but we have no money for it today". Then walk straight out of the shop with absolutely no further comment or discussion. Your child is highly likely to follow you because of the strength of her attachment to you. If you prefer, just pick her up and carry her out, and distract her as soon as you can. "Oh, look at that over there!" Don't try to reason with your child, along the lines of, "You have so many toys at home". This is trying to engage the child's higher brain when it's her lower brain that is in the driving seat.

■ Children over five years old will respond well when given a choice.

With over-fives, their higher brain should have matured enough for you to use a technique involving decision-making: you can offer them a choice. Start by saying, "If you want something special, you've got to do something special". Ask your child whether she would rather give up the toy or help you with some task to earn the money to buy it. Once her higher brain is engaged in decision-making, it naturally calms all that lower brain intensity. What's more, reflecting like this is so good for developing new pathways in the higher brain.

> "Walk straight out of the shop with absolutely no further comment or discussion."

"I'm not leaving without it"

Jessica (aged six) is refusing to leave the toyshop without the furry animals she has found. Her brain is flooded with chemicals that increase her longing for the toys.

Her mother is left managing a storm in the toyshop! The best way out of this situation will be to engage Jessica's higher brain into thinking about the options.

Here, Jessica and her mum have a conversation about pocket money and choices. This breaks the deadlock of "I want" and moves on to "I will think about it".

"If a child has locked her attention onto some activity, it is truly difficult for her to respond to you."

Humour and fun can be very creative ways of managing some of the trying times. For example, if a bored child has moved into horrid screaming around the house, turn the noise into a game.

"Hey, Billy, I've just had an idea! Let's do a BIG NOISE contest! Let's go up to the loft. We each choose to be an animal with a big roar, then we can see who has the biggest roar."[8]

The game can be developed into a story about, say, a dragon or a lion, and you can start to have lots of lovely one-to-one times, playing with your child instead of telling him off. These intense relational times also have real brain-developing powers for your child, as his immature brain systems are emotionally regulated by being in strong contact with an adult's mature brain systems.

When she won't listen to a word you say

There will be times when your child won't come when you call or jump to it when you ask her to do something. This is because key chemical systems in her brain are undeveloped, making her unable to shift attention from one thing to another as easily as an adult can. If your child has locked her attention onto an activity, it is truly difficult for her to respond to you.

So give your child some slack. One thing you can do is to build in a clear disengagement strategy, such as the following: "In five minutes' time I am going to ask you to pack up your toys and to go and clean your teeth". When five minutes are up, say, "I will now count from five to one". If your child does as you ask, give her lots of praise. If she doesn't, simply pick her up and carry her to the bathroom to clean her teeth. Be consistent. Don't move into asking her lots of times to clean her teeth; she will start to desensitize to nagging.

■ **Different rules apply when you need your child to stop immediately.**

Make it very clear what the rules are when you are out and about. Your child should not run off when you say "stop", and she must come back when you call. You could say, "If I need you to come back to me, I will call your name and count from five to one. By 'one' I want you to be back by my side".

If your child ignores you, you could respond: "I can see that you are not quite ready yet for me to let you run around, because you did not come when I called". Then put her in her buggy or use long reins fixed to your wrist – and explain why. There is no need for a raised voice or anger. Your actions will give a clear message to your child that you will not be caught up in her behaviour. Next time you are out, practise this method until your child understands. Every time she comes back well, praise her hugely, saying, "Well done. That was great. You did so well at stopping/coming back when I called". This is likely to produce a lovely cascade of dopamine and opioids in her brain and make her feel pleased with her actions.

Trying times with selfishness

"Our six year old is so selfish. She won't share her toys with the little ones and she never thinks of us. I am sure there is something wrong with her. Maybe it's bad genes." The selfishness of children can be infuriating, but we shouldn't punish them for their lack of consideration. This is because the capacity for concern is largely a sophisticated higher brain function and, as we have seen in previous chapters, children are born with very unfinished higher brains. The capacity to feel and think deeply about another person's emotional pain or stress levels develops slowly over time. Only after many hours of showing your concern for them can you expect your children to feel empathy with you. Sadly, some children have been on the receiving end of so little kindness and concern that they never develop this higher brain function.

Telling tales and name-calling

For a child, telling tales is often far too delicious a proposition to forgo. Child psychologist and author Adele Faber suggests saying something like, "Well I'm not interested in what Sally's doing right now. But I'd love to talk about you".

> "Only after many hours of showing your concern for them can you expect your children to feel empathy with you."

Help your child to express anger and resentment in healthier ways. For example, say: "You know we don't have name-calling in this family. If you have a problem with your sister, tell her what it is".[9] If a child is hurt by another child's behaviour, empathize with her pain: "It was mean of Sally to call you that and it must have really hurt your feelings. It's not true, so ignore her. But how smart of you to come and tell me instead of being mean back".

CONSIDER THIS...

Camilla and Shannon are playing cooperatively here, but they are not always so amicable when it comes to wanting the same toy. Parents often see refusal to share as selfishness, not realizing that having to share toys with a sibling can sometimes trigger deep feelings of having to share a parent. Children don't usually have the words to express this, unless you help them. If you think that asking your child to take turns with a toy is causing a huge amount of pain that can't be stopped with distraction techniques, it may be worth talking to her. Ask her whether she thinks she is getting enough time on her own with Mummy or Daddy (see page 212).

Children at war

When children have an impulse to lash out and fight, your creative parenting can enable them to learn how to reflect and negotiate instead. The wrong reaction from a parent can strengthen the wrong responses in the primitive brain. Shout at children who fight, or ignore them, and they may still be hitting people with words or fists when they grow up.

CONSIDER THIS...

Over time, if a child continues to be attacked by her sibling on a regular basis, without parental intervention, her brain can start to adjust some of its key systems to survive in an aggressive world. The FEAR and RAGE systems can be hard-wired for overactivity, commonly leading to problems with anxiety or anger in later life.

Many parents believe that their children fight more than other children, but the truth is that it is normal for siblings to fight. One study found that 93 percent of seven year olds fought their siblings, and 24 percent of these fought a lot.[10]

That said, fighting can be an uncomfortable reminder that humans do indeed have a primitive, reptilian core to their brains. What's more, because of a child's underdeveloped higher brain, this reptilian core is often in the driving seat. Parent power is so influential that if you treat fighting the wrong way, it can actually strengthen the primitive responses in the brain. If you treat fighting a better way, it will develop the higher brain and naturally inhibit reptilian impulses in your child to lash out when she is feeling competitive, territorial, or threatened in some way.

In short, you have the power to influence whether your child learns how to hurt harder and to be more devious in her physical attacks, or whether she develops and masters those sophisticated human skills of negotiating, planning, and clearly communicating what she needs and wants without using tactics of power and control.

Why do fights happen?

Fights happen because one, or more, of your child's psychological hungers is not being met (see page 117). A child may fight with another child because she is bored and is trying to top up her stimulation levels. She might simply be hungry, which makes her aggressive (see page 113). Overstimulation may result in physiological hyperarousal, which she relieves by biting, kicking, and hitting. She may be angry, frustrated, upset, or bottling up emotions, and because she doesn't have the words to express her feelings she uses her fists. Or perhaps she is being hit by a sibling, or smacked by a parent, and is modelling her hitting behaviour on what she knows at home. She might be being bullied at school, an experience that all too easily moves a child into her own primitive fight-or-flight behaviour in other areas of life.

"A child may fight with another child because she is bored."

How should you respond to fighting?

You need to make sure that the child's higher brain, not the reptilian brain, is activated. There are some vital do's and don'ts involved in this strategy:

■ **Don't meet violence with violence.**

Don't scream, shout, or smack when you see siblings fighting. Such tactics may shock them into temporary obedience or submission, but this response is modelling using rage in

"This isn't funny!"

What started out as a game can very quickly end in lost tempers – these little boys are not sure their play is fun any more. Parents cannot always tell when to intervene, but children's facial expressions are often the clue. Smiles show that the rough and tumble is good-natured. Clenched teeth and an increase in energy usually mean that it is time for parents to step in.

"Children need us to protect them from the hurtful actions of others."

challenging, stressful situations. It could lead to the fight-or-flight part of the brain being hard-wired for an overactive response. The child could also grow up with an explosive temper, or start internalizing her anger and as a result suffer from stress-related illnesses.

Meeting a child's violence with an angry response will also do nothing to help her to develop her higher brain. Rather, fighting is a time for you to help her regulate her overly high levels of bodily arousal, and to calm her down. So your tone of voice in response to the fighting is very important; you should sound firm but calm.

▪ Don't take sides or reward tale-telling.

Unless you witness an unprovoked hurtful act, don't take anyone's word for it. Some children are good at play-acting, putting on a show for their parents, clutching their tummies, and rolling on the floor. If you do take sides, children soon get the idea that if they constantly complain about the "abuse" of a sibling, they earn your loving attention. And, naturally, they delight in seeing their rival punished.

▪ If your child is having a "too big" feeling, help her with it; don't leave her with it.

Putting a raging child in a Time Out room (see page 174) is a short-term solution to fighting. It gives everyone breathing space and time to calm down. If you do this, a child will learn to think twice about biting her sister again, but she is not learning to find better ways of dealing with her anger. Instead, she may be using the time to plot her revenge. So if you use Time Out, think about having a Time In period (see page 172) later on, to help your child work through her feelings and find healthier, more creative ways of managing her anger. Research shows that linking words to feelings through periods of reflection like this can develop new pathways in the higher brain, which will naturally calm primitive impulses to hit and lash out.[11]

Keeping children safe

Children need to have their hurtful actions stopped; they also need us to protect them from the hurtful actions of others. Many adults say that as children they did not have enough protection from aggressive siblings – their parents responding to fights with something like "they're only playing" and not realizing that rivalry had deteriorated into abuse.

Children should have the freedom to resolve their own differences, but only if they are capable of doing this. Some situations are so emotionally charged that children can't resolve them on their own.

What should you do and say in response to fighting that's hurting? Here are some suggestions:

● Separate the two parties, as you would in a dog fight. Say: "Stop now. Separate rooms, please."
Or: "Hold it right there. People are not for hurting. That looks like real fighting. It's not safe for you two to be around each other right now. Sally, go to the kitchen. Jamie, go to the living room."

● Pay attention to the injured party and not the aggressor. Say to the aggressor something like: "Bad choice, Toby, for hitting Sam. I'll now spend time with Sam. You stay here and think about how you could have let Sam know you were angry in a better way."

● Give the children options on how to express their anger. Try: "Hey Jamie, let your sister know with words how angry you are."

● Often, anger is fuelled by hurt, so giving a child a language for hurt is a real gift. Say: "You wish he wouldn't snatch. Seems like you are really cross with him and really hurting because he knocked over your castle."[12]

Make sure you have some clear family rules about quarrelling and fighting and read through them with your children. The rules could include the following:

- There is zero tolerance in this home on fighting that hurts.

- Play-fighting is fine but it has to be agreed by both of you that it really is play that you both enjoy.

- Fighting over a toy means the toy gets taken away until you agree a way of sharing. Ask a grown-up for help with this if you get stuck.

- If you really want to hit out because you are so frustrated or angry, go to a grown-up for help with your feelings.

- Name-calling is not allowed in this family. Go to a grown-up to help you find a really good way of telling your sister/ brother what you would like her/him to do differently.

A lot of bullying in schools comes from children who have been hit by siblings.

Unless parents intervene when appropriate, hitting can spread like wildfire. Many children who have been hit repeatedly by their siblings, without their parents stepping in every time, start bullying other children at school (see page 239). Nearly half of all schoolchildren say they have experienced bullying at some time.

Calling a family meeting about fighting

If hurting-fighting is clearly getting to be an established activity in the home, call a family meeting to discuss it. Make it an occasion that will be marked in the children's minds and show them a clearly written statement of rules about fighting (see box, left). Family meetings give vital psychological messages that feelings can be thought about rather than discharged with fists and teeth. This is also in line with the brain research which shows that putting very strong feelings into words can naturally inhibit the primitive RAGE system

"Unless parents intervene, hitting can spread like wildfire."

in the lower brain.[13] Meetings need ground rules and structure to stop them becoming a free-for-all. A good formula for successful meetings is based on Circle Time – an effective emotional literacy intervention used in primary schools, originated by Jenny Moseley. No one can speak unless they are holding the little teddy (or equivalent). This ensures that children listen to each other and don't interrupt.[14]

If the children are too young to discuss ideas, you can provide the solutions. Even if a child is not happy with a decision, this process will make her feel safe, knowing that you have taken the time to listen, and that you are strong enough to take charge.

Key points

■ **Trying times** with under-fives are often the result of immature brain systems.

■ **It is never OK** to punish a child for exasperating behaviour that is due entirely to undeveloped brain systems.

■ **Before going on an outing,** think how you will engage your child's higher brain in an interesting activity, so that her motoric impulses and primitive lower brain systems don't ruin the day.

■ **If your child is to grow** out of primitive impulses to lash out in rage, she needs lots of one-to-one time with you to help her manage her very intense feelings and for you to find words to help her to think about them.

■ **Cater for your child's** structure hunger, stimulation hunger, and recognition hunger and you will have a great time.

all about
discipline

Discipline is a real art. If you get it right,
it becomes far more than simply managing
behaviour. It will develop your child's social,
moral, and emotional intelligence. If you get it
wrong it can blight a child's life, leaving her with
a heightened level of fear or anger in response
to the world. So it's vital to use discipline
techniques that activate your child's higher
thinking brain, instead of triggering her lower
brain reactions of threat and attack.

Children often behave badly because they
are not very good at speaking about painful
emotions. If you spend time listening to your
child in order to help her with her feelings,
and if you work to improve the health of your
relationship, your child will often stop being
interested in behaving badly.

How not to raise a bully

Over the history of mankind, the way children have been disciplined has played a major role in the perpetuation of human misery. This is because for centuries, the discipline of children has been built on an assumption that a sense of morality is achieved through harsh punishment. Both psychological and neurobiological research has now found this assumption to be entirely wrong.

CONSIDER THIS...

In the UK, 17,000 children (mainly boys) are suspended or expelled from school each year for violence towards other pupils or teachers. Violent, disruptive pupils are the second most frequent cause of teachers leaving the profession. About 100,000 children and young people per year (aged 10–17) are convicted of, or cautioned for, an indictable offence. Reports published in 2004 show that it is now common for schoolchildren to carry knives.

Sculpting the brain of a bully

The risk of bringing up a bully or a thug is largely determined by the type of parenting a child receives. Well-meaning parents often do not realize that disciplining through criticism and commands may actually be changing stress-response systems in the child's brain. This can make the child oversensitive and render the RAGE or FEAR systems over-reactive. This sort of discipline also teaches a child about submission/dominance. From this, a child can all too easily move into submission/dominance in the form of bullying others. This is especially likely if she is smacked as a form of punishment. Research on parental behaviour in the UK shows that 75 percent of parents smack their one year olds; 91 percent of children are smacked; and 10 percent of children have been hit with an implement.[1] Today, the Government has still not outlawed the hitting of children by their parents. Smacking teaches your child it is OK to hit. She may hit her sibling, or kick the cat, or start hitting other children at school. If you smack, you are modelling to her what to do when she is frustrated, which is to lash out.

■ **Let's be clear, we're not talking about occasional episodes of shouting at children.**

Some commands are inevitable and essential, such as shouting "Stop!" to a child who is running into the road or about to put her finger into an electric socket. But if criticism and commands form the bulk of parent–child interactions, it will guarantee for both parent and child a horrid time living together. The child learns all about relationships based on power and control, and all too little about relationships based on warmth, kindness, and cooperation.

When a child lives on a daily basis with the stress of a parent's repeated shouting and angry explosions, the tension from the feelings she is left with can be so awful that it must be discharged. Hitting or bullying another child is a common way of doing this, or for a younger kid, shouting, screaming, biting, hitting, or breaking something. Such children love war games, and are often obsessed with violent computer games where you can shoot and kill to your heart's content.

If a child is repeatedly on the receiving end of criticism, commands, and threats, it will not help his higher brain to develop in ways that are essential for reasoning, planning, and reflecting (see page 18). What is more, this type of parenting can also hard-wire the stress response systems in the brain and the RAGE system in the downstairs brain to be over-reactive.[2] These children then live their lives on a very short fuse. People don't warm to children whose way of being in the world is so ruled by the fight-or-flight mechanisms in the reptilian part of their brain. These children then get a bad reaction from people a lot of the time, which further reinforces their negative view of the world.

■ **So how a child is disciplined is an incredibly serious thing, not only for the child but for society at large.**
Society reaps what it sows in the way it nurtures its children, because stress sculpts the brain to exhibit several antisocial behaviours. "Stress can set off a ripple of hormonal changes that permanently wire a child's brain to cope with a malevolent world. Through this chain of events, violence and abuse pass from generation to generation as well as from one society to the next."[3] Many world leaders who have been disciplined through anger and cruelty go on to treat their

The over-disciplined child can learn to put someone down as she has felt put down, to give orders as she has felt commanded, to shame as she has been shamed, to hit with words as she has felt hit with words.

"Many world leaders who have been disciplined through anger and cruelty go on to treat their own people abominably, or go on to bully other nations."

Case study

Julie's lost children

Julie is having a miserable time as a parent and resorts to frequent criticism, commands, and lectures to discipline her two children. The methods don't work all that well but she had little first-hand experience in her own childhood of the potency of warm touch, hugs, and interactive play.

Mary, aged four, is frightened of her Mummy's shouting. Her sister, Sam, aged twelve, seems to cope better. When Julie shouts at her, she shouts back, but she is a very angry young girl.

The way Julie has disciplined her children may have had enduring effects on both children's brains. The FEAR system in Mary's brain over-reacts to the slightest stress, and there is a danger that she will grow up to be fearful and lack social confidence. Sam has an over-active RAGE system in her downstairs brain. This may be a real problem in her adult work and social life, as she is likely to explode at the smallest frustration.

own people abominably, or go on to bully other nations.[4] As long as we continue to discipline children like this, we will continue to have terrible wars on both the family and the world stage. One very powerful study illustrates the point. Researchers tracked down Germans who, in World War II, risked their own lives by hiding a Jew in their house. When interviewed, the researchers found one distinguishing feature of all these kind people. They had all been socialized in ways that respected their personal dignity.[5]

Violence in adult life

Parenting has a lot to learn from Professor Adrian Raine's sobering research, which involved the brain scans of impulsive murderers. The scans showed that under stress, the murderers had lots of activity in the lower brain and very little in the higher brain (frontal lobes). This means they were unable to reflect, consider, and think about what was happening. This can be the legacy of a childhood where children have not been helped to work though feelings of rage and distress by parents, or offered soothing and calming.[6]

There is a lot of violence in the world, in part because there are a lot of people walking around the planet with poor frontal lobe functions and poor stress-regulating systems. As a result, they are ready to blow at any time.

■ Some people who have not been helped to manage their too strong feelings in childhood end up committing domestic violence.

Most of us feel anger from time to time, perhaps when an unexpectedly high gas bill lands on the doormat or another driver cuts us up in the car, but we manage to over-ride our childish, primitive brain responses and think and behave like adults. For some people, however, these feelings remain overwhelming and unmanageable throughout life, with the result that even small setbacks can trigger the most terrible episodes of family violence.

"I hate playing this game"

Children model their behaviour on the many influences they are exposed to. Violent scenes on TV have been shown to have an effect, but also the way parents choose to correct a child's behaviour can lead him to act in mean or cruel ways. It has been shown that children who have been hit at home are, by the age of four, playing either victim or persecutor roles in their games. On the other hand, children who have not been disciplined harshly tend to play with kindness and cooperation.[7]

Boundaries and behaviour

We have already described how harsh discipline actually hinders socialization, and is far more likely to result in a child becoming a thug than growing up to be a moral citizen. But what of the parents who fail to impose much discipline at all? Society is also peopled with children whose provocative behaviour makes their parents' life a misery.

Some parents are frightened to say a firm "No" because they fear that their child won't like them if they do. It is, however, vital that children are given clear "Nos" if they are ever to develop morally and socially. The child who rarely meets a firm "No" in a parent often ends up feeling more powerful than, and disrespectful towards, her parent. But it is also frightening to a child if she feels that the grown-ups in her life are not in charge. What's more, the lack of parental boundaries over unacceptable behaviour gives the child a very worrying message, that: "It's OK to hurt people, take things from them, swear, treat your mother as a piece of rubbish. Nothing much happens if you do".

The challenge is how to communicate very clearly to children that something is absolutely not acceptable, in ways that engage her higher brain and not the primitive systems of FEAR or RAGE, dominance or submission, deep in the ancient parts of her brain.

Some parents find it difficult to lay down any boundaries at all. Often these are parents who have themselves suffered the legacy of very strict or punitive teachers or parents when they were children. As a result, they are adamant that they will never be like that with their own children, so they swing to the opposite extreme. When the child acts in a way that clearly needs a firm boundary, and an immediate consequence imposed, the parent may say something like "Please don't do that dear. It's not nice" but fail to take any action. The irony is that out of fear of being a bossy, controlling parent, you can get a bossy, controlling child. If there are no immediate consequences for antisocial behaviour, you will get antisocial behaviour.

▐ Here is what can happen if you set no boundaries with your child.

Your child can learn that they can control you, rather than seeing you as being the one in charge. See it from her point of view – if nothing much happens when you hit Mummy or kick the door, why should you want to stop releasing your anger in this way? It can be exhilarating and make you feel very powerful. If you never set clear limits for unacceptable behaviour, your child won't know where the limits are.

The worry of this is that neuroscientists have found that the mere experience of emotion without reflection can result in it becoming an ingrained personality trait.[8] When a five-year-old thug reaches, say, nine or ten, they can be just too big to carry into Time Out (see page 174). At this age, they can seriously hurt you and other family members.

▨ Children need to learn early on that they can't control you.

They need a model of discipline that is assertive, carries conviction, and is firm and clear, without being angry or shaming. Children need to feel absolute conviction in your voice and body movement when you want something to stop, and an immediate consequence if they overstep your boundaries. There should be no discussion. If your voice is flat or weak, your child won't believe you mean it.

Children are not born socialized and considerate of others. They need your help with the raging or controlling impulses in the more primitive parts of the brain, and this chapter is all about giving you the techniques to do it.

▨ When to be emotional...

The first rule is to be very emotional with good behaviour. For example, if your child is playing cooperatively, be lavish with your praise: "Wow, that was great when you let your brother share the toy. Well done for being so kind!"

▨ When to be matter-of-fact...

By contrast, be very matter-of-fact and not at all emotional with bad behaviour. For example, if a five year old splatters his pudding all over the table, say in a really low key voice, "Hey, bad choice. That means you can't watch your DVD today. I hope you choose better next time".

It's very easy for parents to get this the wrong way round, because bad behaviour is usually much more attention-grabbing. They get very emotional when a child is being defiant or irritating, and are matter-of-fact or fail to notice when the child does something good, kind, generous, or creative. Using low-key responses for provocative behaviour

"My Daddy just can't control me."

You need to be able to decide when to tread softly and when to take swift action. You can safely ignore or deal lightly with most things that are not dangerous, damaging, or hurtful. Firm discipline is needed when your child is in danger of causing damage to himself, to others, or to property. You need to be consistent in this from an early age to avoid future problems.

If you give some control to a child in the form of offering him a choice over unimportant things like what to wear, he is less likely to fight you to get some control. For example, instead of shouting, "Put your coat on right now. I will not tell you again", if you ask light-heartedly "Would you rather get ready now or go to school in your pyjamas?" or "Do you think this jacket will be warm enough, or should we find your big coat?", he is more likely to get ready happily, rather than start a fight.

will help to keep your child calm. If you "lose it" with your child, you are in danger of triggering the primitive reptilian parts of her brain, which in the long-run may be damaging to her developing social brain.[9]

Ignore attention-seeking behaviour.

Ignoring is the appropriate response for things like kicking a chair leg or stomping down the stairs very loudly. These attention-seeking misdemeanours generally happen when a child is suffering from stimulation or recognition hunger (see page 117), perhaps because she feels she is losing your attention to a sibling, your mobile phone, or a TV programme. Or she may not be getting enough positive attention from you, such as praise and lovely warm touches.

"Rules, in both family and society, make children and adults alike feel safe."

If you don't manage to ignore minor misdemeanours, a child soon learns that she gets masses of attention for provocative small acts. Often, the clue is the way that your child watches your face expectantly for a delicious display of angry parental feelings! To a child this means a whopping dose of attention in the form of "stop that" or "how dare you". So try not to meet her eyes, and pretend not to see and hear. Instead, think about how to satisfy her stimulation or recognition hunger in creative ways.

Have a clear set of family rules.

A clear set of family rules is a key way of satisfying your child's structure hunger, and will also engage her higher brain. Not having rules, or rewards for keeping to them and penalties for breaking them, is quite frankly crazy. Rules, in both family and society, make children and adults alike feel safe, whereas a lack of them can lead to anarchy and mayhem. Rules help our higher brain to keep in check aggressive feelings and dominating instincts which can so easily be triggered in the old mammalian and reptilian parts of our brain – the lack of them often leads to family members getting very hurt, psychologically and physically.

Rules lift everything out of the personal and into the objective. Rules are all about fairness, and people calm down when they feel things are fair. So make a list of rules and put them up in the home, where all can see. Rules may include items such as no hitting, swearing, or damage to property. Respect others. Ask for help when you are hurting inside, instead of taking it out on someone. Children need to know what the consequences are for breaking a rule, whether you use time out, confiscation of a favourite toy, or imposing a household chore.

Use simple, clear words for young children.

As your children get older, they can appreciate explanations about certain behaviours in terms of fairness, the importance of respecting others, and developing a culture of generosity instead of meanness. But until their higher brain has developed enough, you are wasting your time. So with under-fives, you need to give simple instructions. Get down to their level. Use a clear, authoritative (not angry) voice and say simply, "No", "Stop", "I mean it", and "If you do that again, the consequence will be… If your under-five child is hyperaroused and out-of-control, pick her up and hold her (see page 177). With high levels of physical arousal, she won't be able to focus on what you are saying, however simply it is expressed.

Use choices and consequences.

This is a tried-and-tested way of disciplining children, developed by Foster Cline, whose method of engaging the child's higher thinking brain and not activating the FEAR or RAGE systems in the lower brain, has proved highly successful even with the most destructive and anti-social of children. It is suitable for children aged five and over.[10]

"Children need to know what the consequences are for breaking a rule."

TRY THIS...

Don't reward rude, provocative, or attention-seeking statements with an angry outburst. Be calm and show yourself to be absorbed in whatever else you are doing at the time. This will give a child's statement minimum not maximum impact, and therefore not reward it in any way. For example:

Child: "Your hair is stupid."

Parent: "No kidding" (said with a really low-key voice and with your attention focused elsewhere).

TRY THIS...

Make family rules based on the finest human qualities – goodwill, give and take, a culture of generosity, and respect for others.

Make sure rules have a point and are appropriate; for example, pocket money and privileges have to be earned. Make sure rules are fair – children will be acutely aware of those that are not.

Giving older children a say in family rules is a good idea, and most will be able to make a real contribution to the conversation. But offering premature democracy to under-fives won't work because they don't have the brain maturity to make these types of decisions. Children of this age group tend to see things in black-and-white and move into gruesome punishments for minor sins. For example, when asked by his parents what they should do after baby Eddie had bitten his nanny, Simon (aged five) said, "Put him in the rubbish".

Remember to praise your children when they keep the rules, rather than simply watch out for when they break one.

Providing choices and consequences goes something like this: Tessa is jealous of her sister's new birthday doll. She tries to spoil the doll by stamping on it. Her Mum says that the consequence for Tessa's actions is to help with jobs in the home to get the money to buy another doll. This teaches Tessa that there is a consequence to her behaviour. Alternatively, Tessa's Mum could offer a choice: Tessa can choose to do jobs to buy another doll, or give her sister her own favourite Barbie doll – an exchange that Tessa's little sister would be delighted with. Tessa's Mum refuses to enter into any debate; this strategy avoids giving Tessa masses of attention and rewarding her bad behaviour. Thinking about the choice moves Tessa into her higher thinking brain. Eventually she chooses to do the jobs.

Don't feel you have to come up with an appropriate choice or consequence on the spot. If you pressurize yourself to think quickly, your choices and consequences may end up being crass, pointless, or something that doesn't suit you. So give yourself time. For example, say, "I will have to think up a consequence for what you have done. I'll let you know when I have". However, make sure consequences for behaviour

"Make sure consequences for behaviour happen on the same day."

happen on the same day. Young children don't care about the future; they can't really hold it in mind. So avoid choosing a consequence like, "No cinema trip at the weekend".

■ Reward good behaviour.

Stickers, point systems, and privileges are all types of reward techniques that will engage and develop your child's higher thinking brain, because they involve weighing up the pros and cons of behaving in a certain way. Families who have no clear reward systems sometimes fall into giving the child a diet of criticism with all too little praise. Giving lots of attention for bad behaviour results in more bad behaviour. Lots of attention for good behaviour results in lots of good behaviour. It's a simple formula, but very true.

Let's face it, there is arguably no such thing as unmotivated behaviour. This is largely due to the fact that our brain is designed to seek pleasure and avoid displeasure. As adults, we are motivated to get up to go to work because we get the pleasure of money, job satisfaction, and social contact. So the next time you're surprised that your child doesn't leap at the idea of doing the washing up, remember she is acting normally because she may not see much of a reward in it for herself.

"Lots of attention for good behaviour results in lots of good behaviour. It's a simple formula, but very true."

"Why should I tidy up?"

Mum has asked Susie to tidy before they go to the cinema, but Susie is not interested. She thinks Mum will probably give in and do it if she ignores the request.

Mum says that if Susie does not tidy up, the trip to see the film is off. Hence, in a low-key, but clear way, Mum is using choices and consequences.

There has been no shouting, hitting, or cajoling, but Susie has tidied up. Now Mum is ready to take her to the cinema.

A change of emphasis involves changing threats into promises. So instead of saying in an angry voice, "If you don't tidy your room, there will be no DVD", say in a warm voice, "I promise that if you tidy your room, you can watch your DVD". This simple but vital shift can make all the difference between a family spoilt by endless nagging and highly motivated, helpful children.

Enjoying doing something for the good of others (for example, contributing to the effective running of the home) without needing a tangible reward is a developmental stage. So give your young child a break! At first, she may need rewards, such as a sticker or a point. For others, a big smile and "Well done" from Mummy will be enough. As a child gets older, she will move into more sophisticated forms of motivation, such as pleasure from the sense of achievement gained from cooking a meal for the family, or at an even later developmental stage, the pleasure of doing something out of love, which becomes a far greater pleasure than receiving a gift oneself.

If you want to reward certain behaviours, such as acts of kindness or the ability to share toys well, give the sticker as soon afterwards as possible, so that there is a real connection between what she did and the pleasure of the reward. The accumulation of stickers for a bumper reward is very effective. Making a chart and putting it up on the wall enables your child to see how many stickers she has earned, and is a visual prompt to you to keep praising her for what she has achieved. A good idea for a special treat is something like

"Look what I've done!"

Stickers are great for encouraging and rewarding good behaviour. Let your child put the stickers on a chart so she can see her progress. You could make a "magic carpet". Paint different-sized trees on your chart. Each time your child earns a sticker, the carpet moves up to a higher tree. When it reaches the tallest tree, your child gets a treat.

staying up a bit later at the end of the day, or a special outing to the park with Dad, or a little surprise gift.

For older children or adolescents, rewards can work just as well, but this time points translate into cash. Your child will learn that if she wants pocket money, she must earn it and be careful not to lose it. Earning pocket money is a great practice

"Earning pocket money is a great practice ground for the adult world."

ground for learning to operate well in the adult world. She may be able to earn points by doing chores, and by keeping well to family rules over a period of time, or for acts of kindness. There are also clear penalties for losing points. If the child goes "broke", important items such as her television will be taken from her room; she can then earn them back.

Use thinking words.

When trying to instill socially acceptable behaviour, some parents make the mistake of using fighting words. These are likely to overactivate primitive alarm and stress response systems in her lower brain, which, as we have seen, can lead to personality problems with anger and/or anxiety in later life. Fighting words demand obedience but often incite in the child the opposite: namely, defiance and disobedience.[11]

In contrast, thinking words engage the higher brain. Faced with screaming Little Nero behaviour (see page 128) for example, you might use the following thinking words: "Well, it looks like things aren't going so well for you right now. When you get yourself to the point of being able to ask nicely, I'll be glad to listen". At this point, walk away with not another word. Fighting words would be: "Just another of your bad moods. If you knew what we did for you and we never get any thanks". The former will make him think. The latter is likely to trigger the RAGE system in his lower brain even more.

BRAIN STORY

Using choices and consequences with a defiant child will help to develop her frontal lobes' capacity to reflect, consider, negotiate, and weigh up options. It is important not to use shouting and commands, and to use a calm, quiet voice. Developed frontal lobes have the capacity for:

● reasoning, planning, reflecting, and thinking before acting

● linking and connecting

● negotiation

● problem-solving.

Commands are often an attack on the child's dignity, leaving her feeling shamed or humiliated. Commands teach a child about submission and dominance – the sort of training that can create a bully (see page 160).

A child who is helped with Time In learns that her parent isn't afraid of her big feelings and knows how to handle them. If we don't use Time In, we are in danger of withdrawing from our children when they are most in need of adult understanding. The development of a child's social brain includes the ability to be sensitive to others, empathize, and accurately imagine another person's emotional experience. Children can only develop their social brain if they have had social experiences where someone has been emotionally sensitive to them.

Try some Time In, instead of Time Out

Time In is taking the time to sit with your child after a bout of bad behaviour, to talk together about why she is behaving this way. Time In is not giving attention to bad behaviour, it is giving attention to the feelings that underlie the bad behaviour, so that these can be resolved. Time In acknowledges the fact that so much bad behaviour results from a child having painful feelings which she is not able to manage herself or to describe to you in words. You may need to find a creative way to encourage your child to talk about her feelings, for example, see page 212.

Time Out may be effective in stopping bad behaviour, but putting a child in a room does not give you, as a parent, the opportunity to find out what is making your child behave badly. Time Out is simply about stopping the behaviour, so

"Time In is giving attention to the feelings that underlie bad behaviour..."

the painful feelings that may have triggered it often go underground. As Weininger (an originator of the Time In technique) says about Time Out: "We are in danger of withdrawing from a child just at the very time they need help with their feelings". Over time, using Time In with your child can help her to change from angry, attention-seeking behaviour to a more thoughtful and reflective way of being in the world.[12]

The Thinking Stair or Chair technique

This technique involves providing a place where your child can think about why what she has done is not OK. As well as helping the child to calm down, this technique activates her higher thinking brain. It is a form of Time Out, but is not as severe, because your child is not left behind a closed door. There is less of a feeling of isolation for your child, as she is separate but not removed from the general hubbub of the house. This is less distressing than being confined to a room, but it can be difficult to manage if your child keeps leaving the stair or chair. A typical scenario might be dealt with like this:

- **The first stage is a warning**, delivered in a firm, strong voice and bending down to her level. Say something like, "Sam, there's no swearing in this house. So if you swear again you will have to go and sit on the thinking chair".
- **If she carries on with the bad behaviour move into action.** Gently take her to the stair or chair (see box, below).
- **After the allotted time, come back.** Ask your child if she is ready to play nicely. If she says yes, then bring her back to play. If she repeats the behaviour, repeat the technique.
- **If your child moves off the stair or chair**, keep putting her back. With young children, you can calmly but firmly hold them in the chair, but saying nothing while you do.[13]
- **With an older child, consider Time In** instead. Take the opportunity to talk about the reasons behind her actions.

"Time Out is simply about stopping the behaviour, so the painful feelings that may have triggered it can go underground."

"Why did I do that?"

To use the Thinking Stair or Chair technique, choose a place to sit that is boring, such as a quiet, unused room. The child needs to face the wall. This low level of stimulation offers a boundary to her. Ask your child to spend time thinking about her actions. Explain that she will stay there for, say, eight minutes (one for each year of age), and you will collect her at the end of this time. If she tries to leave the chair or stair, ask her to sit again.

BRAIN STORY

- **Thinking words have** many developmental benefits for your child because they develop your child's higher thinking brain. Research shows that when a child is helped by a thoughtful adult to link words to feelings, brain pathways will form from her higher brain to her lower brain.[14] These pathways are vital for her ability to manage strong feelings or stress well in later life. A vital part of emotional and social intelligence is the ability to find solutions for the stressful times in life when we are thrown into intense states of emotional arousal.

- **Fighting words are bad** for a child's brain because they demand blind obedience but often activate disobedience. If the FEAR system is activated a lot in the name of discipline, a child can suffer from anxiety disorders and social phobias in later life (see page 25).

  Demanding blind obedience will teach children about submission dominance. For some, it will activate the RAGE system in the lower brain. When this happens, a child can be seen to comply at the time, but her RAGE system is like a time-bomb; it can go off at any time in their life. For some, it goes off in the playground and a child can move into bullying. Others contain it until adolescence, when it may manifest itself in self-harm or violence.

Sometimes you need to use Time out.

Time Out is the technique of putting a child in a room on her own when she has been naughty. The parent should stay at the other side of the door, holding on to the handle. This way the child knows she is still there.

The rule is that the child should spend a minute of Time Out for every year of her life so, for example, a five year old will have five minutes of Time Out. This time limit is informed by the fact that any longer could tip a child into a deep fear of abandonment, or move her into damaging states of panic or despair. Time Out tends to activate the SEPARATION DISTRESS system in a child's lower brain (see page 24), which in turn, activates pain centres in the brain. The technique is effective because children come to associate the behaviour which is being punished with pain.

Time Out is particularly appropriate for acts of clear defiance, and for calculated behaviour that causes hurting to others or damage to property. It is particularly apt for times when a child has had enough higher brain thinking

"Time Out is appropriate for calculated hurting or spoiling."

to make a clear decision to move into destructive, hurtful behaviour; for example, "I'm going to spoil my brother's painting because it's better than mine". But as Time Out is discipline through pain (albeit short-lived), it should be used as a last resort. If something is not actually dangerous, damaging, or hurting, consider all your other socializing resources first – ignoring, choices and consequences, or walking away saying, "I don't want to be with you when you are like this".

If you use it discriminately and correctly, there are some brain benefits attached to the Time Out technique. In the long run, the hope is that it will engage your child's higher brain (frontal lobes) in the sense that she will think twice about whether she wants to swear at you, kick her younger brother, or hide her sister's favourite doll.

Parents who over-use Time Out are usually under-using more appropriate techniques.

The worry with Time Out is that it often becomes formulaic and indiscriminate. Because it is so effective from a parent's point of view, it is often used every time a child is slightly non-compliant or whenever a child has a big, loud feeling (see page 29).

For example, it is highly questionable, morally speaking, whether we should use Time Out when a bored child moves into bad behaviour. Shouldn't we take some responsibility and help her to satisfy her stimulation hunger? A bored four year old who has to wait 45 minutes for her lunch, because the service in a restaurant is so bad, is very likely to start blowing bubbles into her orange juice and use her cutlery as drumsticks. Creative parenting means taking a child's psychological hungers for structure, stimulation, and recognition very seriously and making sure we cater for them (see page 117), rather than punishing the child for our own shortcomings in this area. To avoid bad behaviour on a trip due to a child's stimulation hunger, always carry with you crayons and paper or other interesting activities, or play a word game or tell a story.

Follow the rules when you use Time Out.

Sometimes it is appropriate to warn first, "If you don't stop doing that, I will put you in Time Out". Sometimes it is not appropriate to warn; for example, if a child who knows better begins to hurt another child, you need to act swiftly. Scoop her up and put her in Time Out.

When you put the child in the Time Out room, tell her why you are putting her there and for how long. "I am putting you here for six minutes, because it's not OK to hit."

Time Out is appropriate as a last resort when a calm warning from the parent has failed or a child has deliberately hurt someone or destroyed property. Take care not to over-use this technique, both to maintain its impact and to protect your child.

"Time Out is never appropriate for punishing children for having big, painful feelings."

■ **Hold the door shut** and stay at the other side of the door. To avoid activating panic states in your child from fear of abandonment, you need to let her know that you are there. Never lock the door. This can also lead to a state of panic, with the child's brain awash with toxic levels of stress chemicals, which, as we have seen throughout the book, can have long-term damaging effects on her brain.

■ **Don't talk to the child** whilst she is in Time Out. The whole point is withdrawal from you and zero attention for that period of time. Any words from you during that time will just defeat the effect of the technique.

■ **If when your child comes out she swears,** kicks, or hits again, put her back for another session.

"No one understands me"

Before initiating Time Out, consider first whether Time In would be more appropriate. If you spend time listening to your child, you may be able to resolve the areas of conflict that lead to bad behaviour before it occurs again.

When Time Out is never appropriate.

Time Out is never appropriate for punishing children for having big, painful feelings. Most children under five have their moments and will, from time to time, throw themselves on the floor in distress. Little ones may scream when they are dressed (see page 120), or if another child takes a beloved toy car. Loss like this when you are only little will activate the pain systems in the brain, so it is sheer cruelty to put a child in a distressed state into Time Out. If you do, you move into a double failure: you fail to comfort her distress, and punish her for having perfectly natural feelings of pain and loss. A child who experiences inappropriate use of Time Out in this way is receiving the following very worrying psychological messages:

■ **Passionate and painful feelings are not acceptable**. Mummy or Daddy will punish me if I have them. I am only acceptable if I have mild feelings.

■ **I should not ask for help** from Mummy or Daddy when I am struggling with a painful feeling; she might get cross.

We want to train children out of bad behaviour, but we must be careful in doing so that we don't train them out of their passionate emotions and so out of the capacity to feel life fully. Using Time Out in these situations is also very worrying in terms of developing brain systems. The distressed cries of loss, disappointment, and rage need your emotional regulating capacities as a parent. Research shows that if a child is left in a distressed state like this (for example, when taken and left in a Time Out room), high levels of stress chemicals can wash over her brain. She may stop crying, because you are getting angry with her, but research shows that her cortisol levels can remain sky high (see page 54).

Try using the Holding technique.

Holding your child when she is out of control in order to calm her down is not restraint. Rather, it entails providing her with the strong, safe, calm blanket of your enveloping arms. The primary function of Holding is to give your child a sense

Case study

Too much Time Out

Over-use of Time Out can damage parent–child relationships. For example, a six year old who is always being put in Time Out for the slightest offence may start to prefer it to the company of her repeatedly critical mother. One day, Martha was put in Time Out for refusing to finish an over-large portion of spaghetti. As her mother closed the door, she heard Martha say, "Thank goodness; time away from my Mummy who is bad to me".

When her mother opened the door after six minutes to say, "you can come out, Martha". Martha replied, "I don't want to, thanks". She had found some string and was happily making it into a spider's web.

If you have tried firm "Nos" with your child and he is in danger of hurting himself or someone else through his behaviour, then consider using the Holding technique. Holding should be done when you are able to offer real calmness, so your child can benefit from your emotionally regulated body and brain system. A hyperaroused child can sometimes take twenty minutes to calm down. Let him lie in your arms for a while afterwards.

of there being someone big and calm enough to be able to manage their intense feeling storms. When children are feeling "full of wildness that cannot be tamed"[15] and are not helped with their out-of-control hyperaroused states, it can be terrifying for them. Holding is appropriate for situations when a child is in danger of hurting herself, another person, or property, and when a clear "Stop!" isn't working. The child is in such a high state of arousal that she can't hear your words because the verbal centres of her brain are not registering. Under these circumstances, teachers in the UK are legally able to use this technique.[16]

■ **Only use holding if you are calm yourself.**
Holding is done with kindness and firmness. Just as a baby is soothed by being next to your calm body, your child will be calmed, too. Your mature bodily arousal system will regulate the child's immature system.

Never use this technique if you are seething with anger, otherwise you will not be able to calm your child. Also, your child will feel punished and become more hyperaroused by your stress, rather than calmed.

Only use Holding with children who are smaller than you. It is no good for either of you if, in her wild state, a child hurts you or manages to get out of your arms. She will not feel contained and safe if she does. If there is any danger of this, don't use the technique.

There is a clear technique to Holding so that the child feels very safe and "emotionally held". If you improvise, you or your child could get hurt or it just won't calm her down.
■ **Find a place against a wall or sofa** where you can get support. Sit on the floor. Make sure you remove your watch and any jewellery that could hurt your child as she struggles. Take your shoes off.
■ **Visualize yourself as a lovely warm, calm blanket.** Fold your child's arms in front of you and fold your arms on top of hers. Gently, but firmly, hold her arms still. Bend your legs

at the knees and fold them over her legs. This way she cannot kick. In this enveloping blanket, your child will feel safe but not in any way hurt or gripped. If you are doing the technique correctly, you will, after a while, feel very calm too, almost in a meditative state. Give yourself plenty of time.

- **Say to the child, "I am just going to hold you here until you are calm again".** If a child is very out of control and if you are worried about being head-butted or bitten, put a cushion against your chest, or between her chin and your arms.
- **Children may try all manner of things** to get you to let go, saying "I am going to wet myself" or "I need a drink." If she goes into panic or genuine distress, let go. Otherwise, don't be fooled. If you have been, you'll soon know, as she'll go off grinning and triumphant. If she does, just haul her back.
- **Give your child enough time** to reach a state of calm.

CONSIDER THIS...

Before you discipline your child, consider whether he is entirely responsible for his actions. Have you given him enough attention on his own recently? Does he need to get outside to let off some steam? Spending regular one-to-one time with a parent can help to avoid trying times in the first place.

"Visualize yourself as a lovely warm, calm blanket. Gently, but firmly, hold her still."

Step-by-step discipline

The problem with the way most discipline is applied is that it happens on the spur of the moment when parents are enraged by what they see their child doing. Without thought, they may move straight to the top level of censure. A better way is to begin with a low-level boundary, and only move to a stronger one if the one before isn't working:

- **Boundary One.** Parent: "Gemma, please keep the paintbrush on the paper". For a lot of children this is quite enough. Gemma respects the boundary and keeps the paintbrush away from the carpet. But what if she doesn't? Then Gemma is looking for a bigger boundary than this.
- **Boundary Two.** Parent: "Gemma, I really mean it. You must keep the paintbrush on the paper". The parent also puts her hands on Gemma's shoulders. "Gemma, No. Do you understand?" For a lot of children this is quite enough.

"Children want to know that the adults in their life are in charge. Then they can feel safe."

Take time to talk to your child regularly and think about how your relationship can develop and improve. Can you spend more time together, one-to-one? This can help to prevent bad behaviour before it starts.

Gemma doesn't do it again. But imagine Gemma is looking for a bigger boundary than this and begins to paint on the wall.

■ **Boundary Three.** Parent: "Gemma, go and sit in the thinking chair please. After eight minutes, I will come and ask you how you will make up for what you have done". Gemma goes to sit in the chair. She then says she will clean the wall.

■ **Alternative Boundary Three.** Parent: "You'll now have to clean the paint off the wall and spend some time with me cleaning the kitchen cupboards". However, this time Gemma is looking for a bigger boundary still and flies into a rage, with paint flying everywhere.

■ **Boundary Four.** Parent moves into Holding technique. "You seem very intent on making me angry. So I will hold you until you have calmed and are ready to tell me how you will make up for what you have done". Gemma kicks and screams. The parent keeps on holding her. Eventually Gemma and her Mummy agree that she will wash the wall and then help in the kitchen to say she is sorry. Such behaviour would also benefit from some "time in" after it has passed.

■ But why do some children repeatedly look for such a strong boundary?

It can happen because the child has been winning battles early on at age two and three because of weak or no boundaries. All young children need to lose this battle gracefully because if they win, they can feel more powerful than their parents. On one level this may feel very exciting indeed, but it is also very frightening to them. Children like this begin to test you out more and more, looking for stronger and stronger boundaries, because they want to know that the adults in their life are in charge. Then they can feel safe.

If you feel that you have tried everything and your relationship with your child is troubled, then discipline techniques may improve her behaviour, but they won't heal your relationship. A great way forward is to see a parent–child therapist or a family therapist.

Key points

■ **Correcting behaviour** with anger, criticism, and commands can lead to over-sensitive RAGE and/or FEAR systems in your child's lower brain.

■ **Ignoring your** child's bad behaviour, and giving lots of attention to her when she behaves well, always gets a good result.

■ **Time In** is often a better option than Time Out because it helps you understand why your child is behaving badly.

■ **Family rules** and clear boundaries help children to feel secure.

■ **Choices and consequences** engage your child's thinking brain instead of activating fear and rage in her lower brain.

■ **Disciplining your** child in ways that uphold her dignity is a great gift in terms of her future mental health and her social and emotional intelligence.

the chemistry
of love

This chapter looks at love, from the early love between parent and child to loving relationships in adult life. The fact that we can love is one of nature's gifts to us. Love brings exquisite symphonic cascades of chemicals in our brain. These symphonies can make us feel warm, expansive, creative, potent, and deeply content. When we love deeply, we are also intensely alive. The reverse is also true. If we cannot fully love, we cannot fully live.

All about love

Each one of us has foundational genetic systems for the capacity to love, but these systems are "experience dependent". This means that how these genes will be expressed or not expressed depends on the types of experiences we have, and in particular, the types of experiences we have in childhood.

CONSIDER THIS...

The ability to form loving relationships is often established very early in life. Your children will learn about love and kindness with others through your consistent example. In this picture Lisa, aged four, is so tender towards her baby brother because her parents have loved her with tenderness.

In this chapter, I'll be looking at the science of love between parent and child and how it impacts on a child's ability to form rewarding relationships in later life. Your child's first experiences of his relationship with you will have a dramatic influence on how these foundational genetic systems for love and human warmth unfold.

Two types of love

We can love in peace or in torment. Loving in peace means that you associate love with deep states of well-being. The loved one brings to your life security, comfort, and meaning. You see your loved one realistically and have a basic trust in this person. Loving in torment means peaks of excitement marred with jealousy, destructive rage, and fears of both dependency and abandonment. You have a basic mistrust in the other person, which can lead to an impossible need for reassurance as well as clinging behaviour. You may destroy love or run away from it. Whether your child will love in peace or love in torment will be profoundly influenced by the way you love your child now, and the brain chemistries and systems activated as a result.

■ **Loving in peace means that a child will feel very safe in his parent's love.**
This is because that love is a consistent love, not an on-off love. In other words, it will not suddenly move into coldness, indifference, shame, or contempt.

Parents will discipline their child in ways that give him clear boundaries, but do not frighten him or use withdrawal of love to produce obedience.

A parent's love will also be a non-needy love, rather than a suffocating love that overwhelms the child with the parent's unmet emotional needs. It is unconditional, in that it does not depend on achievement or good behaviour or on a child suppressing particular feelings, such as rage or jealousy. It is based on the parent being able to meet the child deeply in pain as well as in joy. A child's love for a parent is not automatic. Just as we cannot command the clouds to move so the sun will shine, parents cannot command love from their child.

"Your child's relationship with you will have a dramatic influence on brain systems for love and human warmth."

■ **Loving in torment means that a child does not feel safe in his parent's love.**

There are a number of reasons why this may be. A child may feel that he could easily lose that love, or that the emotional bond with that parent is fragile or precarious. If a child grows up to love in torment, it can have enduring effects on his ability to sustain loving relationships in his adult life. One or more of the following difficulties may occur:

■ **he may get locked** into a love life that causes endless pain and anguish.

■ **he may only be able** to sustain short-term intimate relationships, which break down after the honeymoon period.

■ **he may only be able** to sustain a "love and run" approach in relationships; he may get close to someone very quickly, and then just as quickly withdraw.

■ **he may be unable** to love in a tender way, or be frightened of intimacy and find reasons why his relationships fail.

CONSIDER THIS...

If your child grows up able to love in peace, in later life he will be able to:

● choose partners well, by walking towards the people who are good for him and away from those who are not
● develop and sustain long-term, fulfilling intimate relationships
● have the vital resources for tenderness, kindness, compassion, and passion
● listen, soothe, and comfort and support the other emotionally
● spontaneously give of himself in the moment to the person he loves
● be loving and sexual at the same time
● feed an intimate relationship with compliments, appreciation, lovely surprises, and being generous in sharing his inner world of thoughts and feelings, even when this feels difficult.

"Loving in peace means that your moment-to moment stream of consciousness, your thoughts and feelings, take you to a warm world inside your head."

■ **his love may be so needy** and desperate that it drives people away, including his own children.
■ **he may muddle up love** with issues of power and control, submission and dominance.
■ **he may not dare to love at all.**

Love chemicals

When you enable your child to love in peace, some wonderful chemical systems will be strongly activated in his brain. Whilst love is a difficult concept to speak about in neuroscientific terms, scientists think it strongly activates a cascade of many positive arousal neurochemicals, comprising particular opioids, oxytocin, and prolactin; they call these the key bonding chemistries.[1]

Warm relationships appear to be all to do with opioid-based processes within the brain. By and large, mammals (including humans) prefer to spend more time with those in whose presence they have experienced high levels of oxytocin, and opioids in their brains.[2] Opioids, in combination with oxytocin and other chemicals produced naturally in both brain and body, are also arguably the key chemicals for well-being and profound states of contentment. In combination, when strongly activated in the brain, they can affect your perception, making you feel that everything is well in the world. Worries no longer take centre stage in your mind.

Loving in peace also means that your moment-to-moment stream of consciousness, your thoughts and feelings, take you to a warm world inside your head. This is because the opioids cascading through your brain make it feel very warm. All mammals have this wonderful brain opioid system.

It is also likely that the finest human qualities – generosity, kindness, compassion, expansiveness towards others (which flow so easily from those people who are able to love in peace) – are also opioid-based. What's more, we treasure people in our lives who strongly activate opioids in our brain. Metaphorically speaking, they make the sun shine. The

"I love being with you"

How you love your child now, the emotional energies and qualities of that love, are directly transferable to your child's relationships with others. If you love in a spontaneously affectionate way, you will be empowering your child to be the same with others. If you delight in your child, and express that openly, she in turn will be able to delight in others. If you express your warmth through fun and play, she will be building up a vital life resource to be fun in her own relationships.

ANIMAL INSIGHTS

It doesn't matter if you are a squirrel, a rabbit, or a big cat. As mammals we all have this wonderful brain opioid system. So we all have the capacity for a profound sense of well-being and contentment. There has been some ground-breaking research about the brain chemistries that trigger bonding behaviours. The research compared mammals who had little oxytocin activity in their brains with those who had a lot. The animals with weak firings of oxytocin in their brains didn't form close relationships and chose to live in isolation. After having sex, they left their mates.

The other mammals, who had a far stronger activation of oxytocin in their brains, had strong preferences for one partner. They also found social contact very rewarding and were far less aggressive. When oxytocin was pumped into the brains of the aggressive, isolated animals, there was a dramatic decrease in aggression.[5]

thought and feeling of these people offers us resilience in times of struggle and suffering. The opioid and oxytocin release from loving in peace can also dramatically diminish our negative feelings, especially feelings of loneliness and isolation, negativity and anger.[3]

Psychological strength

The more warm, unconditional, constant, and physically affectionate your relationship is with your child, the stronger the release of opioids, oxytocin, and prolactin in his brain. As a result, your child is likely to feel increasingly at ease and comfortable with himself. And when he brings to mind your warm presence he will feel very safe in the world. In short, your relationship enables your child to develop psychological strength. Scientists have found that psychological strength is linked to opioids being strongly activated in the brain.[4]

What this means is that for the most part your child will grow up able to:

- think under stress and calm himself down
- be socially confident, warm, and kind
- turn adversity into opportunity
- respond to personal feedback by thinking about what is being said, rather than lashing out with anger or leaving
- move into resolution rather than blame in a conflict.

"We treasure the people in our lives who strongly activate opioids in our brain...they make the sun shine."

All in all, optimally activated opioids and oxytocin in the brain (in combination with other key chemicals) are the foundation stone for our emotional health and may also impact on our ability to succeed in life at whatever activities, jobs, or interests we choose to pursue. When brain researchers gave one group of animals small doses of opioids and another group an opiate antagonist that blocked opioids in their brain, those animals given opioids always turned out to be winners in their play.[6]

In the wider world

The science of secure, loving, parent–child relationships can teach us a great deal about the atrocities on the world stage. We know from studies with other mammals that the strong activation of opioids, oxytocin, and prolactin in their brains makes them feel unaggressive and with no wish to fight. We can infer from this that opioids and oxytocin are powerful anti-aggressive molecules.[7] "Not wishing to fight", whether verbally or physically, is not only of major significance within the family; it also has implications for the way our children conduct themselves and lead their lives as adults, and the effect they will have on the world they inhabit.

■ In the wider world, lack of love leads to low self-esteem and social confidence.

If a child does not feel loved, or does not trust in the constancy of his parent's love, he is psychologically vulnerable. The fear of loss of a parent's love can be so threatening that it sometimes triggers reptilian brain fight-or-flight reactions. Flight makes the child depressed or socially withdrawn. Fight makes him angry and antisocial.

Research shows reduced activation in the child's left frontal lobe (higher brain) as a result of an unresponsive parent.[8] This part of the brain is associated with both positive feelings and social approach behaviour. The child with an emotionally unresponsive parent, and an underactive left frontal lobe, is more likely to have negative feelings about himself and others. He may not want to approach his parents for cuddles, or other children for friendship, as he is too frightened of rejection. These threatened ways of being in the world can endure right into adulthood.

The strong loving-in-peace bond a child develops with her parent is directly related to having enough moments together that trigger the opioids, oxytocin, and prolactin in her brain. A parent who scoops up her child in loving arms when she cries and when she is joyful, throws her up in the air, and showers her with lovely tickles and "raspberries" on her tummy sets the scene for the formation of a deeply loving bond. These simple responses can strongly activate the bonding chemicals.

What makes us care

Another vitally important system in our brain holds the key to our capacity to feel love and warmth towards others. The CARE system, also known as the nurturant system, is one of the seven genetically ingrained emotional systems in the lower brain (see page 19).

An affectionate relationship with a parent, involving lots of cuddles and play, will strengthen the emotional bond between parent and child. The warm physical contact causes the release of oxytocin in the brain. This sensitizes the brain's opioid system, making the child feel calm and securely loved.

Whether we like it or not, we are all genetically programmed to need people. Bonding behaviour is not simply something belonging to childhood; it continues throughout life. We develop strong emotional bonds towards just a few people, usually in a clear hierarchy in terms of strength of bond. Members of our immediate family and sexual partners are likely to be high up the list. We can really like a lot of people, be very fond of them, but we will develop strong emotional bonds to just a few. That is how the CARE system in our brain operates. So when people says, "I love everybody or I love everybody in this group", this is not only sugar-sweet, it is scientifically inaccurate.

Our emotional bonds

The need for strong emotional bonds can be misinterpreted as overdependency, or regressive, infantile need. This is totally wrong. If we deny or try to defend against our genetically programmed need to bond, sooner or later we can move into a feeling of emptiness, a sense of something major missing in our life, hopelessness, and/or depression. And yet, some people try to operate as if they didn't have a CARE system in their lower brain. They may make strong attachments to objects rather than to people; for example, their home, or their computer. They may throw themselves into work, pursuing success and money. At some stage, however, they will find these empty alternatives cannot protect them from feeling a deep sense of meaninglessness about their life.

The CARE system activates many key structures in the lower brain, with accompanying chemistries (see box, below).[9] Other mammals have a CARE system, but their ability to care for their babies differs, particularly due to variance in the oxytocin system in their brains. Because of our larger higher brain, there are also important differences in how our CARE systems operate. When our lower brain CARE system is strongly activated and working in a well-coordinated way with our higher brain, we are able to express love verbally in a delightfully expansive way. We can also express compassion and empathy, and carry out acts of generosity. That said, some primates, like us, prioritize helping another animal in distress above the reward of food. In most reptiles, the CARE system is not developed at all, which is why they tend to produce babies and leave them to fend for themselves.

"Bonding behaviour is not simply something belonging to childhood; it continues throughout life."

BRAIN STORY

The CARE system extends throughout the lower mammalian brain. The structures include:

- anterior cingulate gyrus
- parts of the hypothalamus
- ventral tegmental area (VTA).

Key chemicals in this system include opioids, released from many parts of the brain including the hypothalamus, and prolactin and oxytocin, which are released from the pituitary gland.

When we feel passionate love, the VTA releases dopamine, stimulating a network of pathways in the lower brain and in the frontal lobes, and producing an effect like cocaine. Scientists think the VTA may activate the drive to express caring behaviour.

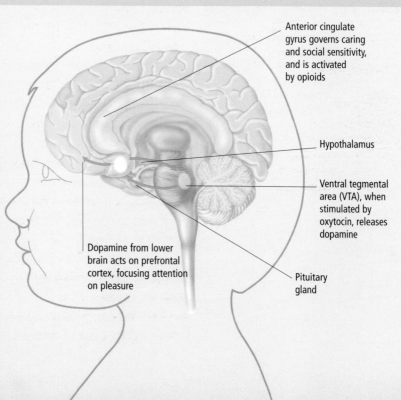

Anterior cingulate gyrus governs caring and social sensitivity, and is activated by opioids

Hypothalamus

Ventral tegmental area (VTA), when stimulated by oxytocin, releases dopamine

Dopamine from lower brain acts on prefrontal cortex, focusing attention on pleasure

Pituitary gland

The first love affair

It's a wonderful gift when you fall in love with your infant and even more amazing if he falls in love with you. In this section I look at how you can have the best chance of forming a deeply fulfilling relationship with your child, full of affection and memorable moments.

CONSIDER THIS...

The first conversations Some parents fall in love with their baby as soon as he is born. For others, it takes a little longer, often because they don't believe a baby is all that interesting until he begins to talk. What they fail to realize is that young babies are capable of the most wonderful conversations (see page 92). And because parents aren't aware of this, their baby loses out on some wonderful early brain-sculpting opportunities.[10]

Beginning around two and a half months, when infants begin to engage strongly with their eyes, you may spend long periods locked in mutual gaze with your new baby. Infants do not do this when looking at other objects; they love to look at faces. The delighted expression on your face will mirror back to your baby just how delightful he is. Children lucky enough to have such beautiful intimate moments with a parent repeatedly, in early life, are rich indeed.

■ **These one-to-one times are also the very foundation stones for a child's self-esteem.**
The ability to light you up is the very basis of your baby's sense of himself as lovely and loveable, as fun to be with, as capable of bringing joy to another. Children who miss out on these early intense, loving one-to-one times are likely to struggle far more with self-esteem in later life. They cannot understand that their blank-faced or unresponsive parent is simply not great at loving or showing love, perhaps due to stress, depression, lack of support, or inhibited parental love in their own childhood, so they are left with the feeling that they are unlovable.

■ **Falling in love with a parent is very important as this love is so often transferred to a love of life.**
Take four-year-old Emma, for example, – she is, quite simply, in love with her Daddy. He has just put some new little pots of jam on the table for breakfast. Emma says with a genuine

THE CHEMISTRY OF LOVE

sense of exhilaration, "Wow, these are the best little pots of jam I have ever seen". Emma has already started transferring her love for her father to a love of life.

Why cuddles are vitally important

"Too big for cuddles now" when your child is no longer a baby or toddler is a grave mistake. Some children with this experience start to drift away from their parents. This is because, without the chain reaction of chemicals activated by physical affection, the emotional bond can weaken. Touch-starved children can reach a defensive point. On the few occasions that cuddles are offered by their parents, they brace

> "From touch-starved childhoods, people can grow up with 'troubled bodies'."

themselves against them or openly reject them. From touch-starved childhoods, people can grow up with "troubled bodies". They can take in a very worrying subliminal message from the fact that their bodies are seemingly so undesirable to the most important people in their lives. Self-harm, smoking, eating disorders, drinking, drug abuse, and bodily neglect can all be testimony to the child short of cuddles, comforting with words and touch, and physical parent–child play.[11]

High-intensity moments

These are moments of real meeting between you and your child, and are key to your child feeling loved and loveable. High-intensity relational moments are times of very strong emotional connection without distraction, and without focusing on some third object, such as a TV or a computer game. For example, your child suddenly flings his arms around you and says "I love you Mummy". You pick him up in response, turn him upside down, and give him a delicious cuddle. He laughs and laughs with glee.

Research shows that societies and families rich in warm physical affection have far fewer problems with anger and aggression, yet in some families there is a steep drop in cuddles and physically playful times after babyhood. This is followed by another steep drop after age five, and then another one when their children reach adolescence. There is a natural moving away from parents in adolescence, but this can start much earlier in parent–child relationships starved of physical affection.[12]

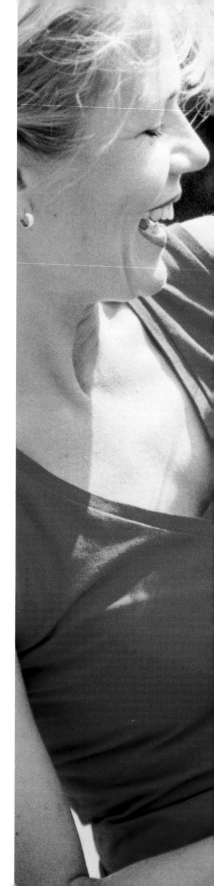

High-intensity moments involve lingering in the sheer intimacy of the moment. They involve reaching out to each other spontaneously. They are moments through which your child feels deeply met in his joy or in his pain. Such childhood moments can become treasured memories in adulthood: "When I was little, my Dad threw me up in the air, let me lay my head on his lap, held me when I cried, and really understood when I was scared."

■ **Children are great teachers of high-intensity relational moments, if we are open to learning.**
They can teach us all about emotional connection or re-teach us about it if we have forgotten. Babies who have been on the receiving end of enough high-intensity relational moments soon became experts. Many babies are superb at intense gaze. They can have real meetings with strangers. So if you are in a café, they will often catch your eye and then you are both into some delicious intimate meeting, across a crowded room. However, if your capacity for intimacy has been blighted or never properly developed in your own childhood, then babies cannot use you in this vital brain-sculpting way.

Some families are fertile grounds for positive high-intensity relational moments; others are not. Some families just get out of the habit of coming together to make something lovely happen. This can particularly be the case as children get older and the family home becomes simply a place of solo activities in different rooms. Sometimes it takes very little to change the culture for the better. When it feels stuck and you can't make headway, think of a period of parent–child counselling or family therapy.

"Some families just get out of the habit of coming together to make something lovely happen."

Questionnaire

How many high-intensity positive relational moments are you having with your child?

You can monitor yourself by doing this assessment. Think of a day recently when you were with your child for several hours. Did any of the following occur?

■ You spontaneously gave your child a cuddle, or some other physically affectionate gesture. She spontaneously gave you a cuddle or kiss and you met this with grace.

■ You spontaneously told your child that she was good at something.

■ You engaged in rough and tumble or gentle and tumble play (see page 104).

■ Your eyes met for a while, with feelings of love or warmth, or you engaged in shared laughter.

■ You shared moments of calm (for example, snuggled up together on the sofa, reading together).

■ Your hellos and goodbyes were lovely moments of connection, rather than rushed non-events.

■ Your child wanted to tell you something important, or simply wanted to chat to you, and you responded with really good, full-attention listening.

If some or most of the above are common occurrences, congratulate yourself. Your way of being with your child will be developing her capacity to love in peace. If they are not common occurrences, don't beat yourself up. See Looking After You (pages 244–269) for ways forward.

High-intensity relational moments are likely to activate opioids in your child's brain. They may also activate dopamine, due to the novelty value of these events. Studies have found a link between psychological strength and the activation of brain opioids, while optimal levels of dopamine are vital for a child to feel intensely alive. What a combination: warmth, well-being, and life force!

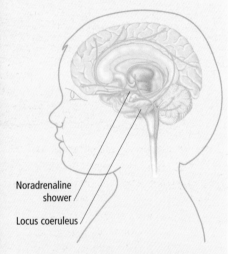

Noradrenaline shower

Locus coeruleus

The locus coeruleus (meaning "blue spot") is a structure deep in the brain stem that is strongly activated when something of significance is happening – a high-intensity relational moment. It then showers the brain with noradrenaline. When this happens, events, thoughts, and impressions are more likely to become fixed in memory. These delightful memories will be important to your child. He will build a strong sense that he is fun to be with and that shared lovely moments with other people make him feel great.

■ "Let's" times are a particular form of high-intensity relational moment.

These are shared activities born out of spontaneity. For a "let's" time to happen with your child, suggest some activity you can do together, such as:

- Let's make a sandcastle
- Let's make a volcano
- Let's make a cake!

This is irresistible to most children. It's also great for young children who are not quite up to making up their own "let's" games and need a little bit of guidance from you first. In "let's" times, you are also modelling the capacity for being "together in fun" in relationships. What a gift for your child to take this capacity into future relationships.

Activities for under-fives

Here are some ideas for high-intensity relational activities you can do with children aged under five. If you have a sense of fun and play, these activities will hopefully be a rich resource of ideas. If, however, you feel uncomfortable around physical play with your child, then they may not be right for you at the moment. If you force yourself to do them, your child will pick up on your awkwardness, anxiety, or flat tone of voice. He may then lose interest because his brain will not be releasing the wonderful bonding chemistries but rather high levels of stress chemicals. If, however, you are at ease with play and touch, you'll know if the activities are right for your child from his squeals of delight and shouts of "again, again!".

■ Play peekaboo and hide-and-seek.

With a baby, place a cloth over your or his face and say, "Where have you gone?" When you or he pulls off the cloth, say delightedly, "Oh, there you are!" Even older children like slightly more sophisticated versions of peekaboo. I have worked with eight year olds and beyond who still enjoy them. Alternatively, with older children, you can play hide-and-seek.

Enter into the spirit of the game and say, "Where have you gone? Has anyone seen Michael?" Children often enjoy the game if you add some absurd suggestions: "Is he on the ceiling?" (look on the ceiling), "Is he under the carpet?" (look under the carpet), "Is he in the plant pot?" (look in the plant pot). End with a huge, delighted hello and, "Oh there you are!" Usually this game brings squeals of delight and requests for more. With under-fives, warn your child when there are just two more games left because an abrupt end to such delight can be experienced as a sudden loss and so can activate the pain centres in his brain. We humans have a genetically programmed painful response when we anticipate a reward and fail to get it.

■ **Try some face-to-face activities.**
Face-to-face contact can deeply enhance parent–child bonds – all these games are played sitting facing each other on the floor. These activities are good for under-fives, and especially if you think your child missed out on a lot of brain-stimulating face-to-face times in his first year of life.

"If a little girl wants to fly, don't say, 'children don't fly'. Instead, pick her up and carry her around above your head…" [13]

■ **Feather or cotton wool ball football.** Place a feather or cotton wool ball on a cushion between you. Mark out your separate goals (perhaps with little sticks) and blow the feather or ball into the other person's goal.
■ **Catch the feathers.** Both of you throw lots of feathers in the air. Both try to catch as many as you can before they fall to the floor. Or each put a feather on the other person's head and play blowing it off and catching it. [14]

CONSIDER THIS…

Hellos and goodbyes can be high-intensity relational moments or weak or failed connections. They can speak so loudly to a child about how much he is loved. Was he missed? Are you delighted to see him? A key neuroscientist speaks at length about the possible adverse effect on brain and body systems of poor parental responsiveness during these reunion experiences. [15]

Do you have enough generosity of spirit, love, and spontaneity next time you greet your child to say hello with open arms and perhaps scoop him up in your arms, showing warmth and delight in your face?

"One of the biggest complaints from adults about their own childhood is the lack of play with their parents."

■ **Blow bubbles** and both try to pop them with your fingers and toes.

■ **Put stickers** on each other's noses, toes, elbows, and tummies.

■ **Try some rough and tumble or gentle romping.**

In chapter 4, we looked at the surprising brain effects of rough and tumble play with children (see page 104). Here are a few ideas:

■ **blow raspberries on your child's tummy.**

■ **pretend to eat his foot.** Go up to him and say something like, "Oh what a lovely foot. I think I will have to eat it." Make lots of lovely fun munching sounds as you do.

■ **chase, catch, and eat.** Children just love to be chased. Say, "I am a hungry lion/crocodile/shark. Ooh, what a yummy delicious little boy to eat." Then chase him. Gauge from the child whether he actually likes being caught and eaten occasionally or whether the fun is in the chase.

Babies and toddlers love to play peekaboo. They enjoy the face-to-face interaction with a parent, and the expressions that you pull! It's their best form of interactive theatre.

Involve your children in day-to-day cooking as well as making special cakes and biscuits. They will enjoy the feeling of creating something worthwhile with you.

Rough and tumble and other physical play, such as chasing and blowing raspberries, is appealing to children of all ages.

■ **upside down boy.** Most children, within the context of a safe, loving relationship, love to be turned upside down or swung around. You will know this if he says, "Again! again!" You can spontaneously go up to him and say, "Ah! I've found an upside down boy" and turn him upside down, holding on to his legs. Make sure, of course, that you hold him really well, over a bed or sofa so the game is safe.

■ **"what have you got in your socks?"** Hold his foot. Say, "I think you've got marbles in your socks". He usually grins and shakes his head. Carry on getting more and more absurd: "Well then, I think you've got snails/sweets/worms in your socks." Perhaps pull off his socks and say, "Oh my goodness, it's toes!"

■ **Mabel the flower.** Take your child's hand and say, "Can I tell you about Mabel the flower (or any other such little fictitious person)?" Draw Mabel on the back of his hand or his arm with your fingers (thereby activating lots of lovely oxytocin in his brain). Tell him an action story about Mabel; for example, Mabel goes fishing or has a tea party in the woods.

■ **telescopes.** This game is suitable for children aged four and over. Give your child a little scroll of paper or an old toilet roll inside and tell him it's a telescope. Explain that telescopes make things look smaller or bigger. As he looks through, be the thing he sees and mime any action he tells you about. He may say, " I can see a tiny green elf mending his shoe", or "I can see an elephant eating the clouds". He can have ten turns on the telescope and then it's your turn.

Let your child lead

One of the biggest complaints from adults about their own childhood is the lack of play with their parents. For so many people, a parent willing to play with them in their childhood has been a proof of love. Many children bemoan the fact that "Mummy is more interested in cleaning than playing".

This said, if you are going to use play actively to strengthen your emotional bond with your child, it needs to be child-led

"Hello funny puppet!"

Play puppets together All you need are puppets or socks with buttons for eyes. Take them exploring around the room. Say, "Oh look, I have found a great hiding place down the side of the sofa" or "Ooh, shall we have tea on the top of this light shade!" You could also make up a song about going exploring. Your child's puppet can follow you around the room, exploring all sorts of nooks and crannies. She might like to take the lead too. This is a wonderful, fun activity that your child will enjoy for its silliness!

play, not play that is dominated by a parent. Sue Jenner, author of *The Parent–Child Game* and a clinical psychologist working for many years at the Maudsley Hospital in London, used child-led play as a key tool in strengthening the emotional bond between parent and child. She repeatedly found that children who were very difficult and badly behaved had all too little child-led play with their parents. So powerful was child-led play that when parents were taught how to do it, children stopped their extremely challenging behaviour and were a delight to be with.

In brain terms, this dramatic shift in behaviour is easy to understand. Child-led play is likely to activate those lovely opioids, which have the power to reduce levels of stress chemicals and have anti-aggressive properties. On a psychological level, child-led play gives vital messages that are key to a child's self-esteem: "My ideas are valuable." "I can make worthwhile things happen."

"Child-led play is likely to activate those lovely opioids, which have the power to reduce levels of stress chemicals."

■ **Parent-dominated play can reduce dopamine levels in a child's brain and activate stress chemicals.**
It can also trigger the RAGE system in a child's lower mammalian brain. This is because we are genetically predisposed to respond with rage to any restriction of our freedom. Parent-controlled play is all about "Do it like this. No, not like that." What's more, there is no emotional connection. Damaging messages from this sort of play include: "My ideas are worthless. I can't make anything good happen." Self-protective children will walk away and lose interest. Compliant ones will continue playing, whilst feeling shut down and controlled.

Child-led play

Child-led play means following your child's play rather than directing it. Try the following ideas:

■ Describe what your child is doing; for example, "Ah, so you are pouring water from the little red watering can into the big red bucket?"

■ Ask to play: "What would you like me to do?"

■ Touch: Gently touch his back or tweak his foot occasionally as you play.

■ Praise: "Wow, that's the best sandcastle I have ever seen!"

Parent-dominated play

Parent-dominated play means leading your child with instructions and corrections. For example, "Nice picture, but you haven't put a door on your shed. It needs a door." Do you recognize yourself in any of the following?

■ Commands: "No, people are supposed to ride in the train. You've drawn them in the engine. Do it like this".

■ Criticisms: "Now try not to be so messy with the dough" or "No, stick it nearer the top".

■ Lessons: "You've drawn the octopus wrong. See – you have missed out two of its legs. Octopuses have eight legs".

■ Negative touch and look: gripping the child's wrist as you say, "Be careful. You're getting paint on the table top". Frowns and glaring eyes.

■ Drowning out: talking over the natural flow of chatter from your child with commands and instructions.[16]

When love is put to the test

Some challenging behaviour is fuelled by a child's genetically programmed need for emotional contact with you. If he feels he has lost the connection, he can act provocatively to try to reconnect. Do we respond with anger or take it as a sign that we are not giving him enough positive relational moments?

CONSIDER THIS...

Children love toys and gadgets with lots of functions. If you press this button, it makes a noise. They particularly like to turn up the volume. If your child is able to make you shout and scream, you become the perfect toy! But if you give your child a positive relational moment instead, the activation of opioids in her brain will outweigh the quick adrenaline fix she gets from winding you up.[17]

A moment of provocation

If parents are not providing enough lovely one-to-ones, a child may resort to getting recognition through provocative approach behaviour. Young children often do ingeniously annoying things to get attention. They will shout in your ear, jump on you, or tie your shoelaces together. It's as if the child is saying: "Mum, I've lost my connection with you. You haven't said anything to me or touched me affectionately for ages now. So I will shout to get a response from you. I know it may be an angry one, but it's better than no response at all".

■ So what do you do? Consider a creative response, not a cross one.

If you respond with a positive relational moment, you can both end the allure of bad behaviour and strengthen the emotional bonds between you. Imagine that you have been on the phone for 20 minutes, during which time you have given your four year old no attention at all. He comes up to you and gives you a little nip on the bottom. You could respond in two ways. Angrily, you say "That's not nice. You do not do that. Right. Time Out." The result: stress chemical release in both his brain and yours. Or you could move into a playful response, likely to release lots of bonding opioids in both your brains. "Ah! A visit from the nipping monster! Yum yum, I'm a crocodile and I love eating nipping monsters" (pretend to eat him). Young children appreciate the absurdity of the situation and will delight in the intensity of the relational moment. You could also try "Car wash". When the annoying approach behaviour happens, pick him up, put him over your knee and say, "Ah, time to wash the car. Here is the car. Put it in the car wash" and do swooshing movements and sounds all over his back. It's a meeting through fun rather than a meeting through anger.

Over time, the child is likely to go straight for a playful or loving approach with you and give the annoying one a miss, which is now so pale and unappealing in comparison. You are also modelling the delight of meeting in joy in a relationship, which sadly some children know so little about.

Hurting too much inside

We are not talking here about responding with a quick cuddle when a child has a cut knee, but rather really connecting with him when he is struggling with a painful emotion. This means taking the time to attempt to understand and then

> "A key part of loving well is the ability to comfort the distress of a loved one."

to find the right words for "what is specific" in the pain of your child.[18] If your child is to love well in later life, your being able to connect on a deep level with his emotional pain is vital. This is because a key part of loving well is, of course, the ability to comfort the distress of a loved one, so that they feel deeply met in their pain.

Take the example of Emily, aged two. She is having a great time in the bath, but it is time for bed. Her Mum lifts Emily out of the bath without warning, and the little girl breaks down into tears of disappointment and rage. Her Mum, however, is great at meeting Emily in her pain. She realizes that she has ruptured Emily from this delightful activity. So she says to her, "I am so sorry, I ended the bath too quickly." Emily looks straight at her and says, "Yes you did." As Mum

Some parents are great at doing exciting activities with their children, vital for developing the brain's SEEKING system (see The Chemistry of Living Life Well, pages 84–109), but they are not so great at helping them with their painful feelings. Interesting activities activate dopamine, not opioids, in the brain, and science points to the fact that dopamine is not key to social bonding.[19] So being good at activities as a parent but without the ability to be emotionally responsive to your child's painful feelings is unlikely to strengthen the love bond between you.

Q Isn't it wrong to reward attention-seeking behaviour?

There are some types of attention-seeking behaviour which need ignoring (such as kicking the chair leg, or talking about poo provocatively), and others which are totally unacceptable (like hurting someone) and need Time Out (see page 174). The danger is applying discipline techniques indiscriminately. Some parents even label a baby's crying as attention-seeking. But crying and the types of behaviour described here are born out of a need for contact with you as his primary emotional regulator. Such behaviour is contact-seeking, not attention-seeking. It's as if the child is saying, "I need contact with you. I've lost that good feeling, and if I find you again I'll feel that all is well in my world".

has met her in her pain, she is no longer in distress. It is feeling alone in one's distress or anguish that activates the pain centres in the brain.

When we focus too much on a child's behaviour and not enough on his emotions, we are in danger of seeing all screams and rages as naughty behaviour in need of modification. In so doing we can fail to respond to real pain. As a result, a child may bring emotional insensitivity and not compassion to his relationships in later life.

■ **If we don't meet a child in his distress, he may learn that people don't get help with painful feelings.**

He may believe that you just deal with painful feelings all by yourself. But in later life this "self-holding" all too often means "holding" with the help of alcohol, nicotine, or some neurotic or physical symptom. Research shows that children are making key decisions as to what to do with their painful feelings as young as the age of one. Emotional development is, in part, the ability to dare to feel the pain of what has happened to you, acknowledge it, and reflect on it, instead of cutting off from it. A child cannot do this without your help.

■ **Let's get real. All parents will "lose it" with their child from time to time.**

As long as it doesn't frighten him, occasional shouting at a child is highly unlikely to have long-term adverse effects on his developing emotional and social brain. But it may break a connection between the two of you. What matters then is whether or not this connection gets mended. Too many unrepaired connections can weaken the love bond between you. If you realize that you were going over the top, or unleashing your stress about something else on to your child, and you acknowledge the child's hurt at your response, this is called interactive or relationship repair.[20] You may sit down with him, cuddle him, and apologize in order to reconnect. This is great modelling for your child, and a vital part of

Case study

Understanding Milly

Milly aged four is upset because she wants to sit in her usual place in the car but today a cousin has taken her seat. In brain terms we know from research that "familiar loved places" as well as familiar loved people can activate opioids in the brain. Not being in her seat in the car can cause an "opioid withdrawal" in the brain, and this is extremely painful. Milly was not warned that this was going to happen, so her dopamine levels will be reduced, too, due to frustration of anticipated rewards, and the RAGE system in her lower brain will also have activated.

Milly's father is tempted to tell Milly to stop fussing. But he tries a different tack. "I know it's really important for you to sit in your usual seat, Milly, and that this is upsetting for you." Milly stops crying and clings to his hand very tightly. Comfort and solace like this can dramatically strengthen the bond between parent and child.

However, Milly's father doesn't give her the seat. Helping children with emotional pain doesn't mean just giving them what they are screaming for.

If your child is screaming his refusal to get out of the bath, or crying for another chocolate biscuit, you don't have to give in to his protests or demands. Setting firm boundaries, and saying "no" in ways which respect the child's dignity (and are not implemented with anger or shaming), will never damage the love-bond between you. Rather, it will add to your child's feeling of security that a parent is in charge.

being able to love in peace in later life. When the going gets tough in his intimate relationships, he is then far more likely to mend moments of conflict than to move into primitive reptilian brain fight-or-flight behaviour, such as lashing out or leaving. Many adult partnerships suffer because neither partner has learned the art of interactive repair.

Repairing the damage

Imagine a familiar scenario. Eric, aged three, is in an elegant restaurant and merrily drives his toy into his spaghetti. He is not being naughty; he hasn't yet grasped the etiquette of restaurants. Feeling embarrassed, Eric's father shouts, "Stop that at once." Eric bursts into tears and, still crying, runs to his Daddy and climbs on his lap. He loves his Daddy very much and so is desperate to mend the broken connection between them. Knowing that he overreacted, his father

"If you always meet your child's love with grace, she can feel that her very goodness is a potent force. "

comforts Eric. This is relationship repair. Eric will not suffer any emotional scars from the event. If broken connections are repeatedly left unrepaired, however, children may start to fear intimate relationships because they are associated with pain.

◼ **Children are also capable of relationship repair.**
It is vital that any acts of relationship repair on behalf of your child are received with grace. He may not use words, but instead may start to help you with something, or draw you a picture, or give you a "present". Responding with grace means going down to his level to get eye contact and thanking him warmly. The problem is that children are often ready to repair at a time when a parent is still angry with them. When this is

the case, it is fine to say, "I'm still too angry with you to respond well to you right now, but I promise I will come and find you when I'm feeling better about things." This way you are not trying to fake a generous response before you are ready to give one.[21]

Being careful with your child's love

When your child reaches out to you with some loving gesture, in that moment he is intensely alive and yet intensely vulnerable. Not only is he wide open to his love being met well, but he is also wide open to shame and humiliation if it's not. Take, for example, the child who smiles adoringly into his mother's eyes and meets only her indifference. He reaches out his little arms towards her, but she brushes him aside, preoccupied with the many stressors in her life. In that moment, it is as if all his passionate feelings just fall into the space between them. We are talking about something utterly bleak here. The thing is that with repeated moments such as this, a child can all too easily come to one of the following conclusions:

- "My love is worthless to my mum, so that makes me basically worthless."
- "I adore my Dad but he doesn't respond so there must be something wrong with me. I must be basically unlovable/ undesirable/uninteresting or even repulsive."

This can cause real problems in terms of self-esteem throughout life. Take the case of Mary, aged seven, whose mother was locked into a depression that affected her ability to love. When Mary was in play therapy, she made up this story: "The little girl was drowned. Her Mummy could have saved her but she didn't because the little girl wasn't pretty enough for her Mummy."

Some children, who feel that their loving is so impotent, move into hating instead. The latter will always guarantee them a reaction within the family and in the wider world, and so give them the sense of potency they are looking for.[22]

"I love you, Mum"

If you always meet your child's love with grace, she can feel that her very goodness is a potent force. So when she comes up to you with that spontaneous cuddle or "I love you Mummy", stop what you are doing, and meet her love with warmth and a very responsive facial expression and tone of voice. Say something like "How lovely!" or "How lucky I am". An unresponsive mother's face can elicit a high-level cortisol response in a child. In some famous research studies in which mothers were asked to keep their faces very still, their infants became very disturbed.[23] Also, by not meeting your child's love with grace, you can inhibit her approach behaviour in later life.

Dealing with broken hearts

What happens when a child suffers pain because of a family break-up or bereavement, or feels he has lost a parent to depression, to drugs or drink, to long-term illness, or to a new baby? This section is about meeting a child's grief or pain in love, and helping to restore well-being.

CONSIDER THIS...

Professor Jaak Panksepp compares the grief of losing a person, or someone's love, to the pain of coming off heroin (which taps into the brain's opioid system artificially).[24]

Coming off heroin
- Psychic pain
- Crying
- Loss of appetite
- Despondency
- Sleeplessness
- Aggressiveness

Coming off a person
- Loneliness
- Crying
- Loss of appetite
- Depression
- Sleeplessness
- Irritability

As we have seen in previous chapters, the opioids that are triggered by being with people we love can make us feel that everything is well with our world. And when we lose that love, or feel that our love is threatened in some way, that feeling of well-being is completely gone.

■ So let's look at what is happening in a grieving child's brain.

Grief can result in the withdrawal of opioids in key parts of the brain, along with reduced levels of other bonding chemicals – oxytocin and prolactin. This causes a marked increase in negative feelings as well as a reduction in positive feelings.[25] When these bonding chemicals are being optimally activated in the brain, they can naturally diminish our anxieties, fear, and stress responses. But when opioids are withdrawn, fear and stress are no longer regulated in the same way and can return with a vengeance.

In a child with a broken heart, the SEPARATION DISTRESS system in the lower mammalian brain is strongly activated (see page 24). This is a system of grief, desolation, loneliness, and often panic, which activates pain centres in the brain. Key to the SEPARATION DISTRESS system is a chemical called glutamate, which plays a vital role in our capacity to form thoughts. Grief can activate overly high levels of glutamate. This can both dramatically increase crying and block you from feeling any of the comforting effects of things such as music and the company of friends.[26]

We know about the pain of broken hearts in childhood from observations of orphaned primates such as chimpanzees, who can die from grief just weeks after losing their mother.[27] They are perfectly capable of physical survival, but their grief is too awful to bear. After the genocide in Rwanda, many children who had seen their parents killed also gave up and died.[28]

Love can be made angry.

We often hear in the news about "love made angry", and when we look closer at the brain chemistry of broken hearts, this is not at all surprising. We have already seen that grief leads

"Grief can result in the withdrawal of opioids in key parts of the brain."

"My world is broken"

A child does not have to experience the loss of a parent through death or divorce to suffer pain. A parent who is physically present but unable to show enough love can break a child's heart, too. On–off parental love (loving one minute, emotionally distant the next) means a rollercoaster for the child in terms of activation of opioids in his brain. He can be locked into a cycle of strong opioid activation followed by extremely painful opioid withdrawal. This cycle awakens an intensity of yearning in a child and often sets up an addiction to that parent. This can lead to loving in torment in later life.[29]

"It is all too easy for society to start to hate children who are locked in anger from a broken heart."

to opioid withdrawal. As opioid systems are involved in the regulation of emotional states, opioid withdrawal means we can feel angry and anxious without being able to regulate our feelings properly. Opioids and oxytocin are also powerful anti-aggression molecules, so their withdrawal can lead to even more anger. In addition, pain in love activates:

- **CRF (corticotropin-releasing factor)** High levels of this stress chemical can block the release of positive arousal chemicals – dopamine, serotonin, and noradrenaline. A reduction in levels of these chemicals can trigger impulsive outbursts of irritation, anger, or rage.
- **Acetylcholine** When opioids are withdrawn, what are known as "opponent forces" are released in the brain. These opponent forces involve the release of high levels of a chemical called acetylcholine. Acetylcholine at optimal levels helps us concentrate and feel alert, but at high levels it makes people angry, hostile, or frequently irritated.

"I want my Dad back "

When a compassionate teacher takes the time to listen and to help a grieving child, it can make all the difference between him thriving and failing to thrive. Sometimes it is easier for a child to talk to a teacher or counsellor than to a parent, because of fears that "it will only upset Mummy if I talk about Daddy leaving".

■ **Many children with broken hearts behave in angry, aggressive ways because of their changed brain chemistry.**

Tragically, it's all too easy for society to start to hate children who are locked in anger from a broken heart, and want to exclude them – from schools or from the wider world in general. Such children need help, not punishment. Hopefully, increasing public knowledge of the dramatic changes in the brain that result from the loss of a beloved parent, or from the loss of their love, will help to improve levels of compassion in society. It may also help to motivate governmental bodies to offer far more counselling and therapy resources for children and young people.

■ **Children with broken hearts don't need to grow up into angry or violent adults.**

If a grieving child has someone in his life who can recognize his pain (even when he's very skilled at disguising it) and offer him comfort, he has every chance of becoming an emotionally stable adult. The awful brain chemistry that can set a child on the road to hostility or real violence in later life doesn't need to happen. The physical comforting of grief will release opioids and oxytocin, deactivating the toxic chemistry in the brain that causes the damage.

This is why it is vital for children who are suffering from the pain of loss (even if on the surface they look just fine) to receive loving attention. Schools, in particular, need to be aware of children who have lost a parent or who they think may be loving in torment at home. Help at the right time for such children can often stop years of misery.

If a child moves into "love made angry" or gets stuck in grief, there can be serious consequences in terms of long-term behaviour problems and learning difficulties. More than 75 percent of people in prison have suffered the pain of broken relationships in childhood.

"The awful brain chemistry that can set a child on the road to hostility doesn't need to happen."

Sibling rivalry

To watch an older child with a new baby can be to witness that child's agony at seeing what was once given to her now going to her sibling. The pain of sibling rivalry, with all its accompanying confusions, should never be underestimated. That feeling of well-being can be completely lost, fuelled by the insidious belief "I'm not as lovable to my Mummy as my little sister".

CONSIDER THIS...

When the excitement and novelty of a new brother or sister begin to fade, painful emotions may begin to surface in the older child:

- feeling that she is on the outside of a couple (mother and new baby)
- feeling that she is the unfavoured one
- feeling unworthy of her mother's love in direct comparison with her rival
- feeling invisible
- feeling that there is not enough love to go round
- feeling that "my place in my mother's mind feels all too precarious. My connection with her is far too fragile."

Sibling rivalry can cover a multitude of feelings in a child, not least the pain of watching the love-duet of her mother with a rival who has equal claim on her affection. Weininger, a psychotherapist, describes the very essence of this pain in love: "There are two people who have what I want and they are giving it to each other and not to me".[30] Brain scans confirm that feeling on the "outside" can activate pain centres in the brain.[31] The aggressive behaviour and impulsivity that comes from sibling pain in love is often due to opioid withdrawal in the brain from this perceived outsider status, the blocking of vital mood-stabilizing systems, and increases in other brain chemicals (see page 209). Hence the occurrence of frequent fighting in families in which one or more children feels the pain of sibling rivalry.

Helping with sibling rivalry

Your child is not going to walk up to you and say, "I think you prefer my brother to me, and that is making me feel so hurt inside". Instead, children's language of feeling is their behaviour.[32] Hence they may show you their pain by hurting their siblings or being defiant or moody.

To help your children, watch them carefully and be acutely vigilant to the times when one child is watching you have a delightful encounter with your other child. If the pain of sibling rivalry is coming out in fighting, talk to your child. If your child finds talking difficult, you might like to have

"Why does he hate me?"

It is vital that parents take sibling rivalry seriously. Potential risks to the development of a twin's or sibling's brain are very real if he has to cope with unexplained hatred whenever his parents' backs are turned. The human brain is designed to be highly adaptive to the environment, particularly in the first years of life, when rapid moulding is going on. The brain of a frequently attacked sibling can all too easily start to adapt itself to survive in a bullying world (see page 234).

a family of puppets in the home for help with expressing difficult feelings. Here's an example of a mother finding a way to talk to her child about her sibling pain.

This mother used hand puppets to stop Laura from being horrid to her baby brother, Georgie. She asked Laura if she would like to do a puppet game and to choose a puppet. Laura chose a seal for herself and a brown bear for Mum. Mum asked her to do a "thumbs up" if the seal got what Laura was feeling right and thumbs down if it was wrong. Mum had a puppet on each hand and conducted the conversation. She used the seal to say, "Hey Brown Bear,

"Be vigilant when one child is watching you have a delightful encounter with your other child."

Case study

The magic stone
When Joe feels angry and ready to lash out because his younger sister has been getting all his mum's attention, he slips a special stone in his mum's pocket. She taught him to do this because she found he was becoming increasingly aggressive towards his sister, but could not find the words to explain how he was feeling.

The stone is a cue to give Joe a special smile, or a special squeeze, and acts as a reminder to her to spend more one-to-one time with him. She praises Joe and says what a great little guy he is for telling her so well about his pain. She responds in such a warm, loving way that opioids, oxytocin, and prolactin are once again activated in his brain. As we have seen, animals with high levels of opioids and oxytocin do not want to fight and, sure enough, Joe stops being horrid to his little sister.

it was so much better before baby Georgie came along. I had you all to myself. Now Georgie is here, it's like I've got this pain in my heart."

Laura put a thumb up in a very definite way. The Bear spoke back, "I am so sorry to hear that you have so much pain in your heart, Little Seal. How brave you are to let me know all this. But you are my very special Seal and baby Georgie can never take the special place in my heart which is just for you. I love you so very much, and am so sorry if I forget sometimes to show you that I do." The bear gave the seal a big cuddle and kissed her on the nose.[33]

Empathy like this is likely to activate opioids in a child's brain, making her feel deeply secure. As a result, Laura no longer has that impulse to be aggressive towards her brother.

It's never too late to fall in love with your child

It is a myth that parents love their children equally. They love them with different intensities and in different ways. If you find you give more love to one child, actively do things to reconnect to the other child in a special way. Timetable in quality one-to-one times each week, such as lovely child-led play or a visit to the park or to the zoo.

Sometimes it's hard to love a child. You may be in a negative lock – meeting in anger or seeing your child as the enemy. Perhaps you were the unfavoured child in your family, and so you are unconsciously repeating this with one of your children now. If this is the case, you need compassion, not criticism. If those bonding brain chemicals are not strongly activated when you are with your child, you won't feel loving towards her. The first step is to understand what might be blocking the CARE system in your lower brain. If you think your childhood is affecting your ability to love, consider seeking parent–child therapy and/or counselling for yourself (see also Looking after You, pages 244–269, for ways forward). Remember, you can fall in love with your child at any time, even if you've had a rocky start.

Key points

■ **To love in peace** throughout life, children need to feel safe in their parents' unconditional love.

■ **If children love in torment**, it can have enduring effects on their ability to have lasting relationships.

■ **One-to-ones** and high-intensity moments with you are the foundation stones of your child's self-esteem.

■ **Letting children** take the lead when you do creative play together helps to reduce challenging behaviour and makes them a joy to be with.

■ **Taking time to understand** your child's painful feelings will deepen the emotional bond between you.

■ **Children with broken hearts** need compassion and understanding to restore their positive brain chemistry.

Your socially intelligent child

The ability to form meaningful human relationships is fundamental to mental health and to happiness. It's the quality of contact we have with other people that is arguably the most important determining factor in quality of life. This is because rich connection with another person means richer connection with ourselves and to life itself. What's more, we can only know ourselves through relationships with others, and we can only develop ourselves through relationships with others.

Developing social skills

Getting along well with people requires social intelligence – it is nothing whatsoever to do with cleverness. There are many very clever people who have poor social intelligence, and as a result they may find it difficult to have a meaningful conversation, to listen well, or to develop long-lasting friendships.

Responding to the emotional cues of others is key to social intelligence. Studies show that eleven year olds who responded well to another child's feelings were significantly more likely to have had a good response to their own feelings from their parents.[1]

Such people may relate in a flat, dull way, devoid of humour, and lacking in any curiosity about the person they are talking to. They may be successful in terms of making money, but are unable to function well in their personal life. What's more, research in the business world shows that the most successful leaders are not the most pushy or determined people, but are those who are the most socially aware of the feelings and needs of others.

There is no social intelligence gene. To become a socially developed human being, your child needs help from you, as we shall see in this chapter.

Learning social skills

Some avenues to social intelligence can be opened up to children by teaching them skills, but many can't. This is because the "social dance" is very subtle and highly complex. You can teach a child simple social skills such as how to ask someone to be your friend, how to talk about your feelings, how to say no, and how to ask for something in a clear way. But social intelligence is far more than this. You can't teach a child how to be moved by another's distress – he either is or he isn't. You can't teach a child how to be emotionally warm – he either is or he isn't. You can't teach a child how to be naturally curious about another person, and to voice that curiosity in such a way that the other person feels valued and interesting. You can't teach a child the capacity to soothe and comfort a person who is in distress. All these wonderful higher human functions will only be possible if he has developed the necessary pathways and complex chemical reactions in his brain, along with a truly embodied response. This development can only take place through particular relationship experiences, and parents are his starting point. It is sometimes the case that adults who have never been on the receiving end of enriching and emotionally responsive "one-to-ones" in childhood can stay developmentally arrested, with the social intelligence of a young child.

Developing social intelligence

Social intelligence involves higher and lower brain pathways working together in a beautifully coordinated way. You, as a parent, will have a powerful influence over whether these vital networking systems will develop well in your child's brain (see page 21).

There are three key areas of social intelligence: the art of relating; the capacity to negotiate, resolve, and be a great team-player; the capacity for compassion and concern. Good parenting can develop all three.

■ You have acquired the art of relating well to other people.

This means that when you are with another person you can accurately read their body language and social cues. This process involves an extraordinary catalogue of subtle responses, reactions, and decisions that are made in milliseconds while scanning the other person's face and body. You have to:
- **recognize their mental state.**
- **gauge your impact on the other person** and adjust your behaviour accordingly. For example, you will sense if the other person is finding you boring, intrusive, or annoying.
- **attend to your own** and the other's emotional reactions at the same time.
- **get the balance right in conversation,** between talking and

Case study

Recovering from hurt

When Sarah was a child, she was constantly shouted at by her depressed mother. Her father was unable to relate well to children, so he had very little quality contact time with Sarah. Most of his exchanges with his daughter were to "bring her into line". Neither parent had the ability to respond sensitively to Sarah's feelings, because their parents had not responded sensitively to their feelings.

From all this, Sarah learnt that relationships are all about power and feelings of hurt and rejection. When Sarah met lovely people in her life, she always drove them away because she tried to control them. She just didn't know another way of being with people. After Sarah was sacked from a good job for bullying her colleagues in the workplace, she realized she needed counselling. With her counsellor, she was able to mourn the fact that she had felt so alone as a child. Sarah was able, over time, to develop warmer, gentler ways of relating. She is now happily married and her children feel very safe and loved by her.

"Being a good team player means giving and taking rather than having your own way."

These boys are only four years old, yet they are already skilled in the art of relating to each other. They can listen to each other well and time their responses. They have a sense of ease in each other's company.

listening, and between showing interest in the other person and sharing information about yourself.

■ **have appropriate body language,** such as not standing too close or too far away.

■ **gauge the subtle timings of dialogue,** of statement and response, avoiding being too quick or slow to respond. This includes not wandering off the topic of conversation.

■ **You are able to negotiate, resolve, and be a good team player.**

This means that when you are with another person you can give and take rather than insist on having things all your own way. You can also:

■ **follow as well as lead.**

■ **listen and run with other people's ideas** as well as express your own.

■ **manage your feelings well** so that you don't spoil your relationships with outbursts of anger, irritation, or anxiety.

■ **say clearly in a non-aggressive,** non-blaming way what you like, don't like, want, and don't want.

■ **in conflict or disagreement,** negotiate and be open to reflecting on a different point of view. You can move to resolution as opposed to blame. All of this makes you really nice to have around!

■ **You have compassion and concern and are able to express it.**

You are deeply moved by human distress and suffering – not just that of people with the same culture, skin colour, beliefs, or religion as you.

■ **You have the courage to feel the pain** of your own suffering and that of others, rather than moving into denial, or being emotionally cut-off in some way.

■ **You are able to soothe and comfort** another person's distress, rather than just giving advice or suggesting that they "get past it" or "pull themselves together".

Q How does parenting have such an impact on a child's social brain?

Powerful relationship experiences in later life can develop the brain systems that are key to social intelligence, but only if your child grows up to be open to them. The problem is that ways of relating established in childhood can so easily become fixed.

If, for example, a child has experienced mainly superficial emotional connections in the family home, she can grow up closed to deeper connections with people in later life. She may simply not know how to develop more meaningful ways of relating to people. If parent–child interactions have frequently been frightening, shaming, or hurtful, the child can grow up deeply mistrustful of people and so push away any overtures offering friendship, kindness, or concern. They just feel too dangerous. What's more, a diet of angry exchanges in childhood can make a child believe that relationships are all about power and control. She may then take this ingrained belief into all her relationships.

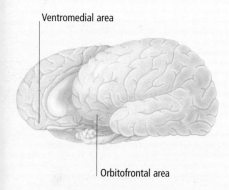

Ventromedial area

Orbitofrontal area

The orbitofrontal and ventromedial areas are regions of the frontal lobes involved in our social intelligence.

The sensitive brain

There are several parts of your child's brain with a key role in social intelligence. With emotionally responsive parenting, new brain pathways will develop in these areas.

First, there is the orbitofrontal part of the higher brain (frontal lobes); see box, left. The setting down of new brain pathways in this area will, over time, enable your child to accurately read, and respond sensitively to, a person's social and emotional cues. Interestingly, this part of the brain is less active in adults and children who are depressed, making it harder for them to be socially sensitive.

New pathways connecting the orbitofrontal area to the lower brain can also enable your child to calm his primitive impulses of fear and anger and regulate his bodily high arousal states. These are called top-down brain pathways.[2] Brain scans of Romanian orphans have shown deficits in this part of the brain – a direct result of their lack of emotionally responsive parenting.

◼ Good parenting can lay down new pathways between the frontal lobes and the cerebellum.

The cerebellum is situated behind the brainstem, at the lowest part of the brain (see page 18). Pathways between this region and the higher brain will enable your child to learn to accurately time his response to what another person is saying, and give it appropriate rhythm and emotional expression. These brain pathways are also likely to enable your child to be more skilled at shifting his attention from one aspect of a conversation to another. Scientists have only recently realized that the cerebellum is involved in social behaviour. Research on children with autism almost always shows malformations in this part of the brain.[4]

◼ The parietal lobes are important, too.

Emotionally responsive parenting may also help to set down important new pathways between a child's parietal lobes and his frontal lobes. The parietal lobes are involved in sensation of movement and navigation of space. These pathways (particularly on the right side of the brain) are responsible for gauging the correct interpersonal space when with another person. This means the ability not to invade someone's private space or appear too distant from them!

■ Why low levels of serotonin can spoil relationships.

The brain chemical serotonin is a major factor in social and emotional intelligence. Optimal levels of serotonin can stabilize mood, reduce aggression, and so play a key role in promoting good relationships. Research studies have shown that monkeys who were highly respected in their group, at the top of their social hierarchy, had optimal levels of

"Low levels of serotonin in the brain are associated with impulsivity."

serotonin.[5] Low levels of serotonin in the brain are associated with impulsive behaviour. If you are unable to inhibit your primitive impulses, frequent angry or anxious outbursts may spoil your relationships. You are also more likely to suffer from bad moods. Children and adults with low levels of serotonin can find it hard to express negative feelings in a calm and diplomatic way.

Serotonin levels are dramatically influenced by human relationships, for better or worse. Research shows that stress in early life can adversely affect the serotonin system in an infant's developing brain, whereas lovely one-to-ones with you can have a positive effect on serotonin levels in your child's ventromedial cortex. By sharing lots of good times with you, your child can be accustomed to optimal levels of serotonin in his brain and this can then become part of who he is, his core personality.

ANIMAL INSIGHTS

Low levels of serotonin in both animals and humans are associated with impulsive behaviour. The person's or animal's emotional responses are not moderated by serotonin, which is a mood-stabilizing chemical. When they get angry it's big, blow-up anger, rather than mild irritation or annoyance. We know that monkeys who have low serotonin are impulsive and aggressive. "Given the opportunity, they will make dangerous leaps from tree to tree that other monkeys won't attempt. They get into frequent fights".[6]

Parenting the social brain

We've seen that positive times with a parent can help develop key pathways in a child's higher brain, and can activate optimal levels of the emotion chemicals that will make him lovely to be around. So how can parents act on that information? Here are a some examples of the vital one-to-ones that help the process.

CONSIDER THIS...

There are some very sensitive babies for whom face-to-face conversations have to be just right. If a sensitive baby finds communication with you worrying in any way whatsoever, he may cut off and withdraw. This may make you pursue him more for a response. As a result, he may then withdraw even more. Both of you can end up feeling hopeless and awful, so make sure that you follow your child's cues (see right).

It all starts with the face-to-face dance in infancy. If you have lots of lovely face-to-face conversations with your infant, pathways will be formed in your child's higher brain which are key to the art of relating.

■ **Research shows that a baby's brain can recognize a face** from the first days of life. In fact, there are certain clusters of brain cells in the frontal lobes just for recognizing and registering faces! "At two or three months an infant will smile when it sees a balloon with eyes painted on it and stop smiling when the balloon face is turned away."[7]

■ **If you use your own social intelligence** when engaged in face-to-face conversation times with your infant, it will be invaluable (see page 92). This means giving your baby time to respond to you, not pushing him to or willing him to respond to you, and being sensitive to times when he needs to look away from you and so not pushing him into re-engaging before he is ready. You should also avoid stressing your baby with too big movements or sounds, or with anxious energy.

Lovely face-to-face times are not only good for a baby's social brain, but they continue to be great for toddlers, under-fives, and even over-fives if they still want them!

■ **Peek-a-boo games** are also great for developing new pathways in your child's social brain.

■ **Joint attentional states in infancy** are times when your infant points to something that he wants you to look at: a view, a bird, a lovely toy. If your infant can do this, it shows he has developed a "theory of mind". This means that he knows that other people are distinct from himself, with different thoughts and feelings to his own. Be really enthusiastic and interested in what he is showing you. One exception is the child with autism (see page 226). Children with autism have problems with joint attentional states and theory of mind. This really hinders their ability to make friendships. There is no clear "other" with whom to form a friendship!

■ **Find accurate words to help your child** link feelings to thought. Avoid long sentences in your response, otherwise the wash of adult words and sophisticated adult sentence construction can make him lose interest. Empathize with his feelings, and use lots of short phrases like, "Too sad for you when you lost the balloon", or "You are so cross now", or "You so wanted the chocolate biscuit."

■ **Build in quality conversation time** every day with your child. Do this through play if he feels easier with this. Ask him how he would like you to play with him and his toys,

"Be really enthusiastic and interested in what your child is showing you."

"You make me feel so happy!"

Having fun together is likely to release optimal levels of dopamine and opioids in your child's brain. As a result, over time, she will come to associate human relationships with feeling good, emotional warmth, and playfulness. These are all key to her being able to develop enriching relationships in life.

As your child grows up, keep listening well to what he is telling you. Some parents are great at talking "at" their child, but they are not good at listening to them. Bend down to his level when he is talking to you, so he can have eye-contact with you as he is telling you this most important thing. Give him time to say it, and respond in age-appropriate language. Use lots of colour in your voice because infants find this delightfully stimulating, whereas flat voices turn them off conversation.

and enjoy following his suggestions for shared play. Alarming statistics show that children, on average, spend only 38 minutes a week in conversation with their parents, in contrast to 21 hours of watching TV. Television will not develop the child's social brain in the ways we have described.[8]

▪ **In your parenting,** show reasoning and calmness at times of conflict and disagreement whenever possible, rather than moving into blame, angry outbursts, or put-downs. This means getting enough emotional support for yourself (see chapter Looking After You, page 244).

▪ **Discipline with a calm firmness,** and by setting clear boundaries and consequences, not with anger (see Behaving Badly, page 110, and All About Discipline, page 158).

When to worry

It's definitely worth getting professional help if your baby is not interested in faces, particularly between two and six months of age, which research shows is the peak time for the face-to-face dance, and a time where masses of networks in the social brain develop.[9] Seek help if:

▪ **during these months, your baby is regularly avoiding eye contact** with you and often staring vacantly into space.

▪ **your baby, after two months, is just too quiet.** He just lies there and does not seem to want your attention.

These may be early signs of a development issue, such as an autistic disorder – for example, autism or Asperger's syndrome. Autism is a problem with the social circuitry of the brain. Although high-functioning individuals with autistic disorders are of normal intelligence, they have abnormalities in social communication and emotional behaviour. As Kanner puts it beautifully, "It strikes at the heart of that which makes us human".[10] Autism prevents a child making deep emotional connections with others. Some people with autism are so socially withdrawn they seem impossible to connect with. Many people think that all forms of autism are a life sentence but recent work in Paris and

Israel is showing that, for some children, it doesn't have to be. The Mifne Centre in Israel has a 75 percent success rate of treating babies with severe forms of autism using three weeks of intensive emotional work with both parents and baby, separately and then together. The baby is given over 300 hours of the most exquisite relational activities with water and bubbles, and one-to-one times with an emotionally responsive adult, using rocking and cooing and the gentlest and most acutely sensitive of human interactions. During this time, it is as if the baby begins to understand, "OK, I get it now – relationships can be wonderful." Many of the Centre's cases are on video and the footage of babies and toddlers "coming back to life" is intensely moving.[11]

It is vital that intervention such as this takes place in the first years of life before the brain undergoes its normal periods of pruning, when underused brain connections are naturally

"The Mifne Centre in Israel has a 75 percent success rate of treating babies with severe autism using three weeks of intensive emotional work."

"Let's make up"

It's a real art for a parent to help children resolve painful clashes when so many primitive lower brain feelings have been activated.

Here a lovely Daddy is helping these two year olds by speaking to them about how painful it has been for both of them to share the toy car.

What a gift for a parent to show children that the most painful conflicts can be resolved.

BRAIN STORY

Human compassion and concern is visible on brain scans. Research shows that when we care about someone in distress, one of the areas of the brain that lights up is the anterior cingulate gyrus (see below) – part of the lower brain's CARE system (see page 190).

In your "brain sculpting" role as a parent, you can influence the establishing of strong communicating pathways between your child's anterior cingulate and his higher brain. This will enhance his ability to both feel and reflect on another person's distress.

Research shows that malfunctions in the anterior cingulate can cause a lack of compassion. Monkeys with a damaged cingulate treat other monkeys as if they were inanimate objects and walk right over them.[12] All too easily, equivalent heartless human acts come to mind.

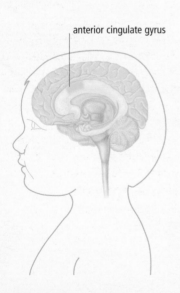

anterior cingulate gyrus

pared away. One period of pruning starts at about two years of age. With some emotionally cut-off children who don't receive intervention, the brain can over-prune or under-prune and a life-long sentence of autism can result.

The legacy of unresponsive parenting

Without emotionally responsive parenting and without enough quality one-to-one time, the parts of a child's social brain that are key to the art of making and developing friendships can remain underdeveloped. This can leave a child with problems forming friendships:

▪ **his timing is off.** He interrupts, comes in too quickly, or comes in too slowly. The conversation feels ruptured, jarring, with a struggle to connect. There is no flow.

▪ **he can't listen well to the other child,** and he can't accurately read the social cues of the other child.

▪ **he fails to accurately read the mental** or emotional state of the other child. He doesn't realize, for example, that the other child is excited, sad, or angry. Feeling emotionally unmet, the other child may walk away and find someone else to play with.

"Without emotionally responsive parenting... a child can have problems forming friendships."

▪ **Nor can he think properly** about the emotional information coming from another child. Researchers working with five year olds found that those whose parents were not responsive to their distress in early life were unable to accurately read distress on the face of another child.[13]

▪ **he has inappropriate body language** and use of space so, for example, other children can feel intruded upon because he comes too close.

■ **As such children grow up,** they may tragically become accustomed to long periods of aloneness, often without understanding why they have so few friends. Or if they do form friendships, these can all too often be short-lived, blighted by a lack of meaningful connections, failed connections, or broken connections.

Sometimes children whose parents have been unresponsive or rather insensitive for too much of the time (because their own parents were emotionally unresponsive or insensitive to them) are lucky enough to develop important relationships with socially sensitive adults other than their parents. These are adults who are prepared to really put the time in. As a result these children do develop brain pathways essential to the art of relating.

Developing compassion and concern

Parenting power that develops a child's capacity for compassion and concern has a profoundly positive impact both on the family stage and in society at large.

Cruelty, be it school bullying or genocide, occurs when people do not have a developed capacity for compassion and concern for vulnerability, distress, or suffering, regardless of the person's colour, creed, or belief system. Many people have concern for those inside their circle of empathy, such as their own family and social, cultural, or religious group, but this does not extend to people outside that circle of contact.

It is vital that governments start to look more closely at the impact of common child-rearing practices on the brain, to insure as much as we can against the continuation of the terrible scale of human suffering around the world. That said, arguably, there is now more hope than ever before. This is because we now know far more about how a child's social brain can be sculpted by emotionally responsive parents, resulting in a developed capacity for compassion and concern. We know far more than ever before, after centuries of appalling cruelty, about how to have a gentler world.

ANIMAL INSIGHTS

Some animals are incapable of compassion and concern towards others who are vulnerable, defenceless, or in distress, because they haven't the brain chemistry and brain anatomical systems required to feel it. Reptiles don't have a developed CARE system in their brains. Many of them produce their young and leave them to fend for themselves.

The female sea turtle, for example, digs a hole in the sand to bury her eggs. A chemical called vasotocin (the reptilian version of our oxytocin) is activated in her brain. Once she has covered her eggs, this "caring" chemical in her brain drops dramatically, so she just wanders off. This means that when her baby turtles are born, their mother is nowhere to be seen. It's just a matter of chance whether the little turtles get to the sea before they are eaten.[14]

Left and right brain

Being deeply moved by the distress of another can only come about if the higher brain is working in a beautifully coordinated way with the CARE system in the lower brain (see page 190). With an under-active CARE system, a person can lose their empathy and move into a place of cold reason.

Ignoring a child in distress can lead him to learning to cut off from others in later life. It is important to be sensitive to a child's emotional pain, and show him compassion for genuine distress at all times.

By consistently helping your child with his difficult feelings, being sensitive to his emotional pain, and showing him compassion for his genuine distress at all times, you will be helping to develop the CARE system in your child's lower mammalian brain. Leaving your child to cry, or cry himself to sleep, is counter to this. Research has shown us how easy it is for a child who has been left to cry to stop crying and in so doing to cut off (see page 62). This can then lead to him cutting off from the pain of others (underactive CARE system in the lower brain).

Brain links

Parenting power can also positively impact on another part of the brain that plays a key role in the capacity for compassion and concern. The left and right sides of our higher brain (frontal lobes) process what is happening to us moment by moment in very different, but equally vital, ways. The left brain houses our verbal centres, for understanding and forming speech. It is key to finding words for feelings. It also registers milder, more positive feelings than the right brain. Without the right brain's input, the left brain is not good at registering emotional pain (our own or other people's).

The right brain is the non-verbal side of the brain. It registers painful feelings very well, and picks up emotional atmospheres very quickly. It has far stronger links with the body than the left side of the brain, so it can pick up very accurately how your body is registering an emotional event.

It also has stronger links than the left brain to the alarm system in your lower brain (the amygdala). Just as the left brain is great at detail, the right brain is great at overview, seeing the whole picture.

A band of nerve tissue called the corpus callosum helps these two sides of the brain (and these two different ways of experiencing what is happening to you) to link up. People with poor social intelligence often have a corpus callosum that functions poorly in emotional processing, so the two sides of the brain don't communicate well with each other.[15]

▪ In infants, there is poor communication between the two sides of the brain.

This is because the corpus callosum is still in a stage of development. So at this age, it's not transferring information well between your child's left and right frontal lobes. This means that your infant will be functioning in a "split-brain" way. As a result, there will be times when he uses lots of words with lots of positive feelings (strong left brain activity). Then suddenly, the next minute, he's "lost it" and he is writhing around on the floor in an intense, wordless state (strong right brain activity), just like a little baby again. As he gets older, with emotionally responsive parenting, your

"As he gets older, with responsive parenting, your child should be more able to find words for strong feelings."

child should be more able to find words (left brain activation) for strong feelings (right brain activation), instead of moving into primitive discharge of those feelings (as in a tantrum). This is due to the development of pathways in the corpus callosum, with its ability to transfer information between these two sides of the brain.

BRAIN STORY

The corpus callosum is an amazing network of fibres enabling communication between the right and left side of the higher brain. The corpus callosum plays a vital role in social intelligence, as it passes information about what we are experiencing in milliseconds from one side of our higher brain to the other. So it helps someone to think and feel clearly about all the things that happen to them.

corpus callosum

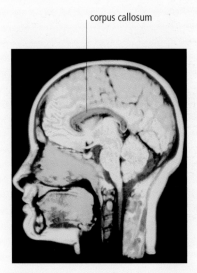

An MRI scan through the head clearly shows the corpus callosum (blue). This band of tissue is composed of nerve fibres (some 300 million in a fully developed adult brain) and functions as an information highway between the two halves of the brain.

"Each time you help your child think about what he is feeling, you are probably helping the development of his corpus callosum."

If you consistently respond with empathy to your child's distress states, she won't need to cut off from her emotional pain, or that of others, and live in a "left brain-dominated" way. Some parents find this easier than others, usually as a result of their own experience as a child.

Once again, you can help influence the ability of your child's right and left brain to communicate well with each other. How? Each time you help your child to think and feel about what he is experiencing, and each time you find the right words for his intense feelings, you are probably helping the development of more sophisticated communication networks in your child's corpus callosum.

■ A poorly functioning corpus callosum may be the cause of a lack of compassion and concern.

Some scientists believe that a key factor in why a person lacks compassion and concern for another is that their corpus callosum is not passing emotional information effectively between the two sides of the brain.[16] Research shows that people who are emotionally cut off from the pain of others are often processing their experiences far more in the left side of their brain than the right. This is called "left hemispheric domination". As one neuroscientist put it, "The left brain has started to act as a subsystem for the mind as a whole".[17] When this happens, a person is far less socially sensitive and emotionally aware. "Left brain-domination" means a person can use words to rationalize away painful feelings, their own and other people's, and justify why it is OK to leave someone in pain and not help them.

As one man, seeing a child howling for his Mummy, said, "I could see that other people were feeling something about that crying child, but I didn't feel anything personally". They may also justify to themselves why it is OK to hurt another human being (world history is rife with examples of this).

As the left brain has far fewer links than the right to the powerful emotion systems in the lower brain and to the body, the "left brain-dominated" person will not be registering the suffering of others very well on a bodily level either.

Many psychologists believe that this lack of compassion can result from a person not receiving enough compassion for their painful feelings in childhood.

Q How can I make sure that my child doesn't grow up socially insensitive to the emotional pain of others?

■ Make sure you discipline your child through calm, firm boundaries and in ways that uphold her dignity. Research shows that with discipline through shaming or anger, a child can all too easily cut off from feelings of hurt and in so doing can lose much of her humanity.[18] (See All About Discipline, page 158)

■ Playground studies have shown that some children from backgrounds where they have not experienced sympathy for their distress have a lack of concern for crying children. Some will even try to "shut them up" by humiliating or attacking them.[19] Children from backgrounds of kindness and concern can show empathy at an early age.

Long-term effects

There are those who argue that bullying is not in the same league as child abuse. But when you look at the long-term effects of severe psychological stress, be it the misuse of power by one child against another or an adult bullying a child in the name of discipline, it is clear they are much the same.

CONSIDER THIS...

In the UK, over 50 percent of all schoolchildren say they have been bullied at some time. Each year, about 20 children in the UK who are being bullied kill themselves. Clearly, as a society, we are both aware and concerned, but arguably when we look at the brain scans of how being bullied can change a child's brain, we are not worried enough.

The problem is that in the early years of life, the human brain moulds itself to adapt to its environment. So, amazingly and tragically, the brain of the bullied child can start to actually alter itself to be more suited to living in a bullying world. This can result in hypervigilance (always being on guard), reptilian brain fight-or-flight defence mechanisms, and overactive RAGE or FEAR systems in the mammalian part of the brain (limbic system).

In some children, it results in emotional coldness and underactive social emotion systems in the lower brain. As with other forms of distress, such as prolonged crying in childhood (see pages 34–63), frequent childhood experiences

"The brain of the bullied child can start to actually alter itself to be more suited to living in a bullying world."

of high stress levels, and stressful relationships, where the child is not comforted to regain a state of calm, can bring about a permanent over-reactivity in key stress response systems in the brain. Moreover, living with intense fear from being bullied at home and/or at school over a prolonged period can start to show itself in actual alterations to key structures in the brain, such as the amygdala (see page 27). After bullying, this part of the brain can become oversensitive and so over-react to minor stressors as if they are big threats. It's called "fear kindling", which means that fear can become an ingrained part of the child's personality. Other studies with bullied children have shown lack of activation in the amygdala, resulting in lack of response to another's fear.[20]

■ If your child is being bullied, it can seriously affect his social confidence and result in long-term changes in the brain.

We have known for a long time that there are likely to be psychological scars from being bullied, but there has usually been hope for recovery – the belief that, with help and support, the bullied child can quickly get over the experience. But now, with the advancement of brain scans, we have a far bleaker picture. The scans show many actual structural and enduring biochemical changes in the brain of the child who has suffered the intense relational stress of psychological abuse. In short, there can be a real cost to the brain itself.

"Fear can become an ingrained part of the child's personality."

"I hate what they do"

When bullying is subtle, it may pass unnoticed. Whispering and name-calling, ostracising and isolating can cause just as much distress and long-term damage to a child's brain as physical assaults. So parents and teachers need to be watchful for signs (see page 239). Schooldays are long, and no child should have to spend her waking hours in a state of fear.

The brain legacy of bullying

For many children who have been bullied, you can see both fight and flight responses in their day-to-day behaviour. A child may develop a dislike of school, or start bedwetting or having other physical symptoms. Scientists have also found a number of worrying changes in the brains of bullied children.

■ **Cell death and/or a reduced activation in the anterior cingulate gyrus.** This area helps moderate the fear response in the brain. It is key to our capacity for empathy.[21]

■ **Long-term alterations in brain circuits and systems** that are to do with managing stress well. A child can develop an over-reactive stress response system in the brain, resulting in being impulsive, aggressive, and/or anxious frequently.

■ **Long-term changes to the adrenaline systems** in the brain. Too much noradrenaline and adrenaline washing over the brain can make you feel anxious and unable to think clearly.

■ **Decrease in blood flow and impairment** in the "cerebellar vermis" in the brain stem. This area controls some of the production and release of noradrenaline and dopamine. Abnormalities here have been associated with ADHD (see page 106), depression, and impaired attention. This area also helps regulate electrical activity in the brain, so when it's not functioning well, more aggression and irritability can result.

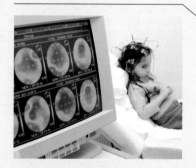

The effects of bullying can be seen in EEG irregularities in the frontal and temporal brain regions. These regions are vital for the management of stress and the regulation of intense feelings.

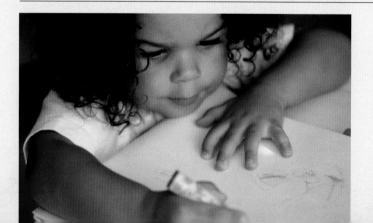

Prolonged stress can cause a reduction in the size of the hippocampus and the amygdala. The hippocampus is very important in memory function, and maltreated people score lower on verbal memory tests. A reduction in the left amygdala is associated with depression, irritability, or hostility.

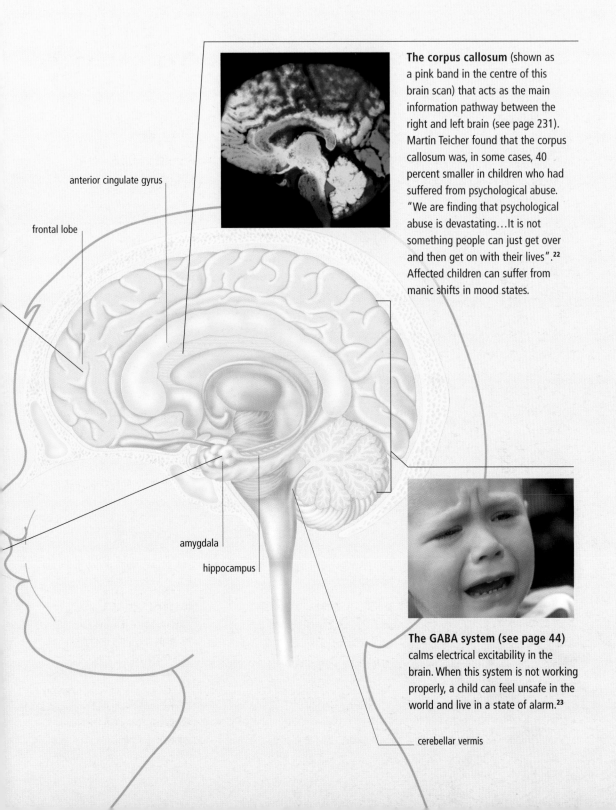

The corpus callosum (shown as a pink band in the centre of this brain scan) that acts as the main information pathway between the right and left brain (see page 231). Martin Teicher found that the corpus callosum was, in some cases, 40 percent smaller in children who had suffered from psychological abuse. "We are finding that psychological abuse is devastating…It is not something people can just get over and then get on with their lives".[22] Affected children can suffer from manic shifts in mood states.

anterior cingulate gyrus

frontal lobe

amygdala

hippocampus

The GABA system (see page 44) calms electrical excitability in the brain. When this system is not working properly, a child can feel unsafe in the world and live in a state of alarm.[23]

cerebellar vermis

Bully-proof your child

Both in school and at home, there are measures that can help protect children from being bullied or becoming bullies. As parents, you can boost your child's self-defences by helping him to develop emotional strength, a lively personality that responds warmly to others, and friendship skills that will last him for life.

Some children who have been bullied suffer from post-traumatic stress disorder. The core arousal system in the brain stem is grossly affected. Children can have problems with sleeping, eating, and breathing, and suffer from headaches and other symptoms. Children like this do not feel safe enough to learn, and school work is often badly affected. Therapy and counselling can help enormously.

What schools can do

When it comes to looking for a suitable school, although you cannot eliminate all risks of bullying there are certain things that can guide your choice. If the head teacher is a very warm person, this is a good indicator from the start. There should also be a watertight and highly effective bullying policy. Many people in the UK like to think we are pretty hot on child protection issues. I would argue that where bullying in schools is concerned we are failing very badly – especially failing the half of all school children who say they have been bullied, many of whom have been bullied at school.

■ **Some schools say that they just cannot properly police the playground or that they don't have the staff to ensure every child's safety.**

If all schools knew the true effects of being bullied on the brain of a child, I think there might be a shift in concern both at school and at government level. I would put CCTV cameras in every school playground (where most bullying occurs). Some would argue this is an infringement of children's rights, yet surely we have a duty to protect every child from the brain damage and often life-long psychological scars that can result from bullying, with all its unbearable feelings of impotence, aloneness, and often terror. That said, some schools appreciate the urgency of putting into place effective bullying policies with an absolute zero tolerance, ensuring that the playground is watched at all times.

If every school is to insure against damaging the brains they are supposed to be developing, bullying at school has to stop, whatever the costs to the government in terms of extra staffing, particularly in the playground. We may not be able to make every child's home a safe, protected place, but we need to do this with our schools.

Be especially wary of relatives, teachers, or friends who fail children by minimizing bullying, saying something equivalent to "they're only teasing" or "boys will be boys".

What you can do at home

Some forms of discipline, such as shouting, shaming, and smacking (see page 160), are bullying by other names. Keep an eye on your own methods of dealing with difficult behaviour, and confront your partner and relatives if you think their treatment of your child comes close to bullying.

> "Be wary of relatives, teachers, or friends who fail children by minimizing bullying, saying 'boys will be boys'."

■ Hold back criticism and give lots of praise.

If parents keep criticizing their child and giving no praise, he will become acclimatized to living in a bullying world. If, in other words, they keep "hitting" their child with words, and that child is being bullied at school, he can all too easily move into thinking, "I deserve this. I'm rubbish", or, "This is normal; the world is so harsh". A child who has known a warm, kind world at home can move far more effectively into asking for help from his parents. This child is far more likely to have an attitude of, "This is not OK; I am a valued and special person. I deserve to be treated well". Schools and homes can do much to help a child realize that he has a right to feel safe in his world and empower him to assert his rights.

CONSIDER THIS...

If you suspect your child is being bullied, watch out for an obsession with war, fighting, and bombing in his play, to the exclusion of all else. Many boys enjoy these activities, but it is the intensity of the fighting and its repetition throughout the day that can be a concern. When a child has a consuming obsession with fighting and war play, it can indicate an attempt at defence against unmanageable feelings of fear and living in a world that has failed him in terms of "making the bullying stop".

● Your child may move into being a bully himself. This is a kind of last-ditch defence. It's a defence of "If you can't beat them, join them".

● Some children who are being bullied develop a school phobia, obsessions, or start bedwetting or having other physical symptoms (part of the overactive FEAR system in the brain).

Q I've found out that my child is being bullied regularly.
What can I do?

If your child has suffered bullying that is persistent rather than being stopped promptly,
consider getting him counselling or therapy. (For organizations that provide it, see Useful
addresses, page 279.) Children are good at acting as if they are just fine, while hiding
feelings of fear and impotence. Many adults still reel from the hurt of being bullied years
ago. Research shows that the effects of bullying, such as changes in the corpus callosum
(the nerve fibres connecting the two halves of the brain), can be partly repaired by such
activities as learning the piano, which helps to integrate right and left brain processing.[24]

▪ Take sibling fighting very seriously.

The contribution of sibling fighting to the bullying epidemic in schools is vastly under-rated (see box, right).[25] When a young child is hurt by his sibling, he hasn't yet developed the frontal lobe capacities to reflect on his emotional experiences. He may simply cut off from his pain but move into primitive fight-or-flight impulses. This can result in him hurting another child, and so a bully is made.

▪ Help your child to develop a confident personality that allows him to cope with the world.

The genes for personality are described as "experience-dependent", which means that, although a child may be genetically predisposed to certain traits, perhaps, to be timid or overanxious or quick to anger, they do not have to be his destiny. Parenting has a great deal to do with helping

> "A person who most people would agree is delightful to be around has optimal arousal ... being full of life and warmth."

to turn such a child into one who is confident about himself and his dealings with the world. Often, the way a person is, and his response to other people, is spoiled by what neuropsychoanalyst Allan Schore calls "being over-aroused or under-aroused inappropriate to the situation". Being over-aroused means getting anxious or angry over things that other people handle well, or having a constantly manic energy that is exhausting to be around. Being under-aroused means the kind of emotional flatness that makes someone seem rather dull. A person who most people would agree is delightful to be around has optimal arousal.[26] This type of person is usually full of life and warmth, whilst also having a real inner calm and ease.

Case study

How bullying begins

Joe is being bullied by his brother Sam, aged seven. Sam is suffering from painful sibling rivalry and isn't being helped with it by his parents. Mum tells them to stop fighting, but in a half-hearted way. When she's not looking, Sam hurts Joe, again and again. Joe sometimes runs to Mum and she gives him a cuddle and tells Sam to stop picking on his little brother. But there is rarely ever a clear and firm consequence for Sam. Sam sometimes gets smacked by his Dad for being mean to Joe, but this endorses his own hitting response.

Every time Joe gets hit, he learns more about hitting, and his brain starts to alter to be more suited to living in a bullying world. He stops asking for help with it from his Mum. One day Joe thumps George, a little boy who is crying in the playground. Instead of feeling powerless like he does with his brother, Joe suddenly feels very strong. George's parents and the school are concerned and tell Joe off, but they just don't have the staff to protect the children properly in the playground. When George goes home, he starts to pick on his toddler brother, and so it goes on – the epidemic spreading from home to school and school to home and back again.

Scientists now know a lot about what happens in the brain of a person who develops an emotionally flat personality. Often, the left frontal lobe (the more rational part of the brain) blocks communication with the frontal lobe on the right-hand side. The right brain registers emotional pain more than the left and has stronger links with the deeply feeling lower brain and the body. People with emotional flatness can also cut themselves off from bodily feeling, often having shallow breathing, lowered levels of adrenaline, and muscular armouring – a holding in and tensing of muscles that dims communication between the brain and the body.[27]

Parenting has a great deal to do with the development of this type of personality. A key factor is not meeting the child in joy. The exuberant child is told to calm down. If he is also not met in emotional pain, he will see strong emotions as too dangerous to feel. The child can cut off from passion itself.

◼ Teach your child the art of making friends.

If you watch children who have formed a special friendship, it is clear that they have developed some key pathways in their social brains. They may not have a wide vocabulary, but they can still possess a sophisticated level of social intelligence. Children who make friends readily are likely to have learned

All children benefit from gentle and sensitive human interactions. Self-esteem and self-confidence begin with feelings of being adored in infancy.

"Children who make friends readily are likely to have learned from adults who are responsive to their emotional needs."

from the example of adults who are responsive to their emotional needs. Parents can contribute to these friendship skills. This can begin by engaging with babies in face-to-face play (see page 92) and in statement and response. As the children grow older, offering them lots of quality talking time further helps them to master the art of friendship.

Key points

- **Meaningful relationships** with other people are fundamental to mental health and long-term happiness.

- **Good parenting** can develop your child's social intelligence, including the ability to relate to others, be a team player, and have the capacity for compassion.

- **Engage with** your child throughout life, starting during early babyhood, with face-to-face conversations and shared play time.

- **Bullying can** have long-term damaging effects on the brain and must be taken very seriously by parents, teachers, and carers.

- **Help your child** to avoid bullying (as bully or victim) by building his confidence and social skills.

looking
after you

Parenting is one of the most stressful jobs
there is. Alongside the wondrous, delightful,
and profoundly fulfilling times, you will also
experience broken sleep and extreme tests of
your patience and temper. Your job is to help
your child with a whole range of feelings,
from tantrums and rage to excitement and joy.
In order to be a calm, loving, and empathic
parent you need to take good care of yourself.
This means recognizing when you're feeling low
and seeking the support and the time you need
to restore mental and physical balance.

Stress-free pregnancy

It's important to look after yourself emotionally as well as physically when you are pregnant. Your emotional state can affect the development of your unborn child's brain. You'll need special support if you are pregnant and feeling stressed, depressed, or anxious.

From seven weeks onwards, pleasure-inducing opioids can be found in the unborn baby's bloodstream. What a great start in life! However, we also know that if the mother is repeatedly very stressed in the last three months of pregnancy, excessively high levels of stress chemicals (cortisol and glutamate) can be transmitted through the placenta into the brain of the unborn baby.

Some research shows that unborn babies who are subjected to overly high levels of stress chemicals can go on to have a reduced capacity to deal with stress as children and as adults. High levels of stress during pregnancy is one of the risk factors for depression and vulnerability to drug-seeking

"A baby who has been stressed before birth can be very unsettled after birth."

in later life.[1] A baby who has been stressed before birth can be a very unsettled baby after birth, and parents may have to work extra hard to regulate their child's painful emotional and physical states. If a stressed baby receives plenty of calming and soothing parenting – of the type described in this book – his ability to handle stress can improve.

In some cases, too much stress during pregnancy has also been shown to affect the genetic unfolding of key emotion chemicals and hormones in the unborn baby. This means that certain key genes don't do what they are supposed to do; they

CONSIDER THIS...

An unborn baby is particularly vulnerable to high levels of maternal stress hormones during the last three months of pregnancy when there is a major growth spurt in its brain. Get as much relaxation and emotional support as you can during this time. Pregnancy massage has been shown to decrease anxiety and stress hormone levels.[2]

don't move to the right place in the brain. In the male foetus, for example, overly high levels of stress in the mother can change the impulses of the hormones testosterone and oestrogen. Research with other mammals shows that male infants may be born with a feminized brain, which can have implications for future sexuality.[3]

Alcohol, drugs, and smoking

If you are highly anxious or stressed out during pregnancy, take a break. A head or foot massage is a good idea. Don't be tempted to resort to drink or drugs (other than any that are prescribed by your doctor). Taking drugs such as cocaine, ecstasy, or speed, or drinking alcohol can change the development of an unborn child's brain. Alcohol also raises the level of cortisol in an unborn child. Research shows that children of alcoholic mothers can have an over-reactive stress response system (see HPA axis, page 40) when they are born.

"If you are highly anxious or stressed out in pregnancy, try a head or foot massage."

"I would like a break"

Feeling tired during pregnancy can have an impact on your existing children. Everyday activities such as work, shopping, and visiting friends can tire you more than you expect and leave you short-tempered. Try to minimize non-essential tasks, and consider shopping via the internet and sharing childcare with family and friends.

Brain scans of children with mothers who drank a lot of alcohol in pregnancy often show a smaller cerebrum (higher brain), with fewer folds. There can also be damage to the cerebellum (which controls coordination and movement), and to the brain stem (responsible for basic processes such as breathing and body temperature). The brain of a child with FAS (fetal alcohol syndrome, caused by the mother's excessive drinking) does not fully develop, resulting in mental and

"Connect with your unborn child"

Celebrating pregnancy can have a profound effect not only on you and your unborn child, but also on the rest of your family. Your sense of well-being will be transmitted to the people around you. And when your baby is born, he is more likely to be calm and easier to settle.

emotional difficulties. Alcohol consumed during the first three months is more dangerous to the unborn child than alcohol consumed later in pregnancy. Most studies agree that if a pregnant mother does not consume more than one alcoholic drink a day, her child will not be affected,[4] but the only way to be totally sure is not to drink alcohol at all during your pregnancy.

■ **If you smoke during pregnancy, you are subjecting your developing baby to harmful nicotine, tar, and carbon monoxide.**

You are also reducing your baby's oxygen supply. Research shows that smoking in pregnancy can also lead to altered structures in some parts of the baby's brain and altered brain functioning, putting the baby at risk of developing behaviour problems and learning difficulties. Pregnant women who smoked more than ten cigarettes a day were significantly more likely to have a child who developed a conduct disorder. Children with mothers who smoked in pregnancy also had a higher risk of alcohol or substance abuse, and of depression, in later life. So make every effort to stop.[5]

Falling in love with your baby...or not

If all goes well during and after delivery, your brain will naturally release high levels of oxytocin (see page 37). This can make you feel blissed out, deeply at one with your baby (and deeply in love), and deliciously lacking in stress. In post-natal depression, the release of early bonding chemicals is blocked but with professional help you can get them flowing again. If not treated, post-natal depression can adversely affect a child's stress hormone levels, sleep, eating, and immune system. Post-natal depression affects about one in every ten mothers, and anti-depressants and/or counselling usually work very well. These get your positive arousal and mood-stabilizing chemicals working properly again and lower stress hormone levels.[6]

Research shows that breastfeeding is great for a mother's mood because it calms the stress response system in her brain. Because the mother feels calm and relaxed, this helps her to calm and soothe her baby. Breastfeeding also gives the baby essential polyunsaturated fatty acids, which can enhance the production of key brain chemicals in the higher brain, namely dopamine and serotonin. However, some studies have shown that both breastfeeding and bottle-feeding, when holding the infant next to your calm body, lower stress hormones, with no significant differences between the two methods.[7]

Now you have children

Along with the joy of parenting comes lots of hard work. Your job is to care not just for your child's physical needs, but also for his emotional and psychological ones. Being constantly on duty can take its toll on you. Responding to the signs of stress in yourself is an essential parenting skill.

After several hours of caring for young children, you may long for peace. If you have a few spare minutes, make an effort to do something that feels self-indulgent. Re-fuelling like this can enable you to stay calm and able to empathize with your children.

A day in the life of a parent

Imagine a typical day of looking after your three-year-old child. He has just got a new toy – a big red bus – and you enthusiastically amplify his delight in it. Then he jumps on top of you and wants 10 minutes of rough and tumble play. You know that this kind of play is great for his brain, so how can you refuse? Next, you give him a biscuit and he is distressed when he breaks it. He bursts into tears because he wants you to mend it. When you explain that you can't, he throws a cup of milk on the floor. Now you need to find a good way to tell him that this isn't acceptable behaviour.

Later, you help your child to come to terms with the fact that he can't bring his pet frog into the living room. You also stop a kicking fight with his brother. You are starting to feel weary, but your child wants you to watch him press the "toot toot" button on his yellow lorry. He looks at you expectantly waiting for you to say "wow", and when you do, it brings a big grin to his face. That smile is lovely for you too, but when he asks you to watch him for the eighteenth time, it's starting to feel a bit wearing. Despite this, you know that attention and praise is so good for establishing positive chemical arousal systems in your child's brain, so you do it again and again. At bedtime, you have to help your child manage his rage about going to bed. And, in addition to all of this, you may also have other children who need you in similar ways.

After several hours spent with young children, you long for peace. So what's happening to you? Well, you can only regulate your child's brain for so long without needing some emotional regulation yourself. In neuroscientific terms, you are biochemically dysregulated. Your bodily arousal system (see page 44) will also be out of balance, adding to your feelings of stress.

Are you dysregulated?

Feeling frazzled, angry, and potentially explosive when your child does something naughty is a sign that you are biochemically dysregulated. Rather than using your higher brain to reflect on the best response, your RAGE system in your lower brain keeps getting triggered. Your higher brain is flooded with stress chemicals and, as a result, you lose the skills of empathy and clear thinking. You feel like screaming!

"Feeling frazzled, angry, and explosive is a sign that you are biochemically dysregulated."

"I know I have to stay calm"

Your role of emotional regulator is to help your child to cope with his unmanageable emotional intensity in order to make it tolerable for him. In so doing, you will be helping him to establish pathways and systems in his brain that will enable him, eventually, to do this on his own. When children have not received effective emotional regulation, later life can be very hard (see page 228).

Food to enhance your mood

Some of the key chemicals that influence your emotions are manufactured from the food you eat. By eating specific foods, and avoiding others, you can help to control or enhance the way you feel, both physically and emotionally. Eating regularly also helps to control your mood and sense of well-being.

Eating a varied, balanced, nutritious diet is important for everyone, especially busy parents. Certain foods are essential for the production of key brain chemicals, and without them, you may feel miserable and tired.

If you know which brain chemicals are manufactured from which foods, it can really add to your potency as a parent. For example, when you find yourself over-reacting to your child's behaviour, ask yourself, "Is my child annoying me because of a stressful situation, or am I short of some key vitamins?"

Emotion chemicals work in symphony, but it's a very sensitive symphony. If one chemical is a bit low, it can affect the others, making you feel miserable. You can make positive changes to the chemical balance in your brain by eating specific foods.

Eating to keep your mood stable

Serotonin is responsible for improving mood, emotional stability, and sleep quality. When people have a low serotonin level, they can feel depressed, aggressive, and anxious.

Tryptophan is the building block from which serotonin is made, and it comes from food. You can make sure you get enough tryptophan by eating plenty of bananas, bread, pasta, and oily fish, such as salmon and mackerel. You can also take fish oil supplements.

For the brain to manufacture serotonin effectively you also need to eat foods that contain vitamins B_6 and B_{12}, and folic acid. Good sources include bananas, avocadoes, fish, vegetables, baked potatoes, chicken, and beef. You can also take vitamin B supplements (the B vitamins all work as a group, so take a supplement that includes B_1, B_2, B_6, and B_{12}). Vitamin B_6 is especially important in serotonin production –

just one milligram too little, per day, can badly affect your emotional state. Research shows that when some depressed people take enough of vitamins B_6 and B_{12}, their depression goes. Sleep quality improves, too. As you get older, you need more of vitamins B_6 and B_{12} because you absorb these vitamins less well with age. B vitamins also contribute to the manufacture and release of GABA, which is a key anti-anxiety chemical in the brain (see page 44).[8]

Food to keep you motivated as a parent

An optimum level of dopamine, in combination with other brain chemicals, is key to ensuring that you have the necessary psychological drive to want to fully engage in life and with your children. When dopamine is strongly activated

"If one chemical is low, it can affect the others, making you feel miserable."

in your brain, it can counteract the negative impact of the minor stressors that are an inevitable part of bringing up children. When dopamine is not optimally activated in your brain, you can feel lethargic, irritable, and depressed, with a lack of motivation to organize interesting things for your children to do that you would also enjoy.

To make dopamine, the brain needs tyrosine, which is present in protein foods such as fish, meat, nuts, and cheese. You also need essential minerals and vitamins. Whilst food can't actually strengthen the activation of dopamine in the brain, it is vital to sustain optimal levels.[9]

Food to help you stay stable under stress

Oily fish contains an omega-3 fatty acid called docosahexaenoic acid (DHA). DHA is a very powerful player in brain chemistry. It forms about half of all the fat in brain cell membranes. It is needed to build and preserve pliable

CONSIDER THIS...

If you feel exhausted, consider whether it is just the broken sleep, or are there other causes? Have you eaten properly? If you don't have a steady supply of glucose to the brain, and enough of the protein needed to form positive arousal chemicals in your brain, you will feel tired.

Have you been indoors all day? A change of environment; being with stimulating, energized people; taking a walk; or doing something interesting to activate your brain's SEEKING system (going to a lively coffee bar or a film) can all raise your dopamine levels.

Don't go to bed stressed. If you do, the high levels of cortisol may wake you up in the early hours. Have a relaxing bath or cuddle with your partner.

"Non-breakfast-eaters are twice as likely to feel depressed and four times as likely to be anxious."

brain cell structures so the brain can work effectively, and so that chemical messages can be sent throughout the brain with ease. DHA has been shown to improve mood by boosting serotonin levels. Once again, DHA is obtained only from your diet. Research on fish oil consumption in different countries has shown that as fish oil consumption goes up, depression rates go down.[10] In fact, the lower your DHA level, the more severe your depression may be. Many people's diets are badly lacking in DHA. So when you eat oily fish or take DHA supplements, the brain is likely to grab most or all of it.

Sardines, salmon, tuna, mackerel, and cold-pressed linseed oil or flaxseed oil are rich in DHA. You can take DHA in the form of a fish oil supplement, but read the label before

"I need breakfast"

A protein-rich breakfast will boost your tyrosine levels, and improve your concentration and problem-solving skills. People who eat a full breakfast are far more effective and creative throughout the day.[11]

The type of carbohydrate that you eat is also important. Wholemeal bread is preferable to white bread, which supplies energy for only about an hour. After this you'll experience a slump in your mood and energy levels. Complex carbohydrates such as oats make your blood glucose levels rise slowly for a few hours, which provides you with sustained energy and can stabilize your mood.

you buy anything because some supplements contain only eicosapentaenoic acid (EHA). You need more DHA as you get older. Also, DHA levels are depleted by alcohol and smoking.

Feeling good throughout the day

The effect of not eating properly or of making poor food choices can have a dramatic effect on your day. If you skip meals, or rely on caffeine or sugary snacks to keep you going, you will feel anxious, irritable, and lacking in energy around your children. The following rules make good sense.

■ **Eat a good breakfast and lunch.** Research shows that non-breakfast-eaters are twice as likely to feel depressed and four times as likely to be anxious as people who eat at the start of the day.[12] Not eating breakfast means that your blood glucose level remains low. Your brain can't function well in this state, and your adrenal glands respond by releasing high levels of adrenaline and cortisol, which can make you feel anxious and on edge.

■ **Avoid sugary snacks and drinks.** Eating biscuits or chocolate, because you haven't had time to feed yourself properly, is the worst thing you can do. After the initial release of pleasure chemicals in your brain, it's downhill all the way. On an empty stomach, sugary food sends your blood sugar levels really high. Your body then releases insulin to drop them down again, but this often means sugar levels fall to a level far lower than before you ate the food. This can make you feel tired and irritable with the children, with all those negative feelings commonly triggered by hypoglycemia.

■ **Snack on fruit or protein.** To give you or your children an energy boost, eat some fruit instead. Fruit has a different sugar in it, called fructose. This does not trigger the insulin release. Carry a banana in your handbag as this snack will boost your levels of tryptophan, the substance needed to make the mood-stabilizing chemical serotonin, and offer you a slow release of sugar into the blood, keeping you going for a while. Nuts can be a good snack too, activating tyrosine,

A protein-rich lunch of meat or fish helps your body to make tyrosine, which will sustain optimal levels of dopamine in your brain. This can make you alert and focused for the rest of the day. If you have a carbohydrate-rich lunch, you may feel sleepy during the afternoon.

which is key to the manufacture of the positive arousal brain chemical dopamine.

■ **Eat carbohydrate foods in the evening.** This activates tryptophan in the brain, a key component in serotonin. Optimal levels of serotonin help regulate sleep. If you want yourself and your children to feel sleepy, avoid high-protein bedtime snacks. They can keep you awake.

■ **Drink six glasses of water a day.** Water is vital to flush out waste products. If you don't drink enough, the waste products stay in your system, making you feel tired, sluggish, and lethargic. Don't use thirst as a barometer of when you need water; by this time, you are already dehydrated.

■ **Consider supplements.** It can be difficult to ensure that your diet has enough of the minerals and vitamins essential to the manufacture of mood-stabilizing and positive arousal brain chemicals – so vital for managing the stress of parenting. As one researcher states, "It would take 46 cups of spinach a day to reach your optimum level of vitamin E, or

"If you want yourself and your children to sleep, avoid high-protein bedtime snacks."

8 cups of almonds". In various parts of the world, including the UK, the daily diet is often lacking in the vital trace element selenium. Low selenium levels are strongly linked to anxiety, low energy, irritability, depression, and fatigue.[13]

Co-enzyme Q_{10} helps convert food into energy. We have lower levels as we get older, so supplements, used carefully, are sometimes necessary. Stress also depletes vital minerals and vitamins.

■ **Drink camomile tea.** Camomile is a mild sedative. It acts on the benzodiazepine receptors in the brain, producing a calming anti-anxiety effect. It is ideal for drinking before bedtime and throughout the day, instead of caffeine drinks such as coffee.

Q What else will help to improve my mood?

Go for a walk in the sunshine. Grey skies are linked to low levels of serotonin in the brain, which can make people feel depressed. Also, reduced exposure to light may result in a deficiency of dopamine; hence you can be less alert, lack get-up-and-go, and suffer from poor concentration. Vitamin D from sunshine is absorbed through the skin, so it is useful to walk outside each day. Low Vitamin D contributes to feelings of depression, and levels can plummet in the winter.

Q Is coffee a bad idea? I need at least four cups a day.

Your child has woken at 6.30 am and you feel tired, so you reach for the coffee to try to feel at least half-human. Caffeine, found in coffee, tea, fizzy drinks, and some painkillers, is the one of the most popular mood-altering drugs. Caffeine can raise your mood and makes you feel more alert, motivated, and energized, because it stimulates noradrenaline, adrenaline, and dopamine in the brain and raises glucose levels. It blocks adenosine, a brain chemical that makes you feel sleepy and helps you to sleep.

Caffeine tolerance varies from person to person and in terms of the time of day. Drink it with food and, in moderation, it can give you a lift. Drink it on an empty stomach and there can be real problems. After the initial high, there will be a drop in glucose levels, leaving you feeling tired, depressed, or easily irritated. Also, the more caffeine you drink, the more you require just to feel normal. It's called "down-regulating".

Why re-fuelling is necessary

Emotional re-fuelling is necessary to bring your brain and body's stress chemicals back to base rate. If you don't emotionally re-fuel, and instead just keep going without a child-free break, you can end up feeling chronically stressed and bad-tempered. This will have a knock-on effect for your children, who will feel stressed by your stress, which can lead to bad behaviour.

Take regular breaks. If you don't take time out for yourself, you may end up feeling irritable, moody, anxious, and prone to anger most of the time. Stress can also damage the quality of your sleep, making you feel tired during the day.

Re-fuelling means quality child-free time doing something relaxing and enjoyable just for you, rather than quick, short-term fixes with side effects, such as alcohol or cigarettes. Any parent, however skilled, who moves into a stoic "soldier-on" mode, without emotional re-fuelling, will end up with a negative brain chemistry and body hyperarousal. Key signs that you need re-fuelling include finding yourself increasingly irritated and short-tempered with the children, with less and less inclination to play with them, spontaneously cuddle them, and praise them. Rather than seeing them as a delight, you start to experience them as a set of demands. With practice you can become skilled at recognizing the signs of biochemical dysregulation in your brain; namely, the rise of stress chemicals and the lowering of positive and mood-stabilizing chemicals such as dopamine and serotonin.

What is emotional re-fuelling?

There are two main types of emotional re-fuelling: auto-regulation and interactive regulation. Auto-regulation means you do something by yourself to change your brain chemistry, such as reading a book, going out for a walk, or relaxing in a lovely warm bath. Interactive regulation means spending quality time with other people, such as your partner or your friends. If we are to stay emotionally healthy as human beings, we need lots of both of these on a regular basis.[14]

Why quick fixes don't work

Some people turn to harmful ways of dealing with the stress of parenting, such as drinking alcohol and smoking cigarettes. Although both of these habits may offer an immediate solution, they can have serious long-term consequences.

■ So why do we find drinking alcohol and smoking so alluring?

Alcohol activates GABA (see page 44), an anti-anxiety system in the brain. It also briefly boosts serotonin and dopamine, so you can feel more socially confident, alert, and relaxed. But too much alcohol can soon lead to the opposite of the desired effect. When you drink too much, your oxytocin, DHA, tryptophan, and glucose levels all fall, so with low blood sugar and low serotonin, you can plummet into a very low mood.

After a few drinks, alcohol can start to seriously deactivate higher brain functions such as our speech and emotion-regulating functions. When this happens, the lower (primitive) brain is left in the driving seat; so it is easy to see how people who drink too much can become angry, violent, or depressed. It is this takeover by the lower brain that accounts for the fact that much domestic violence and child abuse is alcohol-influenced.

■ Smoking triggers acetylcholine (an excitatory brain chemical) and dopamine, and stimulates the adrenal glands, activating adrenalin.

As a result, you feel more alert, motivated, and clear-headed. It also activates niacin, which supports GABA, so you feel less anxious. It slows the heart rate and helps muscles relax. Some research also indicates that the sucking motion of smoking activates oxytocin, just as does a child sucking on a dummy.

But of course, both these quick fixes come with a life-threatening price tag, so you need to find a method of emotional re-fuelling that is not actually bad for your physical or mental health.

CONSIDER THIS...

Getting out of your home for a break can be rewarding for the whole family. Fresh air, sunshine, and space can calm both parents and children. There are many studies showing that physical exercise can release endorphins and dopamine. Exercise also brings down high levels of the stress chemicals adrenaline, noradrenaline, and cortisol. Aerobic exercise can make you feel more alert due to more oxygen to the brain. One study found that sedentary people were more depressed than people who exercised regularly, and had lower levels of endorphins and higher levels of stress hormones.[15]

Restoring balance

You've recognized the signs of stress, low mood, and a negative brain chemistry. Your children are starting to get on your nerves and you feel like exploding at things you normally take in your stride. Now it's time to take action. Here are the activities that can bring down your stress chemicals.

CONSIDER THIS...

Research has shown that the following activities can stimulate oxytocin, an anti-stress chemical:

- meditation
- acupuncture
- massage or physical affection
- yoga
- having a warm bath or jacuzzi
- spending time in light, such as daylight or good artificial lighting.

Activities that calm you down

When you find an activity that calms you down and makes you feel relaxed, it means that your brain is probably releasing the wonderful anti-stress chemical oxytocin. The scientist Uvnas Moberg, who has written extensively about oxytocin, says, "We can choose activities and pursuits that release the oxytocin stored in our own inner medical cabinet. We have this wonderful healing substance inside us and need only to learn the many ways we can draw upon it. This natural healing nectar provides an antidote to the negative effects of a fast-paced lifestyle marked by stress and anxiety"[16] Research shows that oxytocin can:

- have an anti-anxiety effect
- lower blood pressure and pulse rate
- prevent the bloodstream from being flooded with stress hormones
- help the body digest food efficiently
- reduce agitation
- increase sociability.

Once you have found an activity that makes you feel calm, make a point of doing it on a regular basis. For example, have a weekly massage rather than a once-a-month massage, or set aside time for yoga every weekend. This will keep your oxytocin at optimum levels. Alternatively, choose an activity such as sitting in a beautiful garden or park, which will lower bodily hyperarousal and activate the calm and centred branch of your autonomic nervous system (see page 44).

"I feel calm and relaxed"

Yoga can lower blood pressure. Yoga movements calm the body by activating the vagal nerve system (see page 45). Research found that for some people this was more effective than the anti-anxiety drug diazepam in relieving anxiety.[17]

Meditation can lower blood pressure, anxiety, and cortisol levels in long-term meditators. It can also calm the overactive stress response system in the brain, by calming the amygdala (the system in the lower brain that detects threat).[18]

■ **One of the best ways to lower stress levels is to spend time with emotionally warm adults.**

It can be easy to focus on the chemical changes you can get from particular foods or activities, and forget about the ultimate mood changer – being with lovely people. A stimulating conversation with the right person can lower your stress chemical levels and activate optimal levels of dopamine and noradrenaline. Time with a loved one in whose company you feel very safe and at ease can also strongly activate the opioids in the brain, giving you a wonderful feeling of well-being. If it's a physically affectionate relationship, these opioids will have an even deeper effect on you, because of the sensitizing effects of oxytocin on the opioid system. This chemistry is arguably the most emotionally replenishing of all, as we know from the sheer bliss that can come from

"Time with a loved one in whose company you feel very safe can give you a wonderful feeling of well-being."

"A crucial skill is to recognize when you are frazzled."

CONSIDER THIS...

It's important to work out who are the people in your life who emotionally dysregulate you; in other words, who activate high levels of stress chemicals and send your body into a state of hyperarousal. People who commonly emotionally dysregulate other people are those who "talk at you" in lengthy monologues, or who are very anxious or agitated, or who offer little reciprocity in their interactions with you. They rarely, if ever, ask you how you are, or show any curiosity about your life, or they use you as their emotional regulator (or worse, as a therapist), but never show you any empathy for the problems in your life.

luxuriating in the arms of someone we love. So take time to have a comforting phone conversation with a friend, a long lie on the sofa with a loved one, and lots of exchanges full of warmth and laughter. You will be able to meet the most challenging of child behaviour calmly and with the capacity to think well under stress.

As a parent, a crucial skill is to recognize when you are frazzled and emotionally dysregulated and so are in need of the emotionally replenishing qualities of adult company. Every parent needs other adults around if they are to remain calm and in control. Don't wait until you feel isolated, depleted, exhausted, and depressed before you start seeking adult company.

■ **However much you enjoy the company of your children, it's only emotionally aware adults who can give you the emotional regulation you need.**

This is because emotionally aware adults have developed the higher brain functions of compassion, empathy, and concern and the ability to find the words to express it. Such adults may also have developed good vagal tone (see page 45), which means their bodily energy and physical presence is calming to be around, too. In parenting, emotional regulation must always be a one-way process, so it is never appropriate to treat your child as your little confidante or counsellor. It takes children all their time to manage their own feelings without having to manage yours as well.

■ **Sometimes your nearest and dearest are not the best emotional regulators for you.**

They may be people who are biochemically dysregulated for much of the time, because of lack of sufficient emotional regulation in their childhood and no counselling or therapy to change this. As a result, they may be anxious, angry, or depressed for much of the time, so being in their company will not activate the chemicals in your brain which promote a sense of emotional well-being. It's a question of identifying which people in your life can calm and soothe you, and then making sure you get enough time with them.

■ **You'll need special support if your child's strong feelings trigger your own childhood pain.**
Some parents successfully manage to cut off from painful feelings about their own childhood. Then, when they have

"It is never appropriate to treat your child as your little confidante or counsellor."

"It's good to talk to you"

If you are mostly alone with your children, no one is providing you with the vital emotional regulation you need in order to lower your bodily arousal levels. Enjoying time with other adults can change your brain state from stressed to calm; for example, you could join parent groups to meet people.

Cultures in which a family group or whole village bring up a child are very good for the emotional health of both parent and child. The same is true for groups in many animal species.

"A child's intense feelings can trigger emotional pain, which the parent had successfully buried for years."

a child, it all comes flooding back. The child's intense feelings can trigger emotional pain which the parent had successfully buried for years. If this happens, the child's crying or raging tantrums can make you feel desperate or explosive, or want to lash out with words or physically.

If you feel like this often, first check that your emotional state is not due to one or more of the other causes we have looked at for the disruption of the brain's positive chemical balance, such as tiredness, hunger, poor diet, too much coffee, or too much time on your own. If you are sure it's none of these, it may be a childhood memory. Don't expect to have a clear memory of what's being stirred up in you now. In infancy, the brain can store sense memories (for example, sensations, feelings, and images), but it is not yet wired up to be able to store "event memories" – "Mummy did that to me, or said this to me". So, if as a baby you were left screaming and no one came, you won't remember the "event" of this,

"I can't do this all by myself"

You will need special support as an emotional regulator for your children if you are on your own with them for much of the time. A great number of isolation studies show that spending too much time on your own without human interaction causes a drop in positive arousal chemicals and a rise in stress chemicals. One study found that isolation is more of a health risk than smoking.[19]

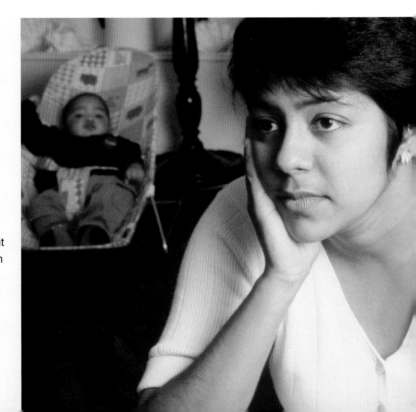

only the sense of desolation and desperation. If you feel like this often, the best thing you can do is seek counselling or psychotherapy (see page 266). If you have labelled your child as "bad" or see him as some kind of enemy with whom you are locked in constant battle, it's also a good idea to get some therapy for you, or parent–child therapy.

■ You will also need special support if you suffer from depression or post-natal depression.

Clinical depression is different from depression as a passing mood that affects most people from time to time. Depression is an illness in which the brain keeps pumping out more and more stress chemicals, and you can't turn the pump off. This then blocks the release of positive arousal brain chemicals. The result is a form of hell-on-earth.[20] The world loses all

"If you think you might be depressed, don't blame yourself, or suffer alone."

its goodness. Not even that lovely smile from your child, or your partner telling you he loves you, makes you feel good. You lose interest or pleasure in all or almost all activities. You can have problems sleeping, or you sleep too much. You have feelings of worthlessness, and excessive and inappropriate guilt. You don't enjoy your children and yet you can be plagued by a dread of something awful happening to them. Clinical depression can also block the CARE system and the PLAY system in the lower brain, which robs you of your maternal feelings and your wish to be playful or physically affectionate with your children.

So if you think you might be depressed, don't blame yourself, or suffer alone. Go to your doctor and explain how you are feeling. Research shows that anti-depressants and counselling or psychotherapy in combination are the most effective treatment.

CONSIDER THIS...

Teachers, like parents, need interactive regulation if they are to emotionally regulate the children in their care. Ideally, all teachers would therefore receive a regular massage and counselling. Also, teaching as part of a team would mean that teachers could bring each other the interactive regulation they need (see page 258).

For many children who haven't received warm, emotionally regulating parenting, school provides a second chance to develop their emotional and social brain. If teachers are chronically stressed, the children in their care don't receive this second chance. These are vital considerations for any government and education system.

■ **Loss or trauma is another reason for needing special support in your role as a parent.**

If you are in pain or under a lot of stress in your life at the moment, your feelings will find their way into your parenting. Perhaps you are reeling from the effects of losing a loved one, or moving home or job. Research shows that trying to brush feelings about major life events under the carpet won't work.

What's more, like it or not, children are barometers for parental stress and anguish. In fact, the right frontal lobe is so acutely aware that it can pick up on emotional atmospheres and suppressed feelings in another person in milliseconds. A child's unspoken reaction to your stress can come out in bad behaviour, in a neurotic symptom (phobia or obsession), or in a bodily symptom such as sleep, food, or bedwetting problems. Some emotionally eloquent children are able to speak about it. As Gemma, age six, said, "It's really difficult to have my feelings when Daddy is having his all the

"Parental emotional baggage can result in children suffering from anxiety"

time". Research shows that parental emotional baggage can all too easily result in children suffering from depression, anxiety, or problems with anger now or in later life.[21] Again, the solution is for you to go for counselling or psychotherapy.

■ **What can therapy do?**

Psychotherapy is a catch-all term for many different types of talking therapy, all of which help you to understand how your own childhood is still affecting you now. Counselling tends to be shorter term and more problem-focused, but can also involve helping you to understand what you are feeling in terms of how you think about yourself and other people in your present and past. If you did not receive enough compassion, understanding, and consistent emotional

Q I find my child's intense emotions really stressful. What can I do?

Some parents find it difficult to bear their child's intense emotions, and may not understand that they are appropriate to the child's age and development. This is usually because of a lack of sufficient emotional regulation in the parent's own childhood, which has left him or her believing that intense feelings are "dangerous". As a result, such parents can find themselves repeatedly wanting their child to have only "nice feelings", punishing developmentally appropriate expressions, and leaving the child to cope with unmanageable feelings by himself. Again, psychotherapy or counselling for the parent is such a gift for the child. It will enable you to manage your child's emotional intensity, rather than giving him the message that passion and excitement are unacceptable.

Spend time with people you care about. Warm, meaningful interactions with others bring your brain chemistry and body arousal level back to an optimum state. Hugs and warm, affectionate touches with your partner trigger the release of oxytocin. This gives you a warm, calm feeling.

regulation from your parents, it's not too late. You can get this from good therapy. The "plasticity" of your higher brain means that it is still able to change, even in adulthood.

■ **Good therapy can offer you powerful emotional interaction through which you can establish effective stress-regulating systems in your brain.**

It can also put an end to habitual negative emotional states, which have caused you to feel repeatedly anxious, angry, or depressed. For some people, therapy enables them to feel truly calm and at peace with themselves for the very first time, due to the activating of opioids and oxytocin.[22]

■ **People often say, "The past is the past". But when you have suffered an agonizing loss, or if you had a painful childhood, this is exactly what it is not.**

The past will only go into the past when it is remembered in the present, with someone who can make it safe for you to think about your early life. This is the role of a counsellor or psychotherapist. Research shows that adults who "own" their emotional pain do not re-enact the emotionally inadequate

"If society values its children it must cherish their parents" ~John Bowlby

parenting they experienced themselves.[23] You can't usually get this level of emotional regulation from a friend, partner, or relative because these relationships are two-way. A therapist is there for you alone.

Perhaps we should finish with a quote from six-year-old Jamie, whose mother needed therapy after the death of her father. One day Jamie said to his schoolteacher, "Today, I am walking on air with my very happy face". When asked why, he said, "Someone's helping my Mummy with all the bad weather in her heart. It was making my family very cold and wet!"

Key points

■ **Be kind to yourself** when you are pregnant – if you are stressed, your unborn baby will be stressed, too.

■ **As a parent** you spend a lot of time regulating your child's emotions. Remember that you also need emotional re-fuelling, with quality child-free time and interactive regulation from calm, soothing adults.

■ **Don't be stoic.** If you keep going despite feeling stressed, your children will sense your negative brain chemistry and this can affect their behaviour.

■ **Find activities that trigger** the release of the brain's natural calming chemicals. These include yoga, massage, meditation, and lying in the arms of someone you love.

■ **If you are really struggling,** talk to your doctor or to a counsellor or a psychotherapist.

References

YOUR CHILD'S BRAIN

1. " Our brains resemble old museums that contain many of the … markings of our evolutionary past, but we are able to keep much of that suppressed by our cortical lid." Panksepp J (1998) *Affective Neuroscience: The Foundations of Human and Animal Emotions*, Oxford University Press, Oxford: 75.

2. Sagan C (2005) *Dragons of Eden: Speculations on the Evolution of Human Intelligence,* Black Dog & Leventhal, New York.

3. MacLean PD (2003) *The triune brain in evolution: Role in paleocerebral functions,* Plenum Press, New York.

4. Sagan C (2005) *Dragons of Eden: Speculations on the Evolution of Human Intelligence,* Black Dog & Leventhal, New York. • Eccles JC (2005) *Evolution of the Brain*, Routledge Books, London.

5. "There is good biological evidence for at least seven innate emotional systems ingrained within the mammalian brain. In the vernacular, they include fear, anger, sorrow, anticipatory eagerness, play, sexual lust and maternal nurturance." Panksepp J (1998) *Affective Neuroscience: The Foundations of Human and Animal Emotions*, Oxford University Press, Oxford: 47. See this book for a complete account of all these systems.

6. Raine A, et al. (1998) Reduced prefrontal and increased subcortical brain functioning assessed using positron emission tomography in predatory and affective murderers, *Behavioural Sciences and the Law* 16: 319-32. • Dawson G, et al. (2000) The role of early experience in shaping behavioral and brain development and its implications for social policy, *Development and Psychopathology* Autumn; 12(4): 695-712.

7. Schore A (2003) *Affect Regulation and Disorders of the Self*, W.W. Norton and Co., New York: 9-13. • Hofer MA (1990) *Early symbolic processes: Hard evidence from a soft place.* • In Gick RA & Bore S (Eds), *Pleasure beyond the pleasure principle*, New Haven; Yale University Press: 55-78.

8. Blunt Bugental D, et al. (2003) The hormonal costs of subtle forms of infant maltreatment, *Hormones and Behaviour* Jan; 43(1): 237-44. • Gunnar MR, et al. (2002) Social regulation of the cortisol levels in early human development, *Psychoneuroendocrinology* Jan-Feb; 27(1-2): 199-220. • Anisman H, et al. (1998) Do early-life events permanently alter behavioral and hormonal responses to stressors? *International Journal of Developmental Neuroscience* Jun-Jul; 16(3-4): 149-64.

9. Beatson J, et al. (2003) Predisposition to depression: the role of attachment, *The Australian and New Zealand Journal of Psychiatry* Apr; 37(2): 219-25. • Gordon M (2003) Roots of Empathy: responsive parenting, caring societies, *The Keio Journal of Medicine* Dec; 52(4): 236-43. • de Kloet ER, et al. (2005) Stress, genes and the mechanism of programming the brain for later life, *Neuroscience and Biobehavioral Reviews* Apr; 29(2): 271-81.

10. Hariri AR, et al. (2000) Modulating emotional responses: effects of a neocortical network on the limbic system, *Neuroreport* Jan 17; 11(1): 43-8. • Barbas H, et al. (2003) Serial pathways from primate prefrontal cortex to autonomic areas may influence emotional expression, *Neuroscience* Oct 10; 4(1): 25.

11. Davidson RJ, et al. (2000) Dysfunction in the neural circuitry of emotion regulation – a possible prelude to violence, *Science* Jul 28; 289(5479): 591-94. • Davidson RJ, et al. (2000) Probing emotion in the developing brain: functional neuroimaging in the assessment of the neural substrates of emotion in normal and disordered children and adolescents, *Mental Retardation and Developmental Disabilities Research Reviews* 2000; 6(3): 166-70.

12. "As the cortex develops, vast numbers of top down neural networks connect with the subcortical area. These top down networks provide the information pathway for inhibiting reflexes and bringing subcortical functions under cortical control. Thus, a vital aspect of the development of the cortex is the inhibitory..." Cozolino, LJ (2002) *The Neuroscience of Psychotherapy: Building and Rebuilding the Human Remain*, W.W. Norton & Co., London. • Lacroix L, et al. (2000) Differential role of the medial and lateral prefrontal cortices in fear and anxiety, *Behavioral Neuroscience* Dec; 114(6): 1119-30.

13. Ito M, et al. (2003) Why "Nurturing the brain" now? *Brain Science Institute* Mar; 35(2): 117-20. • Rosenfeld P, et al. (1991) Maternal regulation of the adrenocortical response in preweanling rats, *Physiology & Behavior* Oct; 50(4): 661-71.

14. Bowlby J (1973) *Attachment and Loss, Volume 2: Separation, Anxiety and Anger*, Hogarth Press, London.

15. Sanchez MM, et al. (2001) Early adverse experience as a developmental risk factor for later psychopathology, *Development and Psychopathology* Summer; 13(3): 419-49. • Preston SD, et al. (2002) Empathy: Its ultimate and proximate bases, *The Behavioral and Brain Sciences* Feb; 25(1): 1-20; discussion 20-71. • Field T (1994) The effects of mother's physical and emotional unavailability on emotion regulation, *Monographs of the Society for Research in Child Development* 59; (2-3): 208-27.

CRYING & SEPARATIONS

1. Panksepp J, et al. (1978) The biology of social attachments: opiates alleviate separation distress, *Biological Psychiatry* Oct 13: 607-18.

2. Kitzinger S (2005) *Understanding your Crying Baby*, Carroll and Brown, London.

3. Leach P (2003) *Your Baby & Child*, Dorling Kindersley, London: 273.

4. Dawson G, et al. (2000) The role of early experience in shaping behavioural and brain development and its implications for social policy, *Developmental Psychology* Autumn; 12(4): 695-712. • Gunnar MR (1989) Studies of the human infant's adrenocortical response to potentially stressful events, *New Directions for Child Development* Fall: 3-18.

5. Gunnar MR, et al. (2002) Social regulation of the cortisol levels in early human development, *Psychoneuroendocrinology* Jan-Feb: 199-220. • Ashman SB, et al. (2002) Stress hormone levels of children of depressed mothers. *Development and Psychopathology* Spring: 333-49. • Blunt Bugental D, et al. (2003) The hormonal costs of subtle forms of infant maltreatment, *Hormones and Behaviour* Jan: 237-44.

6. Zubieta JK, et al. (2003) Regulation of Human Affective Responses by Anterior Cingulate and Limbic and μ-Opioid Neurotransmission, *General Psychiatry* Nov; 60(11): 1037-1172. • Panksepp J (1998) *Affective Neuroscience*, Oxford University Press, New York: 250.

7. Eisenberger NI, et al. (2003) Does rejection hurt? An FMRI study of social exclusion, *Science* Oct: 290-92. • Panksepp J. (2003) Neuroscience. Feeling the pain of social loss, *Science* Oct 10; 302(5643): 237-39.

8. Gerhardt S (2004) *Why love matters: How affection shapes a baby's brain*, Brunner-Routledge, Kings Lynn.

9. Heim C, et al. (1997) Persistent changes in corticotrophin-releasing factor systems due to early life stress: relationship to the pathophysiology of major depression and post-traumatic stress disorder, *Psychopharmacology Bulletin*: 185-92. • Beatson J, et al. (2003) Predispositions to depression: the role of attachment, *The Australian and New Zealand Journal of Psychiatry*, Apr: 219-25. • Plotsky PM, et al. (1998) Psychoneuroendocrinology of depression. Hypothalamic-pituitary-adrenal axis, *The Psychiatric Clinics of North America* June: 293-307.

10. McEwen BS, et al. (1999) Stress and the aging hippocampus, *Neuroendocrinology* Jan: 49-70. • Bremner JD, et al. (1998) The effects of stress on memory and the hippocampus throughout the life cycle: implications for childhood development and aging, *Developmental Psychology* Fall; 10(4): 871-85. • Moghaddam B, et al. (1994) Glucocorticoids mediate and the stress induced extracellular accumulation of glutamate, *Brain Research*: 655, 251-54

11. Bremner JD (2003) Long-term effects of childhood abuse on brain and neurobiology, *Child and Adolescent Psychiatric Clinics of North America* Apr: 271-92. • Rosenblum LA, et al. (1994) Adverse early experiences affect noradrenergic and serotonergic functioning in adult primates, *Biological Psychiatry* Feb 15: 221-27. • Herlenius E, et al. (2001) Neurotransmitters and neuromodulators during early human development, *Early Human Development* Oct: 21-37.

12. Zubieta JK, et al. (2003) Regulation of Human Affective Responses by Anterior Cingulate and Limbic and μ-Opioid Neurotransmission, *General Psychiatry* Nov 60 (11): 1037-1172.

13. Ludington-Hoe SM, et al. (2002) Infant crying: nature, physiologic consequences, and select interventions, *Neonatal Network* Mar 21: 29-36. • Bergman N (2005) More than a cuddle: skin-to-skin contact is key, *The Practising Midwife* Oct; 8(9): 44.

14. Ribble M (1998) Disorganising factors of infant personality, *Americal Journal of Psychiatry*: 459-463. • Uvnas-Moberg K (1998) Oxytocin may mediate the benefits of positive social interaction and emotions, *Psychoneuroendocrinology* Nov: 819-35. • Haley DW, et al. (2003) Infant stress and parent responsiveness: regulation of physiology and behavior during still-face and reunion, *Child Development* Sep-Oct: 1534-46.

15. Caldji C, et al. (2000) The effects of early rearing environment on the development of GABAA and central benzodiazepine receptor levels and novelty-induced fearfulness in the rat, *Neurophsychopharmacology* Mar: 219-29. • Hsu FC, et al. (2003) Repeated neonatal handling with maternal separation permanently alters hippocampal GABAA receptors and behavioural stress responses, *Proceedings of the National Academy of Sciences of the United States of America* Oct 14: 12213-18.

16. Graham YP, et al. (1999) The effects of neonatal stress on brain development: implications for psychopathology, *Development and Psychopathology* Summer: 545-65. • Habib KE, et al. (2001) Neuroendocrinology of Stress, *Endocrinology and Metabolism Clinics of North America* Sep: 695-728; vii-viii. • Levenson RW (2003) Blood, Sweat, and Fears – The Architecture of Emotion, *Annals of the New York Academy of Sciences* 1000: 348-66.

17. Field T (1994) The effects of mother's physical and emotional unavailability on emotion regulation, *Monographs of the Society for Research in Child Development* 59; (2-3): 208-27. • Siniatchkin M, et al. (2003) Migraine and asthma in childhood: evidence for specific asymmetric parent-child interactions in migraine and asthma families, *Cephalalgia* Oct; 23(8): 790-802. • Donzella B, et al. (2000) Cortisol and vagal tone responses to competitive challenge in preschoolers: associations with temperament, *Developmental Psychobiology* Dec;37(4):209-20.

18. Stam R, et al. (1997) Trauma and the gut: interactions between stressful experience and intestinal function, *Gut*. • Alfven G (2004) Plasma oxytocin in children with recurrent abdominal pain, *Journal of Pediatric Gastroenterology and Nutrition* May; 38(5): 513-17. • Jarrett ME, et al. (2003) Anxiety and depression are related to autonomic nervous system function in women with irritable bowel syndrome, *Digestive Diseases and Sciences* Feb; 48 (2): 386-94. • Heaton, K (1999) *Your Bowels*, British Medical Association/Dorling Kindersley, London: 34.

19. Kramer KM, et al. (2003) Developmental effects of oxytocin on stress response: single versus repeated exposure, *Physiology & Behavior* Sept; 79(4-5): 775-82. • Carter CS (2003) Developmental consequences of oxytocin, *Physiology & Behavior* Aug; 79(3): 383-97. • Liu D, et al. (1997) Maternal care, hippocampal glucocorticoid receptors, and hypothalamic-pituitary-adrenal responses to stress, *Science* Sept 12; 277(5332): 1659-62.

20. Jackson D (2004) *When Your Baby Cries*, Hodder-Mobius, London: 99.

21. Murray L, Andrews L (2000) *The social baby: Understanding babies' communication from birth*, CP Publishing, Richmond.

22. Cacioppo JT, et al. (2002) Loneliness and Health: Potential Mechanisms, *Psychosomatic Medicine* May-June: 407-17.

23. Panksepp J (2003) Neuroscience. Feeling the pain of social loss, *Science* 2003 Oct 10; 302(5643): 237-39.

24. Caldji C, et al. Variations in Maternal Care Alter GABA, Receptor Subunit Expression in Brain Regions Associated with Fear, *Neuropsychopharmacology* (2003) 28: 1950-59.

25. Chugani HT, et al. (2001) Local brain functional activity following early deprivation: a study of postinstitutionalized Romanian orphans, *Neuroimage* Dec: 1290-1301.

26. Paul J, et al. (1986) Positive effects of tactile versus kinaesthetic or vestibular stimulation an neuroendochrine and ODC activity in maternally deprived rat pups, *Life Science*: 2081-7. • Sanchez MM, et al. (2001) Early adverse experience as a developmental risk factor for later psychopathology: evidence from rodent and primate models, *Development and Psychopathology* Summer: 419-49. • Kuhn CM, et al. (1998) Responses to maternal separation: mechanisms and mediators, *International Journal of Developmental Neuroscience* Jun-Jul: 261-70.

27. Robertson J, et al. (1969) "John – 17 Months: Nine Days in a Residential Nursery", 16mm film/video: The Robertson Centre. Accompanied by a printed "Guide to the Film" Series: British Medical Association / Concord Film Council.

28. Ahnert L, et al. (2004) Transition to child care: associations with infant-mother attachment, infant negative emotion, and cortisol elevations, *Child Development* May-Jun: 639-50. • Watermura SE, et al. (2002) Rising cortisol at childcare; Relations with nap, rest and temperament, *Developmental Psychobiology* Jan: 33-42. • Dettling AC, et al. (1999) Cortisol levels of young children in full-day childcare centres: relations with age and temperament, *Psychoneuroendocrinology* Jun: 519-36.

29. Hertsgaard L, et al. (1995) Adrenocortical responses to the strange situation in infants with disorganized/disorientated attachment relationships, *Child Development* 66: 1100-06. • Gunnar MR (1989) Studies of the human infant's adrenocortical response to potentially stressful events, *New Directions for Child Development* Fall: 3-18.

30. Belsky J (2001); Emanuel Miller lecture. Developmental risks (still) associated with early child care, *Journal of Child Psychology and Psychiatry, and Allied Disciplines* Oct: 845-59. • Belsky J, et al. (1996) Trouble in the second year: three questions about family interaction, *Child Development* Apr: 556-78.

31. Gunnar MR, et al. (1992) The stressfulness of separation among nine-month-old infants: effects of social context variables and infant temperament, *Child Development* Apr: 290-303. • Dettling AC, et al. (2000) Quality of care and temperament determine changes in cortisol concentrations over the day for young children in childcare, *Psychoneuroendocrinology* Nov: 819-36.

32. Harlow HF, et al. (1979) *Primate Perspectives*, John Wiley, New York/London. • Harlow C (1986) *From learning to love*, Praeger Publications, New York.

33. Ladd CO, et al. (1996) Persistent changes in corticotropin-releasing factor neuronal systems induced by maternal deprivation, *Endocrinology* Apr: 1212-18. • Sanchez MM, et al. (2001) Early adverse experience as a developmental risk factor for later psychopathology: evidence from rodent and primate models, *Development and Psychopathology* Summer: 419-49.

34. Bowlby J (1973) *Attachment and Loss, Volume 2: Separation, Anxiety and Anger*, Hogarth Press, London. • Bowlby J (1979) *The Making and Breaking of Affectional Bonds*, Tavistock, London. • Bowlby J (1988) *A Secure Base: Clinical Applications of Attachment Theory*, Routledge, London.

SLEEP & BEDTIMES

1. Davis KF, et al. (2004) Sleep in infants and young children: part two: common sleep problems, *Journal of Pediatric Health Care* May-Jun; 18(3): 130-7. • Hiscock H, et al. (2004) Problem crying in infancy, *The Medical Journal of Australia* Nov 1; 181(9): 507-12. • Lam P, et al. (2003) Outcomes of infant sleep problems: a longitudinal study of sleep, behavior, and maternal well-being, *Pediatrics* Mar; 111(3): e203-7.

2. Frost J (2005) *Supernanny*, Hodder & Stoughton, London. • Byron T, et al. (2003) *Little Angels*, BBC Worldwide Learning, London.

3. Harrison Y (2004) The relationship between daytime exposure to light and night-time sleep in 6-12 week old infants, *Journal of Sleep Research* Dec; 13(4): 345-52.

4. McKenna JJ, et al. (1993) Infant-parent co-sleeping in an evolutionary perspective: implications for understanding infant sleep development and the sudden infant death syndrome, *Sleep* Apr; 16(3): 263-82. • Field T (1994) The effects of mother's physical and emotional unavailability on emotion regulation, *Monographs of the Society for Research in Child Development* 59;(2-3): 208-27. • Richard C, et al. (1996) Sleeping position, orientation, and proximity in bed sharing infants and mothers, *Sleep* Nov; 19(9): 685-90.

5. McKenna JJ (1986) An anthropological perspective on the sudden infant death syndrome (SIDS). The role of parental breathing cues and speech breathing adaptations, *Medical Anthropology* 10; 9-53. • Bergman N (2005) More than a cuddle: skin-to-skin contact is key, *The Practising Midwife* Oct; 8(9): 44. • Cacioppo JT, et al. (2002) Loneliness and health: potential mechanisms, *Psychosomatic Medicine* May-June; 64(3): 407-17.

6. Bergman, N (2005) More than a cuddle: skin-to-skin contact is key, *The Practising Midwife* Oct; 8(9): 44. • Jackson D (1999) *Three in a bed: The benefits of sleeping with your baby*, Bloomsbury, London

7. Kramer KM, et al. (2003) Developmental effects of oxytocin on stress response: single versus repeated exposure, *Physiology and Behaviour* Sept; 79(4-5): 775-82. • Hofer MA (1996) On the nature and consequences of early loss, *Psychosomatic Medicine* Nov-Dec 58(6): 570-81. • Buckley P, et al. (2002) Interaction between bed sharing and other sleep environments during the first six months of life, *Early Human Development* Feb; 66(2): 123-32.

8. Keller M, et al. (2000) Co-sleeping and children independence; challenging the myths; in McKenna J (Ed.) *Safe Sleeping with Baby: Evolutionary, Developmental and Clinical Perspectives*, University of California Press, California. • McKenna J (2000), Cultural influences on infant and childhood sleep biology and the science that studies it: toward a more inclusive paradigm; in Loughlin J, Carroll J, Marcus C (Eds.) *Sleep in Development and Pediatrics*, Marcel Dekker, New York: 99-230. • McKenna J, et al. (2005) Why babies should never sleep alone: A review of the co-sleeping controversy in relation to SIDS, bedsharing and breast feeding, *Paediatric Respiratory Reviews* 6(2): 134-52.

9. Horne J (1985) *New Scientist* Dec 1985; cited in Jackson D (1999) *Three in a bed: The benefits of sleeping with your baby*, Bloomsbury, London.

10. "Even when asleep, mothers appeared to be aware or sense the presence of their baby in bed with them and at no time was a mother ever observed to roll on her infant, even when sleeping very close together." Jeanine Young (1998), *Bedsharing with Babies; The Facts.* • Jackson D (1999) *Three in a bed: The benefits of sleeping with your baby*, Bloomsbury, London.

11. Gaultier C (1995) Cardiorespiratory adaptation during sleep in infants and children, *Pediatric Pulmonology* Feb; 19(2): 105-17.

12. Kibel MA, et al. (2000) Should the infant sleep in mother's bed? In *Sixth SIDS International Meeting Auckland New Zealand* Feb 8-11. • Farooqi S (1994) Ethnic differences in infant care practices and in the incidence of sudden infant death syndrome in Birmingham, *Early Human Development* Sep 15; 38(3): 209-13.

13. "Nobody understood my questions; the concept of sudden infant death or cot death was apparently unknown among professionals and lay people in such different places as Peking, Hsian, Loyang, Nanking, Shanghai, and Canton. Furthermore I learned that Chinese babies sleep with their mothers... Ever since then I have held the view that even if it happens during the day, cot death is a disease of babies who spend their nights in an atmosphere of loneliness and that cot death is a disease of societies where the nuclear family has taken over." Michael Odent, *Lancet* 1986 Jan 25; cited in Jackson D (1999) *Three in a bed: The benefits of sleeping with your baby*, Bloomsbury, London.

14. Davies DP (1985) Cot death in Hong Kong: a rare problem? *Lancet* 2: 1346-48.

15 and 16. Studies cited in Jackson (1999) *Three in a bed: The benefits of sleeping with your baby*, Bloomsbury, London: 106-30.

17. Bergman N (2005) More than a cuddle: skin-to-skin contact is key, *The Practising Midwife* Oct; 8(9): 44.

18. Latz S, et al. (1999) Co-sleeping in context: sleep practices and problems in young children in Japan and the United States, *Archives of Pediatrics & Adolescent Medicine* Apr; 153(4): 339-46. • Lozoff B, et al. (1996) Co-sleeping and early childhood sleep problems: effects of ethnicity and socioeconomic status, *Journal of Developmental and Behavioral Pediatrics* Feb; 17(1): 9-15.

19. Pantley E (2005) *The No-Cry Sleep Solution*, McGraw-Hill, New York: 327.

20. Pantley E (2005) *The No-Cry Sleep Solution*, McGraw-Hill, New York: 9. • Zhong X, et al. (2005) Increased sympathetic and decreased parasympathetic cardiovascular modulation in normal humans with acute sleep deprivation, *Journal of Applied Physiology* Jun; 98(6): 2024-32.

21. "Infants are observed to be 'staring into space with a glazed look'. The fear or terror involves numbing, avoidance, compliance, mediated by high levels of behaviour-inhibiting cortisol, pain-numbing endogenous opioids, ... dissociation is 'the escape where there is no escape'" Putnam (1997); "a last resort defensive strategy" Dixon (1998). Schore, A (2003) *Affect Regulation and the Repair of the Self*: 66-67, WW. Norton & Co., New York. • Hertsgaard L, et al. (1995) Adrenocortical responses to the strange situation in infants with disorganized/disorientated attachment relationships, *Child Development* 66, 1100-06. • Perry BD, et al. (1995) Childhood trauma, the neurobiology of adaptation, and 'use dependent' development of the brain. How 'states' become 'traits.' *Infant Mental Health Journal* 16: 271-91.

22. Post RM, et al. (1994) Recurrent affective disorder: Roots in developmental neurobiology and illness progression based on changes in gene expression, *Development and Psychopathology* 6: 781-813. • Levine S, et al. (1993) Temporal and social factors influencing behavioral and hormonal responses to separation in mother and infant squirrel monkeys, *Psychoneuroendocrinology* 18(4): 297-306. • Silove D, et al. (1996) Is early separation anxiety a risk factor for adult panic disorder? A critical view, *Comprehensive Psychiatry* May-June; 37(3): 167-79.

23. Bremner JD, Innis RB, Southwick SM, et al. (2000) Decreased benzodiazepine receptor binding in prefrontal cortex in combat-related posttraumatic stress disorder, *The American Journal of Psychiatry* Jul; 157 (7): 1120-6. • Adamec RE, et al. (1997) Blockade of CCK (B) but not CCK (A) receptors before and after the stress of predator exposure prevents lasting increases in anxiety-like behavior: implications for anxiety associated with posttraumatic stress disorder, *Behavioral Neuroscience* Apr; 111(2): 435-49. •Adamec R (1994) Modelling anxiety disorders following chemical exposures, *Toxicology and Industrial Health* Jul-Oct; 10(4-5): 391-420.

24. Ziabreva I, et al. (2003) Mother's voice "buffers" separation-induced receptor changes in the prefrontal cortex of Octodon degus, *Neuroscience* 119(2): 433-41. • Ziabreva I, et al. (2003) Separation-induced receptor changes in the hippocampus and amygdala of Octodon degus: influence of maternal vocalizations, *Journal of Neuroscience* Jun 15; 23(12): 5329-36.

25. Pantley, E (2005) *The no-cry sleep solution*, McGraw-Hill, New York: 327.

26. Field T, et al. (1996) Preschool Children's Sleep and Wake Behavior: Effects of massage therapy, *Early Child Development and Care* 120: 39-44. • Field T, Hernandez-Reif M (2001) Sleep problems in infants decrease following massage therapy, *Early Child Development and Care* 168: 95-104.

THE CHEMISTRY OF LIVING LIFE WELL

1. "Each of us has his or her own....finest drugstore available at the cheapest cost – to produce all the drugs we ever need to run our body–mind." Pert, CB (1997) *Molecules of Emotion*, Simon & Schuster, London: 271

2. Mahler, M (1968) *On Human Symbiosis and the Vicissitudes of Individuation*, International Universities Press, New York.

3. McCarthy MM, et al. (1997) Central nervous system actions of oxytocin and modulation of behavior in humans, *Molecular Medicine Today* 3(6): 269-75 • Uvnas-Moberg K (1997) Physiological and endocrine effects of social contact, *Annals of the New York Academy of Sciences* 15; 807: 146-63 • Zubieta JK, et al. Regulation of Human Affective Responses by Anterior Cingulate and Limbic and μ-Opioid

Neurotransmission, *General Psychiatry* Nov, 60(11): 1037-1172.

4. Heim C, et al. (2001) The role of childhood trauma in the neurobiology of mood and anxiety disorders: preclinical and clinical studies, *Biological Psychiatry* 15; 49(12): 1023-39.

5. Uvnas-Moberg K, et al. (2005) Oxytocin, a mediator of anti-stress, well being, social interaction, growth and healing, *Zeitschrift fur Psychosomatische Medizin und Psychotherapie* 51(1): 57-80 • Kramer KM, et al. (2003) Developmental effects of oxytocin on stress response: single versus repeated exposure, *Physiology & Behavior* 79(4-5): 775-82 • Carter CS (2003) Developmental consequences of oxytocin, *Physiology & Behavior* 79(3): 383-97.

6. Plotsky PM, Thrivikraman KV, Meaney MJ (1993) Central and feedback regulation of hypothalamic corticotrophin–releasing factor secretion, *Ciba Foundation Symposium*: 172: 59-75.

7. Bowlby, J (1979) *The Making and Breaking of Affectional Bonds*, Tavistock, London.

8. Liu D, et al. (1997) Maternal care, hippocampal glucocorticoid receptors, and hypothalamic-pituitary-adrenal responses to stress. *Science* 277(5332): 1659-62 • Caldji C, et al. (2003) Variations in Maternal Care Alter GABAA Receptor Subunit Expression in Brain Regions associated with Fear, *Neuropsychopharmacology* 28: 1950-59 • Scantamburlo G, et al. (2001) Role of the neurohypophysis in psychological stress, *Encephale* May-June 27(3): 245-59.

9. Francis DD, et al. (2002) Naturally occurring differences in maternal care are associated with the expression of oxytocin and vasopressin receptors. *Journal of Neuroendocrinology* 14: 349-53. • Flemming AS, et al. (1999) Neurobiology of mother–infant interactions; experience and central nervous system plasticity across development and generations, *Neuroscience and Biobehavioral Reviews* May: 673-685

10. Panksepp J (2004) *Personal communication.*

11. Depue RA, et al. (1994) Dopamine and the structure of personality: relation of agonist-induced dopamine activity to

positive emotionality, *Journal of Personality and Social Psychology* 66(4): 762-775. • "When lots of dopamine synapses are firing, a person feels as if he or she can do anything." Panksepp J (1998) *Affective Neuroscience*, Oxford University Press, New York: 144 • "There are biological mechanisms behind the most sublime human behaviour." Damasio A (1996) *Descartes' Error*, Papermac, London: 183.

12. Aitken KJ, et al. (1997) Self/other organisation in human psychological development, *Development and Psychopathology* 9: 653-77 • Trevarthen C (1993) The Self born in intersubjectivity: The psychology of an infant communicating; cited in Neisser, U (Ed.) *The Perceived Self: ecological and interpersonal sources of self knowledge*, Press Syndicate of the University of Cambridge: 123 1995.

13. "The unconditionally rewarding and exciting properties of the mother's gaze in these imprinting [on the brain] experiences ...activate...dompaminergic elation (Kelley and Stinus 1984) and dopaminergic arousal in the infant." Cited in Schore 1994. Schore, A (1994) *Affect Regulation and the Origins of the Self – The Neurobiology of Emotional Development*, Lawrence Erlbaum Associates,New Jersey.

14. Schore, A (1997) Early organization of the nonlinear right brain and development of a predisposition to psychiatric disorders, *Development and Psychopathology* 9: 595-631; 603 • Schore, A (1996) The experience-dependent maturation of a regulatory system in the orbital prefrontal cortex and the origin of development psychopathology, *Development and Psychopathology* 8: 59-87

15. Beebe B, et al. (1988) The Contribution of Mother-Infant Mutual Influence to the Origins of Self- and Object Representations, *Psychoanalytic Psychology* 5(4): 305-337.

16. "Everyone looks for that sparkle in friends and lovers to 'make things happen'. Most of all everybody is looking for energy within themselves: the motivation and drive to get up and do something, the endurance, stamina and resolve to carry through..." Brown (1999), op. cit: 2.

17. Panksepp, J (1998) *Affective Neuroscience*, Oxford University Press, New York: 144. • "And when the brain's SEEKING system is

highly activated it 'helps ... [people] to move their bodies effortlessly in search of the things they need, crave and desire." Panksepp J, op.cit.: 53.

18. Depue RA, et al. (1999) Neurobiology of the structure of personality: dopamine, facilitation of incentive motivation, and extraversion, *The Behavioral and Brain Sciences* 22(3): 491-517 • Panksepp J (1998) *Affective Neuroscience*, Oxford University Press, New York: 144.

19. Belz EE, et al. (2003) Environmental enrichment lowers stress-responsive hormones in singly housed male and female rats, *Pharmacology, Biochemistry, and Behavior*: 481-86. • Green TA, et al. (2003) Environmental enrichment decreases nicotine-induced hyperactivity in rats, *Psychopharmacology*: 235-41.

20. "In an experiment with rats, some of the rats were given an enriched environment with climbing tubes and running wheels, novel food and lots of social interaction. Two months later the rats in the enriched environment had an extra 50,000 brain cells in each side of the hippocampus [one of the memory and learning centers in the brain]." Fred Gage Salk, Institute for Biological Studies in La Jolla, California; cited Carper, J (2000) *Your Miracle Brain*, Harper Collins, New York: 31-32.

21. Raine A, et al. (2003) Effects of environmental enrichment at ages 3-5 years on schizotypal personality and antisocial behaviour at ages 17 and 23 years, *The American Journal of Psychiatry*: 1627-35.

22. Morley-Fletcher S, et al. (2003) Environmental enrichment during adolescence reverses the effects of prenatal stress on play behaviour and HPA axis reactivity in rats, *European Journal of Neuroscience* 18(12): 3367-74.

23. Murray, J (2001) TV Violence and Brainmapping in Children, *Psychiatric Times* XV111 (10).

24. Seib HM, et al. (1998) Cognitive correlates of boredom proneness: the role of private self-consciousness and absorption, *The Journal of Psychology* 132 (6): 642-52.

25. Barbalet JM (1999) Boredom and social meaning, *The British Journal of Sociology* 50(4): 631-46.

26. Bar-Onf ME (1999) Turning off the television, *British Medical Journal* April 24.

27. "People take psychostimulants to give them the very sense of vigorously pursuing courses of action that they would get from a healthy SEEKING circuit. Cocaine produces a highly energised state of psychic power and engagement with the world." Panksepp J (1998) *Affective Neuroscience*, Oxford University Press, New York: 118.

28. Gordon N, et al. (2003) Socially-induced brain "fertilization": play promotes brain derived neurotrophic factor transcription in the amygdala and dorsolateral frontal cortex in juvenile rats, *Neuroscience Letters* 341(1-24): 17-20.

29. Panksepp J, et al. (2003) Modeling ADHD-type arousal with unilateral frontal cortex damage in rats and beneficial effects of play therapy, *Brain and Cognition*.

30. Panksepp, J (1993) Rough and Tumble Play: A Fundamental Brain Process. In MacDonald, KB (Ed.) *Parents and Children Playing*, SUNY Press, Albany NY: 147-184. • Ikemoto S, Panksepp J (1992) The effects of early social isolation on the motivation for social play in juvenile rats, *Developmental Psychobiology* May; 25(4): 261-74.

31. Pellegrini A, et al. (1996) The effects of recess timing on children's playground and classroom behaviours, *American Educational Research Journal* 32 (4): 845-64. • Pellegrini A, et al. (1995) A developmental contextualist critique of attention deficit/hyperactivity disorder, *Educational Researcher* 24(1): 13-20.

32. Panksepp J, et al. (2003) Modeling ADHD-type arousal with unilateral frontal cortex damage in rats and beneficial effects of play therapy, *Brain and Cognition*.

33. Beatty WW, et al. (1982) Psychomotor stimulants, social deprivation and play in juvenile rats, *Pharmacology, Biochemistry, and Behavior* Mar; 16(3): 417-22.

34. Bolanos CA, et al. (2003) Methylphenidate treatment during pre- and periadolescence alters behavioral responses to emotional stimuli at adulthood, *Biological Psychiatry* Dec 15; 54(12): 1317-29 • Moll GH, et al. (2001) • Early methylphenidate administration to young rats causes a persistent reduction in the density of striatal dopamine receptors, *Journal of Child and Adolescent Psychopharmacology* Spring, 11(1): 15-24. • Nocjar C, Panksepp J (2002) Chronic intermittent amphetamine pretreatment enhances future appetitive behaviour for drug- and natural- reward: interaction with environmental variables, *Behavioural Brain Research* 128 (2), 22 January: 89-203.

35. Panksepp J, et al. (2003) Modeling ADHD-type arousal with unilateral frontal cortex damage in rats and beneficial effects of play therapy, *Brain and Cognition*.

36. Panksepp, J (1998) *Affective Neuroscience*, Oxford University Press, Oxford: 280.

BEHAVING BADLY

1. Zhong X, et al. (2005) Increased sympathetic and decreased parasympathetic cardiovascular modulation in normal humans with acute sleep deprivation, *Journal of Applied Physiology* Jun; 98(6): 2024-32.

2. Alvarez GG, et al. (2004) The impact of daily sleep duration on health: a review of the literature, *Progress in Cardiovascular Nursing* Spring; 19(2): 56-59. • Zohar D, et al. (2005) The effects of sleep loss on medical residents' emotional reactions to work events: a cognitive-energy model, *Sleep* Jan 1; 28(1): 47-54. • Vgontzas AN, et al. (2001) Chronic insomnia is associated with nyctohemeral activation of the hypothalamic-pituitary-adrenal axis: clinical implications, *The Journal of Clinical Endocrinology and Metabolism* Aug; 86(8): 3787-94.

3. "Research by J. Michael Murphy, of the Department of Psychiatry at Harvard Medical School, documents that a school breakfast improves academic performance, psychological well-being, and behavior...A lack of breakfast took a heavy toll emotionally." Carper J (2000) *Your Miracle Brain*, Harper Collins, New York: 113-14.

4. Teves D, et al. (2004) Activation of human medial prefrontal cortex during autonomic responses to hypoglycemia, *Proceedings of the National Academy of Sciences of the United States of America* Apr 20; 101(16): 6217-21.

5. Richardson AJ, et al. (2005) The Oxford-Durham study: a randomized, controlled trial of dietary supplementation with fatty acids in children with developmental coordination disorder, *Pediatrics* 1115; 1360-66. • Innis SM (2000) The role of dietary n-6 and n-3 fatty acids in the developing brain, *Developmental neuroscience* Sep-Dec; 22(5-6): 474-80 • Wainwright PE (2002) Dietary essential fatty acids and brain function: a developmental perspective on mechanisms, *The Proceedings of the Nutrition Society* Feb: 61-69.

6. Boris M, et al. (1994) Foods and additives are common causes of the attention deficit hyperactive disorder in children, *Annals of allergy* May; 72 (5): 462-68 • Tuormaa TE (1994) The Adverse Effects of Food Additives on Health With a special emphasis on Childhood Hyperactivity, *Journal of Orthomolecular Medicine* 9(4): 225-43 • Feingold BF (1976) Hyperkinesis and learning disabilities linked to the ingestion of artificial food colours and flavours, *Journal of Learning Disabilities* 9: 19-27.

7. "One in five parents think it is OK to smack a toddler for throwing a tantrum. One in ten parents believe that it is OK to smack a toddler for refusing to get into their buggy. 87 percent of parents in the UK shout at their children." All National Society for Prevention of Cruelty to Children (NSPCC) United Kingdom 2003.

8. See Stewart I, Jones V (1987) *T.A. Today*, Lifespace, Nottingham.

9. "To be able to effect something is the assertion that one is not impotent, but that one is an alive functioning human being... It is, in the last analysis, the proof that one Is." Fromm, E. (1973) *The Anatomy of Human Destructiveness*, Cape, London: 31

10. Hariri AR, et al. (2000) Modulating emotional responses: effects of a neocortical network on the limbic system, *Neuroreport* Jan 17; 11(1): 43-48.

11. Denham SA, et al. (2000) Prediction of externalizing behavior problems from early to middle childhood: the role of parental socialization and emotion expression, *Development and Psychopathology* Winter; 12(1): 23-45 • Stuewig J, et al. (2005) The relation of child maltreatment to shame and guilt among adolescents: psychological routes to depression and delinquency, *Child Maltreatment* Nov; 10(4): 324-36 • Aunola K, et al. (2005) The Role of Parenting Styles in Children's Problem Behavior, *Child Development* Nov-Dec; 76(6): 1144-59.

12. Brody GH, et al. (1982) Contributions of parents and peers to children's moral socialization, *Developmental Review* 2: 31-75. • Haley DW, et al. (2003) Infant stress and parent responsiveness: regulation of physiology and behavior, *Child Development* Sep-Oct; 74(5): 1534-46 • Barbas H, et al. (2003) Serial pathways from primate prefrontal cortex to autonomic areas may influence emotional expression, *Neuroscience* Oct 10; 4(1): 25.

13. "The SEEKING system promotes states of eagerness and directed purpose in both humans and animals. The system's dopamine circuits tend to energise and coordinate the functions of many higher brain areas that mediate planning and foresight." Panksepp J (1998) *Affective Neuroscience*, Oxford University Press, New York: 54.

14. Gunnar MR (1989) Studies of the human infant's adrenocortical response to potentially stressful events, *New Directions for Child Development*, Fall (3-18) • Hertsgaard L, et al. (1995) Adrenocortical responses to the strange situation in infants with disorganized/disorientated attachment relationships, *Child Development* 66: 1100-06.

15. Panksepp J (2003) Neuroscience. Feeling the pain of social loss, *Science* Oct 10; 302(5643): 237-39.

16. Pollak SD (2005) Maternal Regulation of Infant Reactivity, *Developmental Psychology* Summer; 17(3): 735-52.

17. Adamec RE (1991) Partial kindling of the ventral hippocampus: identification of changes in limbic physiology which accompany changes in feline aggression and defense, *Physiology & Behavior* Mar; 49(3): 443-53. • "The mere experience of an emotion without the capacity for [thinking] may tend to ingrain the aroused emotion as an [emotional] disposition in the brain." Panksepp J (2001) The Long-term Psychobiological Consequences of Infant Emotions – Prescriptions for the Twenty-First Century, *Infant Mental Health Journal* 22 (1-2) Jan-Apr: 145.

THE TRYING TIMES

1. Cozolino LJ (2002) *The Neuroscience of Psychotherapy: Building and Rebuilding the Human Remain*, W.W. Norton & Co., London: 76 • Schore AN (1997) Early organisation of the non-linear right brain and development of a predisposition to psychiatric disorders, *Development and Psychopathology* 9, 595-631: 607.

2. Panksepp J (1993) Rough and Tumble Play: A Fundamental Brain Process. In MacDonald KB (Ed.) (1993) *Parents and Children Playing*, SUNY Press, Albany, NY: 147-84 • Pellegrini A, et al. (1996) The effects of recess timing on children's playground and classroom behaviours, *American Educational Research Journal* 32 (4): 845-64.

3. Panksepp, J. (1998) *Affective Neuroscience*, Oxford University Press, Oxford: 54, 145, 149.

4. Spangler G, et al. (1994) Maternal sensitivity as an external organizer for biobehavioral regulation in infancy, *Developmental Psychobiology* Nov; 27(7): 425-37. • Feldman R, et al. (1999) Mother-infant affect synchrony as an antecedent of the emergence of self-control, *Developmental Psychology* Jan; 35(1): 223-31.

5. Uvnas-Moberg K, et al. (2005) Oxytocin, a mediator of anti-stress, well-being, social interaction, growth and healing, *Zeitschrift fur Psychosomatische Medizin und Psychotherapie* 51(1):57-80 • Caldji C, et al. (2003) Variations in Maternal Care Alter GABAA Receptor Subunit Expression in Brain Regions associated with Fear, *Neuropsychopharmacology* 28: 1950-59.

6. Gordon N, et al. (2003) Socially-induced brain "fertilization': play promotes brain derived neurotrophic factor transcription in the amygdala and dorsolateral frontal cortex in juvenile rats, *Neuroscience Letters* 341 (1) 24 Apr: 17-20.

7. Zubieta JK, et al. (2003) Regulation of Human Affective Responses by Anterior Cingulate and Limbic and μ-Opioid Neurotransmission, *General Psychiatry* Nov; 60(11): 1037-1172.

8. For other ways to deal with provocation, see Hughes, D (1998) *Building the Bonds of Attachment: Awakening Love in Deeply Troubled Children*, Jason Aronson, New Jersey.

9. Faber A, et al. (1998) *Siblings Without Rivalry*, Collins, New York.

10. Newson J, et al. (1970) *Seven Years Old in the Home Environment*, Penguin, UK.

11. Pennebaker JW (1993) Putting stress into words: health, linguistic, and therapeutic implications, *Behaviour Research and Therapy* Jul; 31(6): 539-48.

12. Parker J, et al. (2002) *Sibling rivalry, sibling love: What every brother and sister needs their parents to know*, Hodder & Stoughton, Chatham.

13. Hariri AR, et al.(2000) Modulating emotional responses: effects of a neocortical network on the limbic system, *Neuroreport* Jan 17; 11(1): 43-48.

14. Moseley J (1996) *Quality Circle Time*, Cambridge LDA.

ALL ABOUT DISCIPLINE

1. Smith M, et al. (1997) Research on parental behaviour, Thomas Coram Research Unit, Institute of Education, University of London.

2. Shea A, et al. (2005) Child maltreatment and HPA axis dysregulation: relationship to major depressive disorder and post traumatic stress disorder in females, *Psychoneuroendocrinology* Feb; 30(2): 162-78.

3. Teicher M (2002) Scars That Won't Heal, *Scientific American* March. • Teicher MH, Andersen SL, Polcari A, et al. (2003) The neurobiological consequences of early stress and childhood maltreatment, *Neuroscience and Biobehavioral Reviews* Jan-Mar; 27(1-2): 33-44. • Teicher M, Anderson S, Polcari A (2002) Developmental neurobiology of childhood stress and trauma, *The Psychiatric Clinics of North America* 25: 297-426.

4. Van der Kolk B (1989) "The Compulsion to Repeat the Trauma: Re-enactment, Revictimization, and Masochism." *Psychiatric Clinics of North America* 12: 389-411 • Gilligan J (1996) *Violence: Our Deadly Epidemic and Its Causes*, G. P. Putnam & Sons, New York: 93 • "Each generation begins anew with fresh, eager, trusting faces of babies, ready to love and create a new world. And each generation of parents ... dominates its children until they become emotionally crippled adults who repeat in nearly exact detail the social violence and domination that existed in previous decades. Should a minority of parents ... begin to provide somewhat more secure, loving early years that allow a bit more freedom and independence, history soon begins to move in surprising new directions and society changes in innovative ways." De Mause L (2002) *The Emotional Life of Nations*, Karnac Books, New York: 97.

5. Oliner S, et al. (1988) *The Altruistic Personality: Rescuers of Jews in Nazi Europe*, The Free Press, New York.

6. Raine A, et al. (1998) Reduced prefrontal and increased subcortical brain functioning assessed using positron emission tomography in predatory and affective murderers, *Behavioural Sciences and the Law* 16: 319-32.

7. Troy M, et al. (1987) Victimisation Among Preschoolers: Role of Attachment Relationship History, *Journal of American Academy of Child and Adolescent Psychiatry* 26: 166-72.

8. "The mere experience of an emotion without the capacity for [thinking] may tend to ingrain the aroused emotion as an [emotional] disposition in the brain." Panksepp J (2001) The Long-term Psychobiological Consequences of Infant Emotions – Prescriptions for the Twenty-First Century, *Infant Mental Health Journal* 22 (1-2) Jan-Apr: 145.

9. Hoffman ML (1994) Discipline and internalization, *Developmental Psychology* 30: 26-28.

10. Cline F, et al. (1990) *Parenting with Love and Logic*, Pinon Press, Colorado Springs.

11. Brody GH, et al. (1982) Contributions of parents and peers to children's moral socialization, *Developmental Review* 2: 31-75.

12. Weninger O (1998) *Time-In Parenting Strategies*, esf Publishers, New York.

13. Frost J (2005) *Supernanny*, Hodder & Stoughton, London. See also some excellent higher-brain-developing discipline in Byron T, Baveystock S (2003) *Little Angels*, BBC Worldwide Learning, London.

14. Hariri AR, et al. (2000) Modulating emotional responses: effects of a

neocortical network on the limbic system, *Neuroreport* Jan 17; 11(1): 43-48. • Pennebaker JW (1993) Putting stress into words: health, linguistic, and therapeutic implications, *Behaviour Research and Therapy* Jul; 31(6): 539-48. • Fossati P, Hevenor et al. (2003) In search of the emotional self: an FMRI study using positive and negative emotional words, *The American Journal of Psychiatry* Nov; 160(11): 1938-45.

15. Philips, A (1999) *Saying No*, Faber & Faber, London.

16. Gentle, safe holding is appropriate in schools if a child is hurting him- or herself or others, or is damaging property, and is so incensed and out of control that all verbal attempts to engage the child have failed. Such necessary interventions are fully in line with guidelines set out in the United Kingdom government document, "New Guidance on the Use of Reasonable Force in School" (DfEE 1998) or Section 550a, Education Act (1996).

THE CHEMISTRY OF LOVE

1. Nelson EE, Panksepp J (1998). Brain substrates of infant-mother attachment: contributions of opioids, oxytocin, and norepinephrine, *Neuroscience and Biobehavioral Reviews* May; 22(3): 437-52 • Panksepp, J. (1998) *Affective Neuroscience: The Foundations of Human and Animal Emotions*, Oxford University Press, Oxford: 249.

2. Panksepp, J. (1998) op cit.: 237.

3. Panksepp, J. (1998) op cit.: 257 • Kalin NH, ET AL. (1995) Opiate systems in mother and infant primates coordinate intimate contact during reunion, *Psychoneuroendocrinology* 20(7): 735-42.

4. Panksepp, J. (1998) op cit.: 293.

5. Carter CS (1998) Neuroendocrine perspectives on social attachment and love, *Psychoneuroendocrinology* Nov; 23(8): 779-881. • Insel TR (1992) Oxytocin: A neuropeptide for affiliation, *Psychoneuroendocrinology* 17:3-35.

6. Panksepp J, et al. (1999) Opiates and play dominance in juvenile rats, *Behavioral Neuroscience* Jun; 99(3): 441-53.

7. McCarthy MM (1990) Oxytocin inhibits infanticide in wild female house mice. *Hormones & Behaviour* 24: 365-75.

8. Dawson G, et al. (1999) Infants of depressed mothers exhibit atypical frontal electrical brain activity during interactions with mother and with a familiar nondepressed adult, *Child Development* Sep-Oct; 70(5): 1058-66. • Dawson G, et al. (1999) Frontal brain electrical activity in infants of depressed and non-depressed mothers; relation to variations in infant behaviour, *Development and Psychopathology* Summer; 11(3): 589-605.

9. For CARE system see Panksepp J (1998) Chapter 13, *Love and the Social Bond in Affective Neuroscience*, Oxford University Press, New York.

10. Aitken KJ, et al. (1997) Self/other organisation in human psychological development, *Development and Psychopathology* 9: 653-77 • Trevarthen C, et al. (2001) Infant intersubjectivity: research, theory, and clinical applications, *Journal of Child Psychology and Psychiatry, and Allied Disciplines* Jan; 42(1): 3-48. • Trevarthen C (1993) The Self born in intersubjectivity: The psychology of an infant communicating; cited in Neisser, U (Ed.) *The Perceived Self: ecological and interpersonal sources of self knowledge*, Press Syndicate of the University of Cambridge, Cambridge:123.

11. Orbach, S (2004) *The Body in Clinical Practice*, Part One: There's no such thing as a body; Part Two: When Touch comes to Therapy. John Bowlby Memorial Lecture in Touch, Attachment and the body. Ed. Kate White, Karnac Books, London.

12. See Montagu A (1971) *Touching: The Human Significance of the Skin*, Harper and Row, London. • Prescott JW (1971) Early somatosensor deprivation as an ontogenetic process in the abnormal development of brain and behaviour, *Proceedings of the Second Conference on Experimental Medicine and Surgery in Primates* (Eds. Goldsmith EI, Mody-Janokowski J, Basel: Karger: 356-75).

13. Adapted from Winnicott DW (1971) *Playing and Reality*, Penguin/Basic, Middx./New York. Winnicott was a famous child psychoanalyst.

14. Lots of these games were originated by Phyllis Booth, With Jernberg, she designed a way of being with children which duplicated those delightful one-to-ones that parents have with their babies. This gives children who have missed out on this vital brain sculpting stage a second chance. Jernberg AM, Booth PB (2001) *Theraplay: Helping parents and children build better relationships through attachment-based play*, Jossey-Bass, San Francisco.

15. Schore A (2003) *Affect Regulation and the Repair of the Self*, WW Norton & Co., New York: 158-174. • Schore A (1996) The experience-dependent maturation of a regulatory system in the orbital prefrontal cortex and the origin of development psychopathology, *Development and Psychopathology* 8: 59-87. • Main M, et al. (1982) Avoidance of the attachment figure in infancy. Descriptions and interpretations. In CM Parkes and Journal of Stevenson-Hinde (Eds) *The place of attachment in human behaviour*, New York Basic Books: 31-59.

16. These diagnostic categories of child led play and parent led play have been adapted from Sue Jenner's parent-child play. Jenner S (1999) *The parent-child game*, Bloomsbury, London.

17. The concept of the parent who becomes the child's favourite toy, by rising to the bait of a child's provocative behaviour, comes from Glasser H, Easley J (1999) *Transforming the Difficult Child*, Nurtured Heart, New York.

18. Hughes D (2005) *Working with Troubled Children*, Lecture Centre for Child Mental Health London, citing Buber M (1987) *I and Thou*, T and T Clark, Edinburgh.

19. "Opioids and oxytocin are bonding chemistries. Dopamine does not appear as important in bonding." Panksepp J (1998) *Affective Neuroscience: The Foundations of Human and Animal Emotions*, Oxford University Press, Oxford: 260.

20. Tronick, EZ (1989) Interactive Repair, Emotions and emotional communication in infants, *The American Psychologist* Feb; 44(2): 112-9. • Butovskaya ML, et al. (2005) The hormonal basis of reconciliation in humans, *Journal of Physiological Anthropology and Applied Human Science* Jul; 24(4): 333-37.

21. See Hughes, D (1998) *Building the Bonds of Attachment: Awakening Love in Deeply Troubled Children*, Jason Aronson, New Jersey, for more exquisite responses to challenging behaviour in children in ways which activate the higher brain rather than the lower brain.

22. "Since the joy of loving seems hopelessly barred to him, he may as well deliver himself over to the joy of hating and obtain what satisfaction he can out of that." Fairbairn WRD (1940) Schizoid Factors in the Personality, *Psychoanalytic Studies of the Personality* (1952), Tavistock/Routledge, London: 27. • Fromm, E (1973) *Anatomy of Human Destructiveness*, Cape, London.

23. Field T (1994) The effects of mother's physical and emotional unavailability on emotion regulation, *Monographs of the Society for Research in Child Development* 59; (2-3): 208-27. • Haley DW, et al. (2003) Infant stress and parent responsiveness: regulation of physiology and behavior during still-face and reunion, *Child Development* Sep-Oct; 74(5): 1534-46.

24. Panksepp J (1998) *Affective Neuroscience*, Oxford University Press, Oxford: 255.

25. Zubieta JK, et al. (2003) Regulation of human affective responses by anterior cingulate and limbic and μ-opioid neurotransmission, *General Psychiatry* Nov 60 (11): 1037-1172.

26. Panksepp J (1998) *Affective Neuroscience*, Oxford University Press, Oxford: 276.

27. Goodall J (1990) *Through a Window: Thirty Years with the Chimpanzees of Gombe*, Weidenfeld and Nicolson, London.

28. "Some of the Rwanda children in the orphanage, after the grief of losing their parents, gave up and died." Glover J (2001) *Humanity: A moral history of the twentieth century*, Pimlico, London.

29. Armstrong-Perlman EM (1991) The Allure of the Bad Object, *Free Associations* 2 (3)23: 343-56.

30. Weninger O (1989) *Children's Phantasies: The Shaping of Relationships*, Karnac Books, London. • Weninger O (1993) *View from the Cradle: Children's Emotions in Everyday Life*, Karnac Books, London.

31. Eisenberger NI, et al. (2003) Does rejection hurt? An FMRI study of social exclusion, *Science* Oct 10;302(5643): 290-92.

32. Jay Vaughan Family Futures Consortium, London. Personal communication 2004.

33. Hughes D (1998) *Building the Bonds of Attachment*, Jason Aronson, New Jersey.

YOUR SOCIALLY INTELLIGENT CHILD

1. Steele M, et al. (2002) Maternal predictors of children's social cognition: an attachment perspective, *Journal of Child Psychology and Psychiatry, and Allied Disciplines* Oct; 43(7): 861-72.

2. "As the cortex develops, vast numbers of top down neural networks connect with the subcortical area.. These top down networks provide the information pathway for inhibiting reflexes and bringing subcortical functions under cortical control. Thus, a vital aspect of the development of the cortex is the inhibitory. This theory is supported by the effects of cortical damage in adults. Individuals with Alzheimer's disease, for example, experience significant cell death in their cortex." Cozolino LJ (2002) *The Neuroscience of Psychotherapy: Building and Rebuilding the Human Remain*, WW Norton & Co., London: 76.

3. Bar-On R, et al. (2003) Exploring the neurological substrate of emotional and social intelligence, *Brain* Aug; 126(8): 1790-800.

4. Critchley HD, et al. (2000) The functional neuroanatomy of social behaviour: changes in cerebral blood flow when people with autistic disorder process facial expressions, *Brain* Nov; 123 (11): 2203-12. • McKelvey JR, et al. (1995) Right-hemisphere dysfunction in Asperger's syndrome, *Journal of Child Neurology* Jul; 10(4): 310-14. • McAlonan GM, et al. (2002) Brain anatomy and sensorimotor gating in Asperger's syndrome, *Brain* Jul; 125(Pt 7): 1594-606.

5. Rosenblum LA, et al. (1994) Adverse early experiences affect noradrenergic and serotonergic functioning in adult primates, *Biological Psychiatry* Feb 15; 35(4): 221-7. • Dolan M, et al. (2002) Serotonergic and cognitive impairment in impulsive aggressive personality disorder offenders; Are there implications for treatment? *Psychological Medicine* 32: 105-17. • "Serotonin supplementation can decrease aggression in animals that have become irritable because of long- term social isolation. In general reduced brain serotonin activity also tends to increase impulsive and acting out forms of behaviour in humans." Panksepp J (1998) *Affective Neuroscience: The Foundations of Human and Animal Emotions*, Oxford University Press, Oxford: 202.

6. Kotulak R (1996) *Inside the Brain: Revolutionary Discoveries of How the Mind Works*, Andrews and McMeel, Kansas City: 85. • Panksepp J (1998) *Affective Neuroscience*, Oxford University Press, Oxford: 202. • "We know that children who have come from angry or violent backgrounds often show lower levels of serotonin." Institute of Juvenile Research, Chicago; cited by Kotulak R (1996), op. cit.: 85.

7. Murray L, et al. (2000) *The social baby: Understanding babies' communication from birth*, CP Publishing, Richmond.

8. Bar-on, ME (1999) Turning off the television, *British Medical Journal* 24; 318(7191): 1152.

9. Stern DN (1985) *The Interpersonal World of the Infant*, Basic Books, New York. • Stern DN (1990) *Diary of a Baby – What Your Child Sees, Feels, and Experiences*, Basic Books, New York.

10. Kanner L (1943) Autistic disturbance of affective contact, *Nervous Child* 2: 217-350.

11. The Mifne Center, PO Box 112 Rosh Pinna 12000, Israel. www.mifne-autism.com Director: Hanna Alonim.

12. De Bellis MD, et al. (2000) N-Acetylaspartate Concentration in the Anterior Cingulate of Maltreated Children and Adolescents With PTSD, *The American Journal of Psychiatry* 157 July:1175-77. • Devinsky O, et al. (1995) Contributions of anterior cingulate cortex to behaviour, *Brain* Feb; 118 (Pt 1): 279-306. • Posner MI, et al. (1998) Attention, self-regulation and consciousness, *Philosophical Transactions of the Royal Society of London. Series B, Biological Sciences* Nov 29; 353(1377): 1915-27.

13. Blair RJ, et al. (2001) A selective impairment in the processing of sad and fearful expressions in children with psychopathic tendencies, *Journal of Abnormal Child Psychology* Dec 29 (6): 491-8. • Blair RJ (1995) A cognitive developmental approach to mortality: investigating the psychopath, *Cognition* Oct 57 (1): 1-29. • Pollak SD, et al. (2000) Recognizing emotion in faces: developmental effects of child abuse and neglect, *Developmental Psychology* Sep; 36(5): 679-88.

14. Panksepp J (1998) *Affective Neuroscience*, Oxford University Press, Oxford: 250.

15. Teicher MH, et al. (1997) Preliminary evidence for abnormal cortical development in physically and sexually abused children using EEG coherence and MRI, *Annals of the New York Academy of Sciences* 821: 160-75. • Teicher MH, et al. (2003) The neurobiological consequences of early stress and childhood maltreatment, *Neuroscience and Biobehavioral Reviews* Jan-Mar; 27(1-2): 33-44. • "We are finding that verbal abuse is devastating... These changes [to the brain] are devastating..." "An underdeveloped corpus callosum inhibits communication between one hemisphere and the other. As a result children could end up 'residing' in one hemisphere rather than moving rapidly and easily from one to the other." Teicher M (2000) Damage Linked to Child Abuse and Neglect, *Cerebrum*: Fall.

16. Teicher M (2002) Scars That Won't Heal, *Scientific American* March. • De Bellis MD, et al. (2002). Brain structures in pediatric maltreatment-related posttraumatic stress disorder: a sociodemographically matched study, *Biological Psychiatry* Dec 1; 52(11): 1066-78. • De Bellis, MD, et al. (2000) N-Acetylaspartate Concentration in the Anterior Cingulate of Maltreated Children and Adolescents With PTSD, *The American Journal of Psychiatry* 157 Jul:1175-77.

17. Siegel DJ (1999) *The Developing Mind*, The Guildford Press, New York.

18. van Goozen SH, et al. (2004) Evidence of fearlessness in behaviourally disordered children: a study on startle reflex modulation, *Journal of Child Psychology and Psychiatry, and Allied Disciplines* May; 45(4): 884-92. • Blair RJ (2001) Neurocognitive models of aggression, the antisocial personality

disorders, and psychopathy, *Journal of Neurology, Neurosurgery, and Psychiatry* Dec; 71(6): 727-31.

19. Troy M, et al. (1987) Victimisation Among Preschoolers: Role of Attachment Relationship History, *Journal of American Academy of Child and Adolescent Psychiatry* 26: 166-72.

20. Blair RJ, et al. (2005) Deafness to fear in boys with psychopathic tendencies, *Journal of Child Psychology and Psychiatry, and Allied Disciplines* Mar; 46(3): 327-36.

21. Singer T, et al. (1994) Empathy for pain involves the affective but not sensory components of pain, *Science* (303) Feb.

22. Teicher MH, et al. (2003) The neurobiological consequences of early stress and childhood maltreatment, *Neuroscience and Biobehavioral Reviews* Jan-Mar; 27(1-2): 33-44. • Teicher MH, et al. (1996) Neurophysiological mechanisms of stress response in children. In Pfeffer CR (Ed.) *Severe stress and mental disturbances in children*, American Psychiatric Press, Washington, DC: 59-84. • Teicher M, et al. (2002) Developmental neurobiology of childhood stress and trauma, *The Psychiatric Clinics of North America* 25: 297-426.

23. Caldji C, et al. (2003) Variations in maternal care alter GABAA receptor subunit expression in brain regions associated with fear, *Neuropsychopharmacology* 28: 1950-59.

24. Schore A (2005) Attachment, Affect Regulation and the Right Brain: Linking Developmental Neuroscience to Pediatrics, *Pediatrics in Review* 26 (6) June.

25. Teicher M (2002) Scars That Won't Heal, *Scientific American* March.

26. Straus MA, et al. (1980) *Behind Closed Doors: Violence in the American Family*, Anchor Books, Garden City, NJ.

27. Schore A (2003) *Affect Dysregulation and Disorders of the Self*, WW Norton & Co., New York: 26.

28. Weinberg I, *Neurosci Biobehav Rev.* 2000 Dec; 24(8): 799-815. • Sierra M, et al. (2002) Autonomic response in depersonalisation disorder, Sep; 59 (9): 833-8. • Lowen A (1975) Bioenergetics, Penguin, London.

LOOKING AFTER YOU

1. de Weerth C, et al. (2003) Prenatal maternal cortisol levels and infant behavior during the first 5 months, *Early Human Development* Nov: 139-51. • Deminiere JM, et al. (1992) Increased locomotor response to novelty and propensity to intravenous amphetamine self-administration in adult offspring of stressed mothers, *Brain Research* Jul 17; 586(1): 135-39. • Watterberg KL (2004) Adrenocortical function and dysfunction in the fetus and neonate, *Seminars in Neonatology* Feb: 13-21.

2. Field T, et al. (1999) Pregnant women benefit from massage therapy, *Journal of Psychosomatic Obstetrics and Gynecology*: 31-38.

3. Williams MT, et al. (1999) Stress during pregnancy alters the offspring hypothalamic, pituitary, adrenal, and testicular response to isolation on the day of weaning. *Neurotoxicology and Teratology* Nov-Dec; 21(6): 653-59. • Panksepp J (1998) *Affective Neuroscience: The Foundations of Human and Animal Emotions*, Oxford University Press, Oxford: 237.

4. Floyd RL et al (2005) Recognition and Prevention of Fetal Alcohol Syndrome, *Obstetrics and Gynecology* Nov 106 (5): 1059-64. • Bookstein FL et al (2005) Preliminary evidence that prenatal alcohol damage may be visible in averaged ultrasound images of the neonatal human corpus callosum, *Alcohol* Jul 36 (3):151-60.

5. Wakschlag LS et al (1997) Maternal smoking during pregnancy and the risk of conduct disorder in boys, *Archives of General Psychiatry* July: 670-76. • Fergusson DM, et al. (1998) Maternal smoking during pregnancy and psychiatric adjustment in late adolescence, *Archives of General Psychiatry* Aug: 721-27.

6. M'bailara K, et al (2005) Baby blues: characterization and influence of psycho-social factors, *Encephale* May-June: 331-36. • Halligan SL, et al. (2004). Exposure to postnatal depression predicts elevated cortisol in adolescent offspring, *Biological Psychiatry* Feb15: 376-81.

7. Heinrichs M et al (2001). Effects of suckling on hypothalamic-pituitary-adrenal axis responses to psychosocial stress in postpartum lactating women, *The Journal of Clinical Endocrinology and Metabolism* Oct: 4798-804.

8. Study conducted at Harvard Medical School and the USDA Human Nutrition Research Center at Tufts University, showing that more than one out of every four depressed patients was deficient in vitamins B6 and B12, and that in many cases symptoms were relieved with vitamin B6 supplements (in doses as low as 10 milligrams a day). Cited in Somer E (1999) *Food and Mood*, Henry Holt, New York.

9. Prasad C (1998). Food, mood and health: a neurobiological outlook, *Brazilian Journal of Medical and Biological Research* Dec: 1517-27.

10. Neki NS, et al. (2004) How brain influences neuro-cardiovascular dysfunction, *The Journal of the Association of Physicians of India*, Mar: 223-30. • Wainwright PE (2002) Dietary essential fatty acids and brain function: a developmental perspective on mechanisms, *The Proceedings of the Nutrition Society* Feb: 61-69.

11. "Just about every measure of thinking ability improves after eating a good breakfast – from math scores and creative thinking to speed and efficiency in solving problems, concentration, recall, and accuracy in work performance." Somer E (1999) *Food and Mood*, Henry Holt, New York: 195.

12. Research by J. Michael Murphy, of the Department of Psychiatry at Harvard Medical School; cited in Carper J (2000) *Your Miracle Brain*, Harper Collins, New York: 113-14.

13. Benton D (2002) Selenium intake, mood and other aspects of psychological functioning, *Nutritional Neuroscience* Dec: 363-74.

14. Seeman TE, et al. (1996) Impact of social environment characteristics on neuroendocrine regulation, *Psychosomatic Medicine* Sep-Oct; 58 (5): 459-71. • Carter CS (1998) Neuroendocrine perspectives on social attachment and love, *Psychoneuroendocrinology* Nov; 23(8): 779-818.

15. Szabo A et al (1993) Psychophysiological profiles in response to various challenges during recovery from acute aerobic exercise, *International Journal of Psychophysiology*. May: 285-92.

16. Uvnas-Moberg, K (2003) *The Oxytocin Factor*, Da Capo Press, Cambridge, MA.

17. Sahasi G, et al. (1989). Effectiveness of yogic techniques in the management of anxiety, *Journal of Personality and Clinical Studies* 5: 51-55.

18. Takahashi T, et al. (2005) Changes in EEG and autonomic nervous activity during meditation and their association with personality traits, *International Journal of Psychophysiology* Feb: 199-207. • Blackwell B, et al. (1976). Transcendental meditation in hypertension. Individual response patterns, *Lancet* 1: 223-26.

19. House JS, et al. (1988) Social relationships and health, *Science* Jul 29 241 (4865): 540-45.

20. Arborelius L, et al. (1999) The role of corticotrophin–releasing factor in depression and anxiety disorders, *The Journal of Endocrinology* Jan; 160 (1): 1-12. • Kathol RG, et al. (1989) Pathophysiology of HPA axis abnormalities in patients with major depression: an update, *The American Journal of Psychiatry* Mar; 146(3): 311-17.

21. Hibbs ED, et al (1992) Parental expressed emotion and psychophysiological reactivity in disturbed and normal children, *The British Journal of Psychiatry* Apr; 160: 504-10. • Ashman SB, et al (2002) Stress hormone levels of children of depressed mothers, *Development and Psychopathology* Spring; 14(2): 333-49.

22. Rottenberg J, et al. (2003) Vagal rebound during resolution of tearful crying among depressed and nondepressed individuals, *Psychophysiology* Jan: 1-6. • Ishii H, et al. (2003) Does being easily moved to tears as a response to psychological stress reflect response to treatment and the general prognosis in patients with rheumatoid arthritis? *Clinical and Experimental Rheumatology* Sep-Oct: 611-16.

23. Phelps JL, et al. (1998) Earned security, daily stress, and parenting: a comparison of five alternative models, *Development and Psychopathology* Winter: 21-38.

Full references, descriptions of studies, and suggested further reading can be found by following the links on www.dk.com/scienceofparenting.

Useful addresses

4Children
Tel: 020 7512 2112
www.4children.org.uk
Gives information on afterschool and out-of-school care in England, Wales, and Scotland.

Association for Family Therapy
Tel: 01925 444 414
Web: www.aft.org.uk
Gives information about family therapy and how to find a therapist in your area.

Association for Post Natal Illness
Tel: 020 7386 0868
www.apni.org
Email: info@apni.org

British Association for Counselling and Psychotherapy (BACP)
Tel: 0870 443 5252
www.bacp.co.uk
Email: bacp@bacp.co.uk
UK's professional association for counsellors and psychotherapists. Use to find a counsellor or therapist in your area.

Bullying Online
www.bullying.co.uk
Email: help@bullying.co.uk
Gives information and advice (including by e-mail) to those affected by bullying.

Centre for Child Mental Health (London)
Tel: 0207 354 2913
www.childmentalhealthcentre.org
Email: info@childmentalhealthcentre.org
Gives information and lectures on neuroscientific and psychological research in child mental health for parents, teachers, and childcare professionals.

Childline
Tel: 0800 1111
www.childline.org.uk
Provides a free 24-hour helpline and support for children and young people.

Cry-sis
Tel: 0845 122 8669
www.cry-sis.org.uk
Email: info@cry-sis.org.uk
Parents helpline – crying/sleepless children.

Dads UK
Helpline: 07092 391489
www.dads-uk.co.uk
National helpline offering suppport to single fathers.

Fathers Direct
www.fathersdirect.com
For all dads, from expectant to experienced.

Gingerbread
Helpline: 0800 018 4318
www.gingerbread.org.uk
Self-help body for single-parent families.

Grandparents' Association
Helpline: 01279 444 964
www.grandparents-association.org.uk
Advice line on all aspects of grandparenting.

Home-Start
Tel: 0800 068 6368
www.home-start.org.uk
Email: support@home-start.org.uk
Provides support and and self-help network for parents of under-fives.

Institute for Arts in Therapy and Education
Tel: 0207 704 2534
www.artspsychotherapy.org
Email: info@artspsychotherapy.org
Offers nationally recognized Masters degree in Integrative Child psychotherapy; also Diplomas in Emotional Literacy for Children and in Parent–Child Therapy.

Institute of Family Therapy
Tel: 0207 391 9150
www.instituteoffamilytherapy.org.uk
Email: ift@psych.bbk.ac.uk
For young people and families with anxiety, depression, and behavioural problems.

It's not your fault
Tel: 0845 7626579
www.itsnotyourfault.org
Offers information and support to young people with divorcing or separating parents.

Kidscape
Tel: 020 7730 3300
Helpline: 08451 205 204
www.kidscape.org.uk
Protects children from bullying or abuse.

Meet-a-Mum Association (MAMA)
Helpline: 0845 120 3746
www.mama.co.uk
Supports mothers and mothers-to-be.

National Society for the Prevention of Cruelty to Children (NSPCC)
Helpline (24 hr): 0808 800 5000

www.nspcc.org.uk
UK's leading child protection charity. Helpline gives advice to anyone concerned about a child at risk of abuse.

One Parent Families Scotland
Tel: 0800 018 5026
www.opfs.org.uk
Email: info@opfs.org.uk
Support for lone parents and their children.

Parentline Plus
Helpline: 0808 800 2222
www.parentlineplus.org.uk
Operates a national freephone helpline to support parents and carers of children.

Pippin (Parents in Partnership – Parent Infant Network)
Tel: 01727 899099
www.pippin.org.uk
Provides structured parenting courses for expectant and new parents.

Relate
Tel: 01788 573241 or 0845 456 1310
www.relate.org.uk
Email: enquiries@relate.org.uk
National network of counselling centres for marriage and family relationship needs.

SureStart
Tel: 0870 000 2288
www.surestart.gov.uk
Government programme to improve health and well-being of families and children.

Traumatic Stress Clinic
Tel: 0207 530 3666
www.traumatic-stress-clinic.org.uk
Offers psychological treatment of children and families following a trauma.

Twins and Multiple Birth Association (TAMBA)
Tel: 0870 770 3305
Web: www.tamba.org.uk
Email: enquiries@tamba.org.uk
Provides information and mutual support for families of twins, triplets, and more.

Young Minds
Tel: 020 7336 8445 (office)
Helpline: 0800 018 2138
Web: www.youngminds.org.uk
Email: info@youngminds.org.uk
National charity for improving children's mental health. Parents' advice line.

Index

A

acetylcholine 210, 259

ACTH (adrenocorticotropin) 40, 41, 79

additives, food 114–15

adenosine 257

ADHD (attention deficit hyperactivity disorder) 105–6, 108, 137

adrenal glands 40, 41, 79, 87, 113, 255, 259

adrenaline 44, 87, 90, 91, 113–14, 202, 236, 255, 257, 259

adrenocorticotropin (ACTH) 40, 41, 79

adult company for parents 261–3, 268

alarm systems 22–5, 27–8, 29, 67

    see also amygdala; specific emotional systems (e.g. RAGE system)

alcohol 44, 72, 247–9, 259

amygdala 27–8, 29, 36, 44, 231, 234–5, 236

anatomy of the brain *see* brain structure

anger *see* fighting; RAGE system; tantrums

anterior cingulate gyrus 22, 191, 228, 236

anxiety 30, 42–3, 80, 143–4

    anti-anxiety chemicals 27, 28, 256

arousal 241–2, 251

    see also hyperarousal

Asperger's syndrome *see* autism

attention deficit hyperactivity disorder (ADHD) 105–6, 108, 137

attention-seeking behaviour 118, 165–6, 166, 167, 202–3, 204

autism 225, 226–8

autonomic nervous system 44–5, 90, 113, 143

autoregulation 258

B

B vitamins 252–3

BDNF (brain-derived neurotrophic factor) 104

bedtime routine 66–7

    see also sleep

behaving badly 111–19, 136, 159, 202–3, 211

    see also discipline; specific bad behaviours (e.g. tantrums)

bereavement response 53, 208–11

big feelings 29–30, 32, 68, 118–19, 155, 242, 267

    right brain activity 230–1, 266

    Time In technique 155, 172, 173, 181

    see also specific feelings (e.g. distress); tantrums

biochemical dysregulation 251, 258, 262

blood sugar (blood glucose) levels 41, 113, 114, 255, 257, 259

blue spot 196

body-to-body contact *see* physical affection

bonding 53, 72, 188, 190, 203, 249

    CARE system 190–1, 214, 228, 229, 230, 265

bonding chemistries 186, 190, 208

    see also specific brain chemicals (e.g. oxytocin)

boredom 48, 101, 102, 132, 139–43, 150, 152, 175

bouncing about 137–9, 143

boundaries and rules 30, 136, 145, 150, 156, 164–8, 179–80, 185, 206

brain cells 20, 21, 22, 96, 227–8

brain chemicals 25–6, 86, 251, 252–7

    see also specific neurochemicals (e.g. oxytocin)

brain–derived neurotrophic factor (BDNF) 104

brain development in childhood 20–5, 28, 30, 104, 116, 117, 227–8

    problems 226–8, 235–7

    see also brain sculpting

brain–gut studies 45

brain hemispheres 22

    see also left and right brains

brain pathways (networks) 11, 25, 28, 122, 137, 155, 174, 222–3, 229, 242

    top-down 29, 32, 222

brain sculpting 9, 20, 22, 31, 42–3, 90, 121, 125, 160–3, 194

brain stem 19, 196, 236, 248

brain structure 18–19, 22

    cells *see* brain cells

    emotional *see* mammalian brain

evolution 16–17, 18, 21, 36, 50

frontal lobes *see* higher brain

higher *see* higher brain

limbic system *see* mammalian brain

mammalian *see* mammalian brain

neo-cortex *see* higher brain

rational *see* higher brain

reptilian *see* reptilian brain

    see also specific parts of the brain (e.g. corpus callosum)

brain systems *see* specific systems (e.g. RAGE system)

breakfast 113, 254, 255

breastfeeding 249

breathing techniques 46

broken-hearted children 208–11, 215

bullying 153, 156, 160–3, 229, 235

    bully-proofing 238–42, 243

    little Nero tantrums 121, 125, 128–32, 133

    long-term effects 22, 234–7, 243

    statistics 10, 160, 234, 238

    see also fighting; violence

C

cafés and restaurants 137, 139, 175, 206

caffeine 257

calming and comforting *see* soothing

camomile tea 256

car journeys 141–3, 205

car seats 120

car wash game 203

carbohydrates 67, 254, 255, 256

CARE system 119, 190–1, 214, 228, 229, 230, 265

cerebellar vermis 236

cerebellum 19, 222, 248

cerebrum 117

challenging behaviour *see* behaving badly

child-led play 199–200, 201, 215

childcare 52–3, 54–9

childrearing *see* parenting

chocolate and sweets 67, 114, 255

choices and consequences technique 125, 126, 145, 148–9, 166, 167–8, 169, 171, 181

Acknowledgments

Over the eight years of writing and researching this book, some great minds and hearts have supported me. I wish in particular to express my gratitude to the following people:

Professor Jaak Panksepp who for many years has been correcting the text of this book and in the nicest possible way, ensuring that I properly represent the science. It has been a great privilege and honour to learn from such an eminent scientist, whose work is key to the emotional well-being of children.

Elaine Duigenan, an extremely talented photographer working in London and New York, who took many of the photos in this book. Elaine has a gift to fully enter into a child's experiencing of the moment, powerfully representing the full range of their feeling states from intense joy to intense pain. She shows children just as they are, rather than looking through a sugar-coated lens, and in so doing reassuring parents about the normality of those inevitable testing times as well as the delight.

Professor Allan Schore (University of California at Los Angeles, David Geffen School of Medicine). It is only right that I declare that I am not the first to make the "Everestian climb" into this vast area of scientific study. Allan is! In his many books, he has integrated an awesome mass of brain research on parent–child interaction, brilliantly applying it to psychopathology and psychotherapy. At the start of my journey I received some vital tutoring from him, and this book owes a lot to his groundbreaking psychoneurobiological models.

Eleanore Armstrong-Perlman, Past Chair of the Guild of Psychotherapists and Fairbairnian psychoanalytic scholar. I thank her for her invaluable help on the chapter, "Chemistry of Love", and for her outstanding empathy for the suffering of children. She has helped me to speak for the babies.

Dr Dan Hughes (author: *Building the Bonds of Attachment*), who appears from time to time through the lines of this book. I've gained

such a lot from him both personally and professionally. It is always a profoundly moving experience to watch him reaching unreachable children with his neuroscientifically grounded PACE model (play, acceptance, curiosity and empathy).

The late Sue Fish, a key founder of Integrative Child Psychotherapy in the UK. Her capacity for high intensity relational moments with both children and adults are testimony to all the studies in this book about the long-term brain benefits of human warmth, shared play, compassion and touch.

All those at The Centre for Child Mental Health: Charlotte Emmett, Ruth Bonner, and latterly Eleanor Cole, whose work on this book has meant it was largely a high dopamine experience of togetherness, rather than an isolated slog!

Brett Kahr, Senior Clinical Research Fellow in Psychotherapy and Mental Health and **Sir Richard Bowlby**, President of the Centre for Child Mental Health, who both bring so much richness and inspiration to our work in disseminating the latest child mental health research.

My mother Muriel Sunderland, whose love of knowledge, psychology and education has inspired my own.

The Goring Hotel London, whose staff exemplify all that is best in English charm and finesse, during my many writing visits to this enriching environment.

Esther Ripley, Senior Editor at Dorling Kindersley for all her sophisticated higher brain skills when the birth of a book such as this is unutterably complex, and Anne Fisher and Jo Grey for their design expertise.

Graeme Blench (Co-Director, Centre for Child Mental Health) for his unending support to me both personally and professionally.

And finally I want to thank all the scientists and psychologists referred to in this book, whose findings will help us to move towards a better world for our children.

Publishers acknowledgments

DK publishing would like to thank:

Sue Bosanko for the index and Katie John for proofreading and editorial assistance.

Illustrator: Joanna Cameron

The children and parents who have acted as models for photography. We wish to point out that names have been changed and captions, quotations and case histories bear no relation to the actual children and adults, pictured in this book.

Picture credits
The publisher would like to thank the following for their kind permission to reproduce their photographs:

(Key: a-above; b-below/bottom; c-centre; l-left; r-right; t-top)

Alamy Images: Finn Roberts 36cl; 140; Aflo Foto Agency 259; BananaStock 235; Andy Bishop 250; blickwinkel 223; Photick - Image and Click 209; Brandon Cole Marine Photography 229; Paul Doyle 212; Elvele Images 237br; Fotofacade 152; John T. Fowler 148t; Garry Gay 40bl; Tim Graham 267; Image Source 232; image100 204; Christina Kennedy 213; Motoring Picture Library 247; Photofusion Picture Library 153; Medical-on-Line 264; Pegaz 154; cbp-photo 99; Photo Network 123b; John Powell Photographer 124, 166; Bubbles Photolibrary 234; RubberBall 233; Profimedia.CZ s.r.o. 147; thislife pictures 120bc, 260; Westend61 219, 266-267; Janine Wiedel Photolibrary 210, 211; Brand X Pictures 214; University of Southern California: Susan Lynch, Brain and Creativity Institute, University of Southern California / Dr Antonio Damasio, Professor of Psychology, Neuroscience and Neurology, and Director, Institute for the Neurological Study of Emotion, Decision-Making, and Creativity, University of

Southern California 24; Corbis: 75, 158, 188, 189, 194-195; Patrick Bennett 230; Hal Beral 17clb; Rolf Bruderer 256-257; Jim Craigmyle 102b; Goupy Didier 20cl; Kevin Dodge 220; Pat Doyle 224; Laura Dwight 120br, 170; Jim Erickson 126tl; Tom Galliher 18bl; Françoise Gervais 240; John Henley 30t, 238; Gavriel Jecan 70; Ronnie Kaufman 190; Michael Keller 254; LWA-Sharie Kennedy 242; Tim Kiusalaas 244; Bob London 125tr; Simon Marcus 168t; Roy McMahon 175; Gideon Mendel 160; Bill Miles 78cl; Jeffry W. Myers 74; Tim Pannell 268; JLP/Jose L. Pelaez 225; Jose Luis Pelaez, Inc. 207; Gavin Kingcome Photography 89; ROB & SAS 2-3, 181; George Shelley 8t; Ariel Skelley 9b; Tom Stewart 32t; LWA-Dann Tardif 180, 185tr; Kennan Ward 17cb, 88; Larry Williams 198bl; Jennie Woodcock; Reflections Photolibrary 163; Claude Woodruff 4-5, 14bl; Grace/zefa 157; K. Mitchell/zefa 199; LWA-Dann Tardif/zefa 23t; Pete Leonard/zefa 64; Tim O'Leary/zefa 197; Virgo/zefa 136; Elaine Duigenan: 10, 11t, 12b, 17crb, 19t, 25t, 26, 29, 31t, 34, 37, 42, 43t, 46, 51, 55t, 59, 60tl, 84, 86, 90, 92, 93, 96, 97, 98, 100, 103, 105, 106, 108, 112, 115, 116, 118, 119, 120, 121, 122, 129, 130, 131, 133, 134, 137, 138, 139, 141, 142, 145, 146, 149, 151, 161, 164, 169, 173, 176, 177, 178, 182, 184cl, 187, 192, 193, 198bc, 198br, 200-201, 202, 203, 205, 215, 226, 227, 227bl, 227br, 239, 251, 253, 258; Getty Images: Walther Bear 132cl; The Image Bank 236bl; Uwe Krejci 13b; Elyse Lewin 14bl; Ghislain & Marie David de Lossy 110; Gavin Kingcome Photography 1c, 89; Yellow Dog Productions 95; Harry Sheridan 89; Jerome Tisne 11; Jane Goodall: 50; Onur Guentuerkuen: 7t; H.F. Harlow: 58; Royalty Free Images: Alamy Images 49tr; Corbis 129cr; Science Photo Library: AJ PHOTO / HOP AMERICAIN 236cr; Scott Camazine 41; Scott Camazine & Sue Trainor 231, 237tc; CNRI 117; Sovereign, ISM 104; Sidney Moulds 40cra; Harry T. Chugani, M.D. Children's Hospital of Michigan, Wayne State University, Detroit, Michigan, USA: 52l; Zefa Visual Media: P. Leonard 122
All other images © Dorling Kindersley
For further information see: www.dkimages.com